Air Fryer Cookbook for Beginners

....

Easy, Quick, Delicious, Affordable, and Irresistible Air Fryer Recipes for Everyday.

Ray Beasley

Copyright © 2023 by   All rights reserved.

The content contained within this book may not be reproduced, duplicated, or transmitted without direct written permission from the author or the publisher. Under no circumstances will any blame or legal responsibility be held against the publisher, or author, for any damages, reparation, or monetary loss due to the information contained within this book, either directly or indirectly.

Legal Notice: This book is copyright protected. It is only for personal use. You cannot amend, distribute, sell, use, quote or paraphrase any part, or the content within this book, without the consent of the author or publisher.

Disclaimer Notice: Please note the information contained within this document is for educational and entertainment purposes only. All effort has been executed to present accurate, up to date, reliable, complete information. No warranties of any kind are declared or implied. Readers acknowledge that the author is not engaged in the rendering of legal, financial, medical, or professional advice. The content within this book has been derived from various sources. Please consult a licensed professional before attempting any techniques outlined in this book. By reading this document, the reader agrees that under no circumstances is the author responsible for any losses, direct or indirect, that are incurred as a result of the use of the information contained within this document, including, but not limited to, errors, omissions, or inaccuracies.

Table of Contents

Table of Contents 3

Chapter 1: Introduction 7
History of the Air Fryer 7
Benefits of the Air Fryer 7
Features of the Air Fryer 7
Tips for Using the Air Fryer 8
Cleaning and Maintenance of the Air Fryer 8

Chapter 2: Measurement Conversions 9
BASIC KITCHEN CONVERSIONS & EQUIVALENTS 9

Chapter 3: Bread And Breakfast Recipes 10
Avocado Tempura 11
Easy Corn Dog Cupcakes 11
Carrot Orange Muffins 11
Black's Bangin' Casserole 11
Ham And Cheddar Gritters 11
Thyme Beef & Eggs 12
Buttery Scallops 12
Ham And Egg Toast Cups 12
Puffed Egg Tarts 12
Spinach Bacon Spread 12
Simple Cinnamon Toasts 13
Classic Hash Browns 13
Breakfast Frittata 13
Favorite Blueberry Muffins 13
Banana-blackberry Muffins 13
Cream Cheese Danish 14
Crispy Fish Sticks 14
Asparagus And Bell Pepper Strata 14
Western Frittata 14
Cheesy Mustard Toasts 15
Potato Bread Rolls 15
Breakfast Burrito With Sausage 15
Simple Cherry Tarts 16
Zucchini Muffins With Cinnamon 16
Cinnamon Rolls With Cream Cheese Glaze 16
Hash Browns 17
Not-so-english Muffins 17
Herbed Omelet 17
Yummy Bagel Breakfast 17
Chocolate Chip Scones 17
Egg In A Hole 18
Coconut & Peanut Rice Cereal 18
Blueberry Scones 18
Vodka Basil Muffins With Strawberries 18
Parmesan Spinach Muffins 18
Almond-pumpkin Porridge 19
Spinach With Scrambled Eggs 19
English Breakfast 19
Jalapeño And Bacon Breakfast Pizza 19
Bread Boat Eggs 19
Spinach Eggs And Cheese 19
Cheesy Cauliflower "hash Browns" 20
Mozzarella Rolls 20
Pita And Pepperoni Pizza 20
Spinach And Mushroom Mini Quiche 20

Chapter 4: Appetizers And Snacks Recipes 21
Home-style Buffalo Chicken Wings 22
Thyme Sweet Potato Chips 22
Beef Steak Sliders 22
Crispy Paprika Chips 22
Stuffed Baby Bella Caps 22
Glazed Chicken Wings 23
Peppery Chicken Meatballs 23
Potato Chips 23
Buffalo Cauliflower Wings 23
Stuffed Jalapeno Poppers 23
Spiced Sweet Potato Fries 24
Zucchini Chips 24
Crispy Fried Pickle Chips 24
Ranch Broccoli With Cheddar 24
Roasted Jalapeño Salsa Verde 24
Garlicky Radish Chips 25
Salmon Bites With Coconut 25
Cheesy Green Dip 25
Herby Breaded Artichoke Hearts 25
Uncle's Potato Wedges 25
Mustard Pork Meatballs 26
Crab Cake Bites 26
Fried Dill Pickle Chips 26
Shrimp Pirogues 26
Middle Eastern Roasted Chickpeas 27
Bacon Tater Tots 27
Bacon-y Cauliflower Skewers 27
Bbq Chips 27
Salmon Nachos 27
Lemony Pear Chips 28
Popcorn Chicken Bites 28
Bacon With Chocolate Coating 28
Fried String Beans With Greek Sauce 28
Fried Ranch Pickles 28
Thick-crust Pepperoni Pizza 29
Barbecue Chicken Nachos 29

Cucumber Sushi 29	Ham And Cheese Sliders 31
Caponata Salsa 29	Crispy Curried Sweet Potato Fries 31
Prosciutto Mozzarella Bites 30	Garlic Spinach Dip 31
Sweet Plantain Chips 30	Cheesy Jalapeño Poppers 31
Cheesy Hash Brown Bruschetta 30	Indian Cauliflower Tikka Bites 32
Savory Sausage Balls 30	Chives Meatballs 32
Spicy Cocktail Wieners 31	Spicy Turkey Meatballs 32

Chapter 5: Vegetarians Recipes 33

Easy Cheese & Spinach Lasagna 34	Zucchini Tamale Pie 38
Eggplant Parmesan 34	Green Bean Sautée 38
Parmesan Portobello Mushroom Caps .. 34	Bell Pepper & Lentil Tacos 39
Mushroom, Zucchini And Black Bean Burgers ... 34	Rice & Bean Burritos 39
Tofu & Spinach Lasagna 35	Vegetable Burgers 39
Spiced Vegetable Galette 35	Mushroom Lasagna 39
Mushroom And Fried Onion Quesadilla 35	Layered Ravioli Bake 40
Golden Breaded Mushrooms 36	Italian-style Fried Cauliflower 40
Savory Herb Cloud Eggs 36	Pizza Dough 40
Caramelized Carrots 36	Falafels 40
Stuffed Mushrooms 36	Chewy Glazed Parsnips 40
Gourmet Wasabi Popcorn 36	Crustless Spinach And Cheese Frittata 41
Brussels Sprouts With Balsamic Oil 37	Two-cheese Grilled Sandwiches 41
Cauliflower Pizza Crust 37	Vegan Buddha Bowls(1) 41
Breadcrumbs Stuffed Mushrooms 37	Zucchini & Bell Pepper Stir-fry 41
Roasted Vegetable, Brown Rice And Black Bean Burrito 37	Curried Potato, Cauliflower And Pea Turnovers 41
Bengali Samosa With Mango Chutney 37	Portobello Mini Pizzas 42
Kale & Lentils With Crispy Onions 38	

Chapter 6: Beef, pork & Lamb Recipes 43

Italian Sausage Rolls 44	Stress-free Beef Patties 49
Moroccan-style Steak With Salad 44	Mushroom And Beef Meatloaf 49
Pork Tenderloins 44	Sun-dried Tomato Crusted Chops 50
Sriracha Pork Strips With Rice 44	Indian Fry Bread Tacos 50
Kochukaru Pork Lettuce Cups 45	Air-fried Pork With Wine Sauce 50
Garlic Beef Cubes 45	Jerk Pork Butt Pieces 51
Rib Eye Steak Seasoned With Italian Herb 45	Potato And Prosciutto Salad 51
Garlic Fillets 45	Greek-style Pork Stuffed Jalapeño Poppers 51
Beef & Mushrooms 45	Spinach And Mushroom Steak Rolls 51
Spinach And Provolone Steak Rolls 46	Montreal Steak 51
Beef Loin With Thyme And Parsley ... 46	Double Cheese & Beef Burgers 52
Beef And Mushroom Meatballs 46	Grilled Pork & Bell Pepper Salad 52
Mediterranean-style Beef Steak 46	Delectable Pork Chops 52
Cheeseburger-stuffed Bell Peppers 46	Simple Pork Chops 52
Tender Pork Ribs With Bbq Sauce 47	Breaded Pork Cutlets 52
Crumbed Golden Filet Mignon 47	Cheeseburger Sliders With Pickle Sauce 53
Balsamic Marinated Rib Eye Steak With Balsamic Fried Cipollini Onions 47	Beef And Bean Chimichangas 53
	Air Fried Grilled Steak 53
Beef Chuck With Brussels Sprouts 47	Flavorful Espresso-grilled Pork Tenderloin 53
Lemon-garlic Strip Steak 48	Garlic Beef Meatloaf 53
Crispy Lamb Shoulder Chops 48	Mustard Pork 54
Delectable Beef With Kale Pieces 48	Steak Fingers 54
Baharat Lamb Kebab With Mint Sauce 48	Pork Tenderloin With Apple Juice 54
Tacos Norteños 49	Beef Chuck Cheeseburgers 54
Chinese-style Lamb Chops 49	Sweet-and-sour Polish Sausage 54
Cheese Beef Roll 49	

Chapter 7: Poultry Recipes 55

Seasoned Chicken Breast 56	Garlic Turkey With Tomato Mix 56
Hawaiian Pineapple Chicken Kebabs 56	Spinach And Feta Chicken Meatballs 56

Chicken Wings With Lemon Pepper 57
Mushroom & Turkey Bread Pizza 57
Mexican-inspired Chicken Breasts 57
Butter And Bacon Chicken 57
Jerk Chicken Kebabs 57
Cheddar Chicken Fajitas 58
Buttermilk-fried Drumsticks 58
Sage & Paprika Turkey Cutlets 58
Spicy Pork Rind Fried Chicken 58
Crunchy Chicken Strips 59
Spicy Honey Mustard Chicken 59
Gingery Turkey Meatballs 59
Basic Chicken Breasts(2) 59
Buffalo Chicken Sandwiches 59
The Ultimate Chicken Bulgogi 59
Spicy Coconut Chicken Wings 60
Sweet Marinated Chicken Wings 60
Tuscan Stuffed Chicken 60
Chicken Wings With Sauce 61
Rich Turkey Burgers 61
Asian Meatball Tacos 61
Breaded Homestyle Chicken Strips 61
Grilled Chicken Pesto 62

Crispy Chicken Strips 62
Breaded Chicken Patties 62
Cheesy Chicken-avocado Paninis 62
Italian Chicken Parmesan 62
Crispy Chicken Nuggets With Turnip 63
Glazed Chicken Drumsticks With Herbs 63
Spiced Duck Legs 63
Crunchy Chicken And Ranch Wraps 63
Mexican Sheet Pan Dinner 64
Garlic Chicken 64
Kale & Rice Chicken Rolls 64
Katsu Chicken Thighs 64
Chicken Tenders With Veggies 65
Healthy Vegetable Patties 65
Coconut Chicken With Apricot-ginger Sauce 65
Parmesan-lemon Chicken 66
Garlic Chicken Popcorn 66
Fancy Chicken Piccata 66
Easy Asian Turkey Meatballs 66
Herb-roasted Turkey Breast 67
Chipotle Drumsticks 67
Creamy Chicken Tenders 67
Tempero Baiano Brazilian Chicken 67

Chapter 8: Fish And Seafood Recipes 68

Blackened Shrimp Tacos 69
Easy Air Fried Salmon 69
Crispy Cod Sticks 69
Fish And Vegetable Tacos 69
Healthy Salmon With Cardamom 69
Mahi Mahi With Cilantro-chili Butter 69
Fish Tacos With Hot Coleslaw 70
Lemon-roasted Salmon Fillets 70
Super Crunchy Flounder Fillets 70
Cajun Flounder Fillets 71
Snow Crab Legs 71
Garlic-lemon Steamer Clams 71
Asian Steamed Tuna 71
Potato Chip-crusted Cod 71
Fish Sticks For Kids 71
Crispy Sweet-and-sour Cod Fillets 72
Salmon On Bed Of Fennel And Carrot 72
Tuna Wraps 72
Snapper Scampi 72
Mayonnaise Salmon With Spinach 72
Air Fried Cod With Basil Vinaigrette 73
Coconut Shrimp 73
Garlic-lemon Scallops 73

Parmesan White Fish 73
Yummy White Fish 74
Crabmeat-stuffed Flounder 74
Garlic Tilapia Fillets 74
Country Shrimp "boil" 74
Great Cat Fish 75
Roasted Prawns With Firecracker Sauce 75
Typical Crab Cakes With Lemon Wedges 75
Old Bay Lobster Tails 75
Crab Rangoon 75
Timeless Garlic-lemon Scallops 76
Masala Fish 'n' Chips 76
Smoked Paprika Cod Goujons 76
Lobster Tails 76
Caribbean Skewers 76
Panko-breaded Cod Fillets 77
Quick Shrimp Scampi 77
Sea Bass With Potato Scales And Caper Aïoli 77
Outrageous Crispy Fried Salmon Skin 77
Fish Mania With Mustard 77
Blackened Catfish 78
Chili-lime Shrimp 78

Chapter 9: Vegetable Side Dishes Recipes 79

Salmon Salad With Steamboat Dressing 80
Shallots Almonds Green Beans 80
Cheese Broccoli With Basil 80
Yellow Squash And Zucchinis Dish 80
Roasted Broccoli And Red Bean Salad 80
Rutabaga Fries 81
Roasted Ratatouille Vegetables 81
Crispy Herbed Potatoes 81
Mozzarella Cabbage Wedges 81

Roasted Broccoli 81
Roasted Salsa 81
Grilled Lime Scallions 82
Golden Garlicky Mushrooms 82
Sweet And Spicy Tofu 82
Prosciutto Mini Mushroom Pizza 82
Roasted Butternut Squash With Cranberries 83
Fried Eggplant Slices 83
Stuffed Peppers With Cottage 83

Dijon Roasted Purple Potatoes 83	Stuffed Peppers 87
Glazed Carrots 84	Fried Brussel Sprouts 87
Beef Stuffed Bell Peppers 84	Kidney Beans Oatmeal In Peppers 87
Garlic Parmesan–roasted Cauliflower 84	Moroccan Cauliflower 87
Potato Wedges 84	Asparagus Wrapped In Pancetta 87
Roasted Potatoes And Asparagus 84	Swiss Vegetable Casserole 87
Crunchy Roasted Potatoes 85	Turmeric Cauliflower Rice 88
Baked Shishito Peppers 85	Green Beans And New Potatoes 88
Pork Tenderloin Salad 85	Roasted Bell Peppers 88
Stuffed Bell Peppers With Mayonnaise 85	Garlic-parmesan Popcorn 88
Roasted Fennel Salad 85	Smashed Fried Baby Potatoes 88
Ricotta & Broccoli Cannelloni 86	Easy Homemade Veggie Burger 89
Mint Lemon Squash 86	Sweet Corn Fritters With Avocado 89
Sweet Butternut Squash 86	Garlicky Vegetable Rainbow Fritters 89
Healthy Caprese Salad 86	Roasted Asparagus 89
Lush Vegetables Roast 86	Cheese Spinach 90

Chapter 10: Desserts And Sweets Recipes **91**

Cherry Cheesecake Rolls 92	Maple Cinnamon Cheesecake 96
Fudgy Chocolate Brownies 92	Berry Tacos 97
Pecan Snowball Cookies 92	Rustic Berry Layer Cake 97
Pineapple Chips With Cinnamon 92	Strawberry Pastry Rolls 97
Fruity Oatmeal Crisp 92	Healthy Berry Crumble 97
Apple-blueberry Hand Pies 93	Lava Cakes 98
Cheese Muffins With Cinnamon 93	Peanut Butter-banana Roll-ups 98
Strawberry Donuts 93	Vanilla Cupcakes With Chocolate Chips 98
Black Forest Pies 93	Enticing Grain-free Cakes 98
Lemony Apple Butter 94	Almond Pecan Muffins 99
Pineapple Galette 94	Marshmallow Pastries 99
Oreo-coated Peanut Butter Cups 94	Cinnamon And Pecan Pie 99
Gingerbread 94	Vanilla Butter Cake 99
Enticing Cappuccino Muffins 95	Blueberry Vanilla Muffins 100
Cinnamon Almonds 95	Mango Cobbler With Raspberries 100
Eggless & Vegan Cake 95	Black And Blue Clafoutis 100
Orange-chocolate Cake 95	Coconut-custard Pie 101
Wild Blueberry Sweet Empanadas 96	Party S´mores 101
Hot Coconut 'n Cocoa Buns 96	Strawberry-rhubarb Crumble 101
Creamy Cheesecake Bites 96	Vanilla Coconut Pie 101

Recipes Index **102**

Chapter 1: Introduction

The Air Fryer has emerged as a culinary game-changer, revolutionizing the way we prepare and enjoy our favorite dishes. With its unique blend of history, benefits, features, usage tips, and maintenance guidelines, the Air Fryer has become an essential appliance in kitchens worldwide.

History of the Air Fryer

The concept of air frying can be traced back to the early 2000s when kitchen appliance manufacturers began exploring healthier alternatives to traditional deep frying. The desire to reduce oil consumption and create lighter, yet still delicious, versions of fried foods was the driving force behind the invention of the Air Fryer.

The technology behind the Air Fryer is based on convection cooking, which uses hot air circulation to cook food quickly and evenly. This innovative approach was developed as a response to the increasing health consciousness of consumers who sought to enjoy the crispiness and flavors of fried foods without the excess oil and calories.

Over the years, various companies have refined and perfected the Air Fryer, making it more accessible to households. Today, it has become a kitchen staple, enabling home cooks to prepare a wide range of dishes with a fraction of the oil traditionally used in frying.

Benefits of the Air Fryer

The Air Fryer offers a multitude of advantages that cater to modern lifestyles and health-conscious consumers:

1. **Healthier Cooking:** Perhaps the most prominent benefit, the Air Fryer allows you to enjoy crispy and delicious fried foods with significantly less oil, reducing the intake of unhealthy fats and calories.
2. **Time Efficiency:** With its rapid hot air circulation, the Air Fryer cooks food faster than conventional ovens, making it a time-saving solution for busy individuals and families.
3. **Versatility:** Beyond air frying, many Air Fryer models can roast, bake, grill, and even reheat food, providing a versatile cooking experience in a single appliance.
4. **Energy Efficiency:** The Air Fryer consumes less energy compared to traditional ovens, contributing to reduced electricity bills and environmental sustainability.
5. **Crispy Results:** The high-temperature cooking capability of the Air Fryer ensures that food comes out crispy on the outside while remaining tender on the inside.
6. **Ease of Use:** Most Air Fryers feature user-friendly digital controls and pre-set cooking programs, making them accessible to cooks of all skill levels.

Features of the Air Fryer

The Air Fryer is equipped with a range of features that make it a must-have in modern kitchens:

- **Temperature Control:** Adjustable temperature settings allow you to fine-tune the cooking process for different recipes, ensuring optimal results.
- **Timer Function:** A timer function allows you to set precise cooking times, preventing overcooking or burning.
- **Cooking Basket:** The cooking basket, often with a non-stick coating, holds the food and allows hot air to circulate evenly for consistent cooking.
- **Digital Interface:** Many Air Fryers feature a digital display and intuitive controls for easy operation.
- **Pre-Set Programs:** Some models come with

Air Fryer Cookbook for Beginners

pre-set cooking programs for popular dishes, simplifying the cooking process.

Tips for Using the Air Fryer

To maximize your Air Fryer's potential, consider the following tips:

Preheat: Preheat your Air Fryer for a few minutes before adding food to ensure even cooking and crispy results.

1. **Don't Overcrowd:** Avoid overcrowding the cooking basket to allow proper air circulation and ensure even cooking.
2. **Shake or Flip:** Shake the basket or flip food halfway through cooking to ensure uniform browning and crispiness.
3. **Oil Application:** Use a spray bottle to lightly coat food with oil, or apply oil sparingly with a brush to achieve the desired level of crispiness.
4. **Experiment:** Don't hesitate to experiment with different recipes, cooking times, and temperatures to find your preferred results.

Cleaning and Maintenance of the Air Fryer

Proper cleaning and maintenance are crucial to prolong the life of your Air Fryer:

- **Regular Cleaning:** After each use, allow the Air Fryer to cool, then remove the cooking basket and other removable components for cleaning. Many parts are dishwasher-safe for easy cleanup.
- **Exterior Cleaning:** Wipe down the exterior of the Air Fryer with a damp cloth to remove any grease or residue.
- **Air Vent Maintenance:** Check and clean the air vents to ensure proper air circulation, which is essential for efficient cooking.
- **Storage:** Store your Air Fryer in a dry place when not in use to prevent dust and debris from accumulating.

In conclusion, the Air Fryer has emerged as a transformative kitchen appliance, offering a healthier and more convenient way to enjoy fried foods and a wide range of other dishes. With its numerous benefits, versatile features, and straightforward usage and maintenance guidelines, the Air Fryer has earned its place as a staple in modern kitchens. Discover the joy of cooking with less oil, reduced cooking times, and delicious results by adding an Air Fryer to your culinary repertoire.

Chapter 2: Measurement Conversions

BASIC KITCHEN CONVERSIONS & EQUIVALENTS

DRY MEASUREMENTS CONVERSION CHART
3 TEASPOONS = 1 TABLESPOON = 1/16 CUP
6 TEASPOONS = 2 TABLESPOONS = 1/8 CUP
12 TEASPOONS = 4 TABLESPOONS = 1/4 CUP
24 TEASPOONS = 8 TABLESPOONS = 1/2 CUP
36 TEASPOONS = 12 TABLESPOONS = 3/4 CUP
48 TEASPOONS = 16 TABLESPOONS = 1 CUP

METRIC TO US COOKING CONVERSIONS
OVEN TEMPERATURES
120 °C = 250 °F
160 °C = 320 °F
180° C = 360 °F
205 °C = 400 °F
220 °C = 425 °F

LIQUID MEASUREMENTS CONVERSION CHART
8 FLUID OUNCES = 1 CUP = 1/2 PINT = 1/4 QUART
16 FLUID OUNCES = 2 CUPS = 1 PINT = 1/2 QUART
32 FLUID OUNCES = 4 CUPS = 2 PINTS = 1 QUART = 1/4 GALLON
128 FLUID OUNCES = 16 CUPS = 8 PINTS = 4 QUARTS
= 1 GALLON

BAKING IN GRAMS
1 CUP FLOUR = 140 GRAMS
1 CUP SUGAR = 150 GRAMS
1 CUP POWDERED SUGAR = 160 GRAMS
1 CUP HEAVY CREAM = 235 GRAMS

VOLUME
1 MILLILITER = 1/5 TEASPOON
5 ML = 1 TEASPOON
15 ML = 1 TABLESPOON
240 ML = 1 CUP OR 8 FLUID OUNCES
1 LITER = 34 FL. OUNCES

WEIGHT
1 GRAM = .035 OUNCES
100 GRAMS = 3.5 OUNCES
500 GRAMS = 1.1 POUNDS
1 KILOGRAM = 35 OUNCES

US TO METRIC COOKING CONVERSIONS
1/5 TSP = 1 ML
1 TSP = 5 ML
1 TBSP = 15 ML
1 FL OUNCE = 30 ML
1 CUP = 237 ML
1 PINT (2 CUPS) = 473 ML
1 QUART (4 CUPS) = .95 LITER
1 GALLON (16 CUPS) = 3.8 LITERS
1 OZ = 28 GRAMS
1 POUND = 454 GRAMS

BUTTER
1 CUP BUTTER = 2 STICKS = 8 OUNCES = 230 GRAMS = 8 TABLESPOONS

WHAT DOES 1 CUP EQUAL
1 CUP = 8 FLUID OUNCES
1 CUP = 16 TABLESPOONS
1 CUP = 48 TEASPOONS
1 CUP = 1/2 PINT
1 CUP = 1/4 QUART
1 CUP = 1/16 GALLON
1 CUP = 240 ML

BAKING PAN CONVERSIONS
1 CUP ALL-PURPOSE FLOUR = 4.5 OZ
1 CUP ROLLED OATS = 3 OZ 1 LARGE EGG = 1.7 OZ
1 CUP BUTTER = 8 OZ 1 CUP MILK = 8 OZ
1 CUP HEAVY CREAM = 8.4 OZ
1 CUP GRANULATED SUGAR = 7.1 OZ
1 CUP PACKED BROWN SUGAR = 7.75 OZ
1 CUP VEGETABLE OIL = 7.7 OZ
1 CUP UNSIFTED POWDERED SUGAR = 4.4 OZ

BAKING PAN CONVERSIONS
9-INCH ROUND CAKE PAN = 12 CUPS
10-INCH TUBE PAN =16 CUPS
11-INCH BUNDT PAN = 12 CUPS
9-INCH SPRINGFORM PAN = 10 CUPS
9 X 5 INCH LOAF PAN = 8 CUPS
9-INCH SQUARE PAN = 8 CUPS

Chapter 3: Bread And Breakfast Recipes

Avocado Tempura

Servings: 4
Cooking Time: 20 Minutes
Ingredients:
- ½ cup breadcrumbs
- ½ tsp. salt
- 1 Haas avocado, pitted, peeled and sliced
- Liquid from 1 can white beans or aquafaba

Directions:
1. Set your Air Fryer to 350°F and allow to warm.
2. Mix the breadcrumbs and salt in a shallow bowl until well-incorporated.
3. Dip the avocado slices in the bean/aquafaba juice, then into the breadcrumbs. Put the avocados in the fryer, taking care not to overlap any slices, and fry for 10 minutes, giving the basket a good shake at the halfway point.

Easy Corn Dog Cupcakes

Servings: 6
Cooking Time: 30 Minutes
Ingredients:
- 1 cup cornbread Mix
- 2 tsp granulated sugar
- Salt to taste
- 3/4 cup cream cheese
- 3 tbsp butter, melted
- 1 egg
- ¼ cup minced onions
- 1 tsp dried parsley
- 2 beef hot dogs, sliced and cut into half-moons

Directions:
1. Preheat air fryer at 350°F. Combine cornbread, sugar, and salt in a bowl. In another bowl, whisk cream cheese, parsley, butter, and egg. Pour wet ingredients to dry ingredients and toss to combine. Fold in onion and hot dog pieces. Transfer it into 8 greased silicone cupcake liners. Place it in the frying basket and Bake for 8-10 minutes. Serve right away.

Carrot Orange Muffins

Servings: 12
Cooking Time: 12 Minutes
Ingredients:
- 1½ cups all-purpose flour
- ½ cup granulated sugar
- ½ teaspoon ground cinnamon
- 2 teaspoons baking powder
- ¼ teaspoon baking soda
- ½ teaspoon salt
- 2 large eggs
- ¼ cup vegetable oil
- ⅓ cup orange marmalade
- 2 cups grated carrots

Directions:
1. Preheat the air fryer to 320°F.
2. In a large bowl, whisk together the flour, sugar, cinnamon, baking powder, baking soda, and salt; set aside.
3. In a separate bowl, whisk together the eggs, vegetable oil, orange marmalade, and grated carrots.
4. Make a well in the dry ingredients; then pour the wet ingredients into the well of the dry ingredients. Using a rubber spatula, mix the ingredients for 1 minute or until slightly lumpy.
5. Using silicone muffin liners, fill 6 muffin liners two-thirds full.
6. Carefully place the muffin liners in the air fryer basket and bake for 12 minutes (or until the tops are browned and a toothpick inserted in the center comes out clean). Carefully remove the muffins from the basket and repeat with remaining batter.
7. Serve warm.

Black's Bangin' Casserole

Servings: 4
Cooking Time: 40 Minutes
Ingredients:
- 5 eggs
- 3 tbsp chunky tomato sauce
- 2 tbsp heavy cream
- 2 tbsp grated parmesan cheese

Directions:
1. Preheat your fryer to 350°F
2. Combine the eggs and cream in a bowl.
3. Mix in the tomato sauce and add the cheese.
4. Spread into a glass baking dish and bake for 25-35 minutes.
5. Top with extra cheese.
6. Enjoy!

Ham And Cheddar Gritters

Servings: 6
Cooking Time: 12 Minutes
Ingredients:
- 4 cups water
- 1 cup quick-cooking grits
- ¼ teaspoon salt
- 2 tablespoons butter
- 2 cups grated Cheddar cheese, divided
- 1 cup finely diced ham
- 1 tablespoon chopped chives
- salt and freshly ground black pepper
- 1 egg, beaten
- 2 cups panko breadcrumbs
- vegetable oil

Directions:
1. Bring the water to a boil in a saucepan. Whisk in the grits and ¼ teaspoon of salt, and cook for 7 minutes until the grits are soft. Remove the pan from the heat and stir in the butter and 1 cup of the grated Cheddar cheese. Transfer the grits to a bowl and let them cool for just 10 to 15 minutes.

2. Stir the ham, chives and the rest of the cheese into the grits and season with salt and pepper to taste. Add the beaten egg and refrigerate the mixture for 30 minutes. (Try not to chill the grits much longer than 30 minutes, or the mixture will be too firm to shape into patties.)
3. While the grit mixture is chilling, make the country gravy and set it aside.
4. Place the panko breadcrumbs in a shallow dish. Measure out ¼-cup portions of the grits mixture and shape them into patties. Coat all sides of the patties with the panko breadcrumbs, patting them with your hands so the crumbs adhere to the patties. You should have about 16 patties. Spray both sides of the patties with oil.
5. Preheat the air fryer to 400°F.
6. In batches of 5 or 6, air-fry the fritters for 8 minutes. Using a flat spatula, flip the fritters over and air-fry for another 4 minutes.
7. Serve hot with country gravy.

Thyme Beef & Eggs

Servings: 1
Cooking Time: 25 Minutes
Ingredients:
- 2 tbsp butter
- 1 rosemary sprig
- 2 garlic cloves, pressed
- 8 oz sirloin steak
- Salt and pepper to taste
- ⅛ tsp cayenne pepper
- 2 eggs
- 1 tsp dried thyme

Directions:
1. Preheat air fryer to 400°F. On a clean cutting board, place butter and half of the rosemary spring in the center. Set aside. Season both sides of the steak with salt, black pepper, thyme, pressed garlic, and cayenne pepper. Transfer the steak to the frying basket and top with the other half of the rosemary sprig. Cook for 4 minutes, then flip the steak. Cook for another 3 minutes.
2. Remove the steak and set it on top of the butter and rosemary sprig on the cutter board. Tent with foil and let it rest. Grease ramekin and crack both eggs into it. Season with salt and pepper. Transfer the ramekin to the frying basket and bake for 4-5 minutes until the egg white is cooked and set. Remove the foil from the steak and slice. Serve with eggs and enjoy.

Buttery Scallops

Servings: 2
Cooking Time: 8 Minutes
Ingredients:
- 1 lb jumbo scallops
- 1 tbsp fresh lemon juice
- 2 tbsp butter, melted

Directions:
1. Preheat the air fryer to 400°F.
2. In a small bowl, mix together lemon juice and butter.
3. Brush scallops with lemon juice and butter mixture and place into the air fryer basket.
4. Cook scallops for 4 minutes. Turn halfway through.
5. Again brush scallops with lemon butter mixture and cook for 4 minutes more. Turn halfway through.
6. Serve and enjoy.

Ham And Egg Toast Cups

Servings: 2
Cooking Time: 5 Minutes
Ingredients:
- 2 eggs
- 2 slices of ham
- 2 tablespoons butter
- Cheddar cheese, for topping
- Salt, to taste
- Black pepper, to taste

Directions:
1. Preheat the Air fryer to 400°F and grease both ramekins with melted butter.
2. Place each ham slice in the greased ramekins and crack each egg over ham slices.
3. Sprinkle with salt, black pepper and cheddar cheese and transfer into the Air fryer basket.
4. Cook for about 5 minutes and remove the ramekins from the basket.
5. Serve warm.

Puffed Egg Tarts

Servings: 4
Cooking Time: 42 Minutes
Ingredients:
- 1 sheet frozen puff pastry half, thawed and cut into 4 squares
- ¾ cup Monterey Jack cheese, shredded and divided
- 4 large eggs
- 1 tablespoon fresh parsley, minced
- 1 tablespoon olive oil

Directions:
1. Preheat the Air fryer to 390°F
2. Place 2 pastry squares in the air fryer basket and cook for about 10 minutes.
3. Remove Air fryer basket from the Air fryer and press each square gently with a metal tablespoon to form an indentation.
4. Place 3 tablespoons of cheese in each hole and top with 1 egg each.
5. Return Air fryer basket to Air fryer and cook for about 11 minutes.
6. Remove tarts from the Air fryer basket and sprinkle with half the parsley.
7. Repeat with remaining pastry squares, cheese and eggs.
8. Dish out and serve warm.

Spinach Bacon Spread

Servings: 4
Cooking Time: 10 Minutes
Ingredients:
- 2 tablespoons coconut cream
- 3 cups spinach leaves

- 2 tablespoons cilantro
- 2 tablespoons bacon, cooked and crumbled
- Salt and black pepper to the taste

Directions:
1. Combine coconut cream, spinach leaves, salt, and black pepper in a suitable baking pan.
2. Transfer the baking pan into your air fryer and cook at 360 degrees F/ 180 degrees C for 10 minutes.
3. When cooked, transfer to a blender and pulse well.
4. To serve, sprinkle the bacon on the top of the mixture.

Simple Cinnamon Toasts

Servings: 4
Cooking Time: 4 Minutes
Ingredients:
- 1 tablespoon salted butter
- 2 teaspoons ground cinnamon
- 4 tablespoons sugar
- ½ teaspoon vanilla extract
- 10 bread slices

Directions:
1. Preheat the air fryer to 380ºF (193ºC).
2. In a bowl, combine the butter, cinnamon, sugar, and vanilla extract. Spread onto the slices of bread.
3. Put the bread inside the air fryer and bake for 4 minutes or until golden brown.
4. Serve warm.

Classic Hash Browns

Servings: 4
Cooking Time: 20 Minutes
Ingredients:
- 4 russet potatoes
- 1 teaspoon paprika
- Salt
- Pepper
- Cooking oil

Directions:
1. Peel the potatoes using a vegetable peeler. Using a cheese grater, shred the potatoes. If your grater has different-size holes, use the area of the tool with the largest holes.
2. Place the shredded potatoes in a large bowl of cold water. Let sit for 5 minutes. Cold water helps remove excess starch from the potatoes. Stir to help dissolve the starch.
3. Drain the potatoes and dry with paper towels or napkins. Make sure the potatoes are completely dry.
4. Season the potatoes with the paprika and salt and pepper to taste.
5. Spray the potatoes with cooking oil and transfer them to the air fryer. Cook for 20 minutes, shaking the basket every 5 minutes (a total of 4 times).
6. Cool before serving.

Breakfast Frittata

Servings: 2
Cooking Time: 25 Minutes
Ingredients:
- 4 cooked pancetta slices, chopped
- 5 eggs
- Salt and pepper to taste
- ½ leek, thinly sliced
- ½ cup grated cheddar cheese
- 1 tomato, sliced
- 1 cup iceberg lettuce, torn
- 2 tbsp milk

Directions:
1. Preheat air fryer to 320ºF. Beat the eggs, milk, salt, and pepper in a bowl. Mix in pancetta and cheddar. Transfer to a greased with olive oil baking pan. Top with tomato slices and leek and place it in the frying basket. Bake for 14 minutes. Let cool for 5 minutes. Serve with lettuce.

Favorite Blueberry Muffins

Servings: 8
Cooking Time: 25 Minutes
Ingredients:
- 1 cup all-purpose flour
- ½ tsp baking soda
- 1/3 cup granulated sugar
- ¼ tsp salt
- 1 tbsp lemon juice
- 1 tsp lemon zest
- ¼ cup milk
- ½ tsp vanilla extract
- 1 egg
- 1 tbsp vegetable oil
- ¼ cup halved blueberries
- 1 tbsp powdered sugar

Directions:
1. Preheat air fryer at 375ºF. Combine dry ingredients in a bowl. Mix ¼ cup of fresh milk with 1 tsp of lemon juice and leave for 10 minutes. Put it in another bowl with the wet ingredients. Pour wet ingredients into dry ingredients and gently toss to combine. Fold in blueberries. Spoon mixture into 8 greased silicone cupcake liners and Bake them in the fryer for 6-8 minutes. Let cool onto a cooling rack. Serve right away sprinkled with powdered sugar.

Banana-blackberry Muffins

Servings: 6
Cooking Time: 20 Minutes
Ingredients:
- 1 ripe banana, mashed
- ½ cup milk
- 1 tsp apple cider vinegar
- 1 tsp vanilla extract
- 2 tbsp ground flaxseed
- 2 tbsp coconut sugar
- ¾ cup flour
- 1 tsp baking powder
- ½ tsp baking soda

- ¾ cup blackberries

Directions:
1. Preheat air fryer to 350°F. Place the banana in a bowl. Stir in milk, apple vinegar, vanilla extract, flaxseed, and coconut sugar until combined. In another bowl, combine flour, baking powder, and baking soda. Pour it into the banana mixture and toss to combine. Divide the batter between 6 muffin molds and top each with blackberries, pressing slightly. Bake for 16 minutes until golden brown and a toothpick comes out clean. Serve cooled.

Cream Cheese Danish

Servings: 4
Cooking Time: 10 Minutes
Ingredients:
- 1 sheet frozen puff pastry dough, thawed
- 1 large egg, beaten
- 4 ounces full-fat cream cheese, softened
- ¼ cup confectioners' sugar
- 1 teaspoon vanilla extract
- ½ teaspoon lemon juice

Directions:
1. Preheat the air fryer to 320°F.
2. Unfold puff pastry and cut into four equal squares. For each pastry, fold all four corners partway to the center, leaving a 1" square in the center.
3. Brush egg evenly over folded puff pastry.
4. In a medium bowl, mix cream cheese, confectioners' sugar, vanilla, and lemon juice. Scoop 2 tablespoons of mixture into the center of each pastry square.
5. Place danishes directly in the air fryer basket and cook 10 minutes until puffy and golden brown. Cool 5 minutes before serving.

Crispy Fish Sticks

Servings: 4
Cooking Time: 10 Minutes
Ingredients:
- 8 ounces cod fillet
- 1 egg, beaten
- ¼ cup coconut flour
- ¼ teaspoon ground coriander
- ¼ teaspoon ground paprika
- ¼ teaspoon ground cumin
- ¼ teaspoon Pink salt
- ⅓ cup coconut flakes
- 1 tablespoon mascarpone
- 1 teaspoon heavy cream
- Cooking spray

Directions:
1. Roughly chop the cod fillet. Then transfer into a blender.
2. Place in coconut flour, paprika, cumin, egg, salt, and ground coriander. Then mix the mixture together until smooth.
3. Then place the mixture into a bowl.
4. Place the fish mixture onto lined parchment paper and then shape into flat square.
5. Cut the square into sticks.
6. Whisk mascarpone and heavy cream together in a separate bowl.
7. Sprinkle the fish sticks with the mascarpone mixture and coat with coconut flakes.
8. At 400 degrees F/ 205 degrees C, heat your air fryer in advance.
9. Using cooking spray, spray the air fryer basket.
10. Place the fish sticks evenly inside the air fryer basket.
11. Cook the fish sticks in the preheated air fryer for 10 minutes.
12. Halfway through cooking, flip the fish sticks to the other side.
13. When cooked, remove from the air fryer and serve with your favorite dip.

Asparagus And Bell Pepper Strata

Servings: 4
Cooking Time: 14 To 20 Minutes
Ingredients:
- 8 large asparagus spears, trimmed and cut into 2-inch pieces
- ⅓ cup shredded carrot (see Tip)
- ½ cup chopped red bell pepper
- 2 slices low-sodium whole-wheat bread, cut into ½-inch cubes
- 3 egg whites
- 1 egg
- 3 tablespoons 1 percent milk
- ½ teaspoon dried thyme

Directions:
1. In a 6-by-2-inch pan, combine the asparagus, carrot, red bell pepper, and 1 tablespoon of water. Bake in the air fryer for 3 to 5 minutes, or until crisp-tender. Drain well.
2. Add the bread cubes to the vegetables and gently toss.
3. In a medium bowl, whisk the egg whites, egg, milk, and thyme until frothy.
4. Pour the egg mixture into the pan. Bake for 11 to 15 minutes, or until the strata is slightly puffy and set and the top starts to brown. Serve.

Western Frittata

Servings: 1
Cooking Time: 19 Minutes
Ingredients:
- ½ red or green bell pepper, cut into ½-inch chunks
- 1 teaspoon olive oil
- 3 eggs, beaten
- ¼ cup grated Cheddar cheese
- ¼ cup diced cooked ham
- salt and freshly ground black pepper, to taste
- 1 teaspoon butter
- 1 teaspoon chopped fresh parsley

Directions:

1. Preheat the air fryer to 400°F.
2. Toss the peppers with the olive oil and air-fry for 6 minutes, shaking the basket once or twice during the cooking process to redistribute the ingredients.
3. While the vegetables are cooking, beat the eggs well in a bowl, stir in the Cheddar cheese and ham, and season with salt and freshly ground black pepper. Add the air-fried peppers to this bowl when they have finished cooking.
4. Place a 6- or 7-inch non-stick metal cake pan into the air fryer basket with the butter using an aluminum sling to lower the pan into the basket. (Fold a piece of aluminum foil into a strip about 2-inches wide by 24-inches long.) Air-fry for 1 minute at 380°F to melt the butter. Remove the cake pan and rotate the pan to distribute the butter and grease the pan. Pour the egg mixture into the cake pan and return the pan to the air fryer, using the aluminum sling.
5. Air-fry at 380°F for 12 minutes, or until the frittata has puffed up and is lightly browned. Let the frittata sit in the air fryer for 5 minutes to cool to an edible temperature and set up. Remove the cake pan from the air fryer, sprinkle with parsley and serve immediately.

Cheesy Mustard Toasts

Servings: 4
Cooking Time: 15 Minutes
Ingredients:
- 4 bread slices
- 2 tablespoons cheddar cheese, shredded
- 2 eggs, whites and yolks, separated
- 1 tablespoon mustard
- 1 tablespoon paprika

Directions:
1. Set the temperature of Air Fryer to 355°F.
2. Place the bread slices in an Air fryer basket.
3. Air Fry for about 5 minutes or until toasted.
4. Add the egg whites in a clean glass bowl and beat until they form soft peaks.
5. In another bowl, mix together the cheese, egg yolks, mustard, and paprika.
6. Gently, fold in the egg whites.
7. Spread the mustard mixture over the toasted bread slices.
8. Air Fry for about 10 minutes.
9. Serve warm!

Potato Bread Rolls

Servings: 5
Cooking Time: 20 Minutes
Ingredients:
- 5 large potatoes, boiled and mashed
- Salt and ground black pepper, to taste
- ½ teaspoon mustard seeds
- 1 tablespoon olive oil
- 2 small onions, chopped
- 2 sprigs curry leaves
- ½ teaspoon turmeric powder
- 2 green chilis, seeded and chopped
- 1 bunch coriander, chopped
- 8 slices bread, brown sides discarded

Directions:
1. Preheat the air fryer to 400°F (204°C).
2. Put the mashed potatoes in a bowl and sprinkle on salt and pepper. Set to one side.
3. Fry the mustard seeds in olive oil over a medium-low heat in a skillet, stirring continuously, until they sputter.
4. Add the onions and cook until they turn translucent. Add the curry leaves and turmeric powder and stir. Cook for a further 2 minutes until fragrant.
5. Remove the pan from the heat and combine with the potatoes. Mix in the green chilies and coriander.
6. Wet the bread slightly and drain of any excess liquid.
7. Spoon a small amount of the potato mixture into the center of the bread and enclose the bread around the filling, sealing it entirely. Continue until the rest of the bread and filling is used up. Brush each bread roll with some oil and transfer to the basket of the air fryer.
8. Air fry for 15 minutes, gently shaking the air fryer basket at the halfway point to ensure each roll is cooked evenly.
9. Serve immediately.

Breakfast Burrito With Sausage

Servings: 6
Cooking Time: 35 Minutes
Ingredients:
- 2 tbsp olive oil
- Salt and pepper to taste
- 6 eggs, beaten
- ½ chopped red bell pepper
- ½ chopped green bell pepper
- 1 onion, finely chopped
- 8 oz chicken sausage
- ½ cup salsa
- 6 flour tortillas
- ½ cup grated cheddar

Directions:
1. Warm the olive oil in a skillet over medium heat. Add the eggs and stir-fry them for 2-3 minutes until scrambled. Season with salt and pepper and set aside.
2. Sauté the bell peppers and onion in the same skillet for 2-3 minutes until tender. Add and brown the chicken sausage, breaking into small pieces with a wooden spoon, about 4 minutes. Return the scrambled eggs and stir in the salsa. Remove the skillet from heat. Divide the mixture between the tortillas. Fold up the top and bottom edges, then roll to fully enclose the filling. Secure with toothpicks. Spritz with cooking spray.
3. Preheat air fryer to 400°F. Bake the burritos in the air fryer for 10 minutes, turning them once halfway through cooking until crisp. Garnish with cheddar cheese. Serve.

Air Fryer Cookbook for Beginners

Simple Cherry Tarts

Servings: 6
Cooking Time: 10 Minutes
Ingredients:
- For the tarts:
- 2 refrigerated piecrusts
- ⅓ cup cherry preserves
- 1 teaspoon cornstarch
- Cooking oil
- For the frosting:
- ½ cup vanilla yogurt
- 1 ounce cream cheese
- 1 teaspoon stevia
- Rainbow sprinkles

Directions:
1. Place the piecrusts on a flat surface. Make use of a knife or pizza cutter, cut each piecrust into 3 rectangles, for 6 in total. I discard the unused dough left from slicing the edges.
2. In a suitable bowl, combine the preserves and cornstarch. Mix well.
3. Scoop 1 tablespoon of the preserve mixture onto the top ½ of each piece of piecrust.
4. Fold the bottom of each piece up to close the tart.
5. Press along the edges of each tart to seal using the back of a fork.
6. Sprinkle the breakfast tarts with cooking oil and place them in the air fryer.
7. Cook for almost 10 minutes
8. Allow the breakfast tarts to cool fully before removing from the air fryer.
9. To make the frosting:
10. In a suitable bowl, mix the yogurt, cream cheese, and stevia. Mix well.
11. Spread the breakfast tarts with frosting and top with sprinkles, and serve.

Zucchini Muffins With Cinnamon

Servings: 8
Cooking Time: 20 Minutes
Ingredients:
- 6 eggs
- 4 drops stevia
- ¼ cup Swerve
- ⅓ cup coconut oil, melted
- 1 cup zucchini, grated
- ¾ cup coconut flour
- ¼ teaspoon ground nutmeg
- 1 teaspoon ground cinnamon
- ½ teaspoon baking soda

Directions:
1. At 325 degrees F/ 160 degrees C, preheat your air fryer.
2. Add all the recipe ingredients except zucchini in a suitable bowl and mix well.
3. Add zucchini and stir well.
4. Pour batter into the silicone muffin molds and place into the air fryer basket.
5. Cook muffins for 20 minutes.
6. Serve and enjoy.

Cinnamon Rolls With Cream Cheese Glaze

Servings: 8
Cooking Time: 9 Minutes
Ingredients:
- 1 pound frozen bread dough, thawed
- ¼ cup butter, melted and cooled
- ¾ cup brown sugar
- 1½ tablespoons ground cinnamon
- Cream Cheese Glaze:
- 4 ounces cream cheese, softened
- 2 tablespoons butter, softened
- 1¼ cups powdered sugar
- ½ teaspoon vanilla

Directions:
1. Let the bread dough come to room temperature on the counter. On a lightly floured surface roll the dough into a 13-inch by 11-inch rectangle. Position the rectangle so the 13-inch side is facing you. Brush the melted butter all over the dough, leaving a 1-inch border uncovered along the edge farthest away from you.
2. Combine the brown sugar and cinnamon in a small bowl. Sprinkle the mixture evenly over the buttered dough, keeping the 1-inch border uncovered. Roll the dough into a log starting with the edge closest to you. Roll the dough tightly, making sure to roll evenly and push out any air pockets. When you get to the uncovered edge of the dough, press the dough onto the roll to seal it together.
3. Cut the log into 8 pieces slicing slowly with a sawing motion so you don't flatten the dough. Turn the slices on their sides and cover with a clean kitchen towel. Let the rolls sit in the warmest part of your kitchen for 1½ to 2 hours to rise.
4. To make the glaze, place the cream cheese and butter in a microwave-safe bowl. Soften the mixture in the microwave for 30 seconds at a time until it is easy to stir. Gradually add the powdered sugar and stir to combine. Add the vanilla extract and whisk until smooth. Set aside.
5. When the rolls have risen, Preheat the air fryer to 350°F.
6. Transfer 4 of the rolls to the air fryer basket. Air-fry for 5 minutes. Turn the rolls over and air-fry for another 4 minutes. Repeat with the remaining 4 rolls.
7. Let the rolls cool for a couple of minutes before glazing. Spread large dollops of cream cheese glaze on top of the warm cinnamon rolls, allowing some of the glaze to drip down the side of the rolls. Serve warm and enjoy!

Hash Browns

Servings: 2
Cooking Time: 30 Minutes
Ingredients:
- 2 large russet potatoes, peeled
- 2 cups cold water
- 1 tablespoon olive oil
- ½ teaspoon salt

Directions:
1. Grate potatoes into a bowl filled with cold water. Let soak 10 minutes. Drain into a colander, then press into paper towels to remove excess moisture.
2. Dry the bowl and return potatoes to it. Toss with oil and salt.
3. Preheat the air fryer to 375°F. Spray a 6" round cake pan with cooking spray.
4. Pour potatoes into prepared pan, pressing them down.
5. Cook 20 minutes until brown and crispy. Serve warm.

Not-so-english Muffins

Servings: 4
Cooking Time: 10 Minutes
Ingredients:
- 2 strips turkey bacon, cut in half crosswise
- 2 whole-grain English muffins, split
- 1 cup fresh baby spinach, long stems removed
- ¼ ripe pear, peeled and thinly sliced
- 4 slices Provolone cheese

Directions:
1. Place bacon strips in air fryer basket and cook for 2 minutes. Check and separate strips if necessary so they cook evenly. Cook for 4 more minutes, until crispy. Remove and drain on paper towels.
2. Place split muffin halves in air fryer basket and cook at 390°F for 2 minutes, just until lightly browned.
3. Open air fryer and top each muffin with a quarter of the baby spinach, several pear slices, a strip of bacon, and a slice of cheese.
4. Cook at 360°F for 2 minutes, until cheese completely melts.

Herbed Omelet

Servings: 4
Cooking Time: 20 Minutes
Ingredients:
- 10 eggs, whisked
- ½ cup cheddar, shredded
- 2 tablespoons parsley, chopped
- 2 tablespoons chives, chopped
- 2 tablespoons basil, chopped
- Cooking spray
- Salt and black pepper to the taste

Directions:
1. Mix all ingredients except the cheese and the cooking spray together in a bowl until whisked well.
2. Before cooking, heat your air fryer to 350 degrees F/ 175 degrees C.
3. Grease the baking pan with cooking spray.
4. Pour the egg mixture inside the pan.
5. Cook in your air fryer for 20 minutes.
6. Serve on plates.

Yummy Bagel Breakfast

Servings: 5-6
Cooking Time: 6 Minutes
Ingredients:
- 2 bagels, make halves
- 4 teaspoons butter

Directions:
1. On a flat kitchen surface, plug your air fryer and turn it on.
2. Preheat your air fryer for about 4-5 minutes to 370 degrees F/ 185 degrees C.
3. Gently coat your air frying basket with cooking oil or spray.
4. Place the bagels to the basket.
5. Transfer the basket in the air fryer. Let it cook for the next 3 minutes.
6. Remove the basket; spread the butter over the bagels and cook for 3 more minutes.
7. Serve warm!

Chocolate Chip Scones

Servings: 8
Cooking Time: 15 Minutes
Ingredients:
- ½ cup cold salted butter, divided
- 2 cups all-purpose flour
- ½ cup brown sugar
- ½ teaspoon baking powder
- 1 large egg
- ¾ cup buttermilk
- ½ cup semisweet chocolate chips

Directions:
1. Preheat the air fryer to 320°F. Cut parchment paper to fit the air fryer basket.
2. Chill 6 tablespoons butter in the freezer 10 minutes. In a small microwave-safe bowl, microwave remaining 2 tablespoons butter 30 seconds until melted, and set aside.
3. In a large bowl, mix flour, brown sugar, and baking powder.
4. Remove butter from freezer and grate into bowl. Use a wooden spoon to evenly distribute.
5. Add egg and buttermilk and stir gently until a soft, sticky dough forms. Gently fold in chocolate chips.
6. Turn dough out onto a lightly floured surface. Fold a couple of times and gently form into a 6" round. Cut into eight triangles.
7. Place scones on parchment in the air fryer basket, leaving at least 2" space between each, working in batches as necessary.
8. Brush each scone with melted butter. Cook 15 minutes until scones are dark golden brown and crispy on the edges, and a toothpick inserted into the center comes out clean. Serve warm.

Egg In A Hole

Servings: 4
Cooking Time: 10 Minutes
Ingredients:
- 4 slices white sandwich bread
- 4 large eggs
- ½ teaspoon salt
- ¼ teaspoon ground black pepper

Directions:
1. Preheat the air fryer to 350°F. Spray a 6" round cake pan with cooking spray.
2. Place as many pieces of bread as will fit in one layer in prepared pan, working in batches as necessary.
3. Using a small cup or cookie cutter, cut a circle out of the center of each bread slice. Crack an egg directly into each cutout and sprinkle eggs with salt and pepper.
4. Cook 5 minutes, then carefully turn and cook an additional 5 minutes or less, depending on your preference. Serve warm.

Coconut & Peanut Rice Cereal

Servings: 4
Cooking Time: 15 Minutes
Ingredients:
- 4 cups rice cereal
- 1 cup coconut shreds
- 2 tbsp peanut butter
- 1 tsp vanilla extract
- ¼ cup honey
- 1 tbsp light brown sugar
- 2 tsp ground cinnamon
- ¼ cup hazelnut flour
- Salt to taste

Directions:
1. Preheat air fryer at 350ºF. Combine the rice cereal, coconut shreds, peanut butter, vanilla extract, honey, brown sugar, cinnamon, hazelnut flour, and salt in a bowl. Press mixture into a greased cake pan. Place cake pan in the frying basket and Air Fry for 5 minutes, stirring once. Let cool completely for 10 minutes before crumbling. Store it into an airtight container up to 5 days.

Blueberry Scones

Servings: 8
Cooking Time: 15 Minutes
Ingredients:
- ½ cup cold salted butter, divided
- 2 cups all-purpose flour
- ½ cup granulated sugar
- 1 teaspoon baking powder
- 1 large egg
- ½ cup whole milk
- ½ cup fresh blueberries

Directions:
1. Chill 6 tablespoons butter in the freezer 10 minutes. In a small microwave-safe bowl, microwave remaining 2 tablespoons butter 30 seconds until melted.
2. Preheat the air fryer to 320°F. Cut parchment paper to fit the air fryer basket.
3. In a large bowl, mix flour, sugar, and baking powder.
4. Add egg and milk and stir until a sticky dough forms.
5. Remove butter from freezer and grate into bowl. Fold grated butter into dough until just combined.
6. Fold in blueberries. Turn dough onto a lightly floured surface. Sprinkle dough with flour and fold a couple of times, then gently form into a 6" round. Cut into eight triangles.
7. Place scones on parchment in the air fryer basket, leaving at least 2" of space between each, working in batches as necessary.
8. Brush each scone with melted butter and cook 15 minutes until scones are dark golden brown and crispy on the edges, and a toothpick inserted into the center comes out clean. Serve warm.

Vodka Basil Muffins With Strawberries

Servings: 6
Cooking Time: 20 Minutes
Ingredients:
- ½ cup flour
- ½ cup granular sugar
- ½ tsp baking powder
- ⅛ tsp salt
- ½ cup chopped strawberries
- ¼ tsp vanilla extract
- 3 tbsp butter, melted
- 2 eggs
- ¼ tsp vodka
- 1 tbsp chopped basil

Directions:
1. Preheat air fryer to 375ºF. Combine the dry ingredients in a bowl. Set aside. In another bowl, whisk the wet ingredients. Pour wet ingredients into the bowl with the dry ingredients and gently combine. Add basil and vodka to the batter. Do not overmix and spoon batter into six silicone cupcake liners lightly greased with olive oil. Place liners in the frying basket and Bake for 7 minutes. Let cool for 5 minutes onto a cooling rack before serving.

Parmesan Spinach Muffins

Servings: 4
Cooking Time: 15 Minutes
Ingredients:
- 2 eggs, whisked
- Cooking spray
- 1 and ½ cups coconut milk
- 1 tablespoon baking powder
- 4 ounces baby spinach, chopped
- 2 ounces parmesan cheese, grated
- 3 ounces almond flour

Directions:
1. Grease the muffin molds with cooking spray.
2. Mix the whisked eggs, coconut milk, baking powder, baby spinach, parmesan cheese, and almond flour together in a mixing bowl.
3. Transfer onto the greased molds.
4. Cook in your air fryer at 380 degrees F/ 195 degrees C for 15 minutes.
5. When the cooking time is up, serve on plates.
6. Enjoy your breakfast.

Almond-pumpkin Porridge

Servings: 4
Cooking Time: 10 Minutes
Ingredients:
- 1 cup pumpkin seeds
- 2/3 cup chopped pecans
- 1/3 cup quick-cooking oats
- ¼ cup pumpkin purée
- ¼ cup diced pitted dates
- 1 tsp chia seeds
- 1 tsp sesame seeds
- 1 tsp dried berries
- 2 tbsp butter
- 2 tsp pumpkin pie spice
- ¼ cup honey
- 1 tbsp dark brown sugar
- ¼ cup almond flour
- Salt to taste

Directions:
1. Preheat air fryer at 350ºF. Combine the pumpkin seeds, pecans, oats, pumpkin purée, dates, chia seeds, sesame seeds, dried berries, butter, pumpkin pie spice, honey, sugar, almond flour, and salt in a bowl. Press mixture into a greased cake pan. Place cake pan in the frying basket and Bake for 5 minutes, stirring once. Let cool completely for 10 minutes before crumbling.

Spinach With Scrambled Eggs

Servings: 2
Cooking Time: 10 Minutes
Ingredients:
- 2 tablespoons olive oil
- 4 eggs, whisked
- 5 ounces (142 g) fresh spinach, chopped
- 1 medium tomato, chopped
- 1 teaspoon fresh lemon juice
- ½ teaspoon coarse salt
- ½ teaspoon ground black pepper
- ½ cup of fresh basil, roughly chopped

Directions:
1. Grease a baking pan with the oil, tilting it to spread the oil around. Preheat the air fryer to 280ºF (138ºC).
2. Mix the remaining ingredients, apart from the basil leaves, whisking well until everything is completely combined.
3. Bake in the air fryer for 10 minutes.
4. Top with fresh basil leaves before serving.

English Breakfast

Servings: 2
Cooking Time: 30 Minutes
Ingredients:
- 6 bacon strips
- 1 cup cooked white beans
- 1 tbsp melted butter
- ½ tbsp flour
- Salt and pepper to taste
- 2 eggs

Directions:
1. Preheat air fryer to 360°F. In a second bowl, combine the beans, butter, flour, salt, and pepper. Mix well. Put the bacon in the frying basket and Air Fry for 10 minutes, flipping once. Remove the bacon and stir in the beans. Crack the eggs on top and cook for 10-12 minutes until the eggs are set. Serve with bacon.

Jalapeño And Bacon Breakfast Pizza

Servings: 2
Cooking Time: 10 Minutes
Ingredients:
- 1 cup shredded mozzarella cheese
- 1 ounce cream cheese, broken into small pieces
- 4 slices cooked sugar-free bacon, chopped
- ¼ cup chopped pickled jalapeños
- 1 large egg, whisked
- ¼ teaspoon salt

Directions:
1. Place mozzarella in a single layer on the bottom of an ungreased 6" round nonstick baking dish. Scatter cream cheese pieces, bacon, and jalapeños over mozzarella, then pour egg evenly around baking dish.
2. Sprinkle with salt and place into air fryer basket. Adjust the temperature to 330°F and set the timer for 10 minutes. When cheese is brown and egg is set, pizza will be done.
3. Let cool on a large plate 5 minutes before serving.

Bread Boat Eggs

Servings: 4
Cooking Time: 10 Minutes
Ingredients:
- 4 pistolette rolls
- 1 teaspoon butter
- ¼ cup diced fresh mushrooms
- ½ teaspoon dried onion flakes
- 4 eggs
- ½ teaspoon salt
- ¼ teaspoon dried dill weed
- ¼ teaspoon dried parsley
- 1 tablespoon milk

Directions:
1. Cut a rectangle in the top of each roll and scoop out center, leaving ½-inch shell on the sides and bottom.
2. Place butter, mushrooms, and dried onion in air fryer baking pan and cook for 1 minute. Stir and cook 3 moreminutes.
3. In a medium bowl, beat together the eggs, salt, dill, parsley, and milk. Pour mixture into pan with mushrooms.
4. Cook at 390°F for 2minutes. Stir. Continue cooking for 3 or 4minutes, stirring every minute, until eggs are scrambled to your liking.
5. Remove baking pan from air fryer and fill rolls with scrambled egg mixture.
6. Place filled rolls in air fryer basket and cook at 390°F for 2 to 3minutes or until rolls are lightly browned.

Spinach Eggs And Cheese

Servings: 2
Cooking Time: 40 Minutes
Ingredients:

- 3 whole eggs
- 3 oz cottage cheese
- 3-4 oz chopped spinach
- ¼ cup parmesan cheese
- ¼ cup of milk

Directions:
1. Preheat your fryer to 375°F.
2. In a large bowl, whisk the eggs, cottage cheese, the parmesan and the milk.
3. Mix in the spinach.
4. Transfer to a small, greased, fryer dish.
5. Sprinkle the cheese on top.
6. Bake for 25-30 minutes.
7. Let cool for 5 minutes and serve.

Cheesy Cauliflower "hash Browns"

Servings:6
Cooking Time: 24 Minutes
Ingredients:
- 2 ounces 100% cheese crisps
- 1 steamer bag cauliflower, cooked according to package instructions
- 1 large egg
- ½ cup shredded sharp Cheddar cheese
- ½ teaspoon salt

Directions:
1. Let cooked cauliflower cool 10 minutes.
2. Place cheese crisps into food processor and pulse on low 30 seconds until crisps are finely ground.
3. Using a kitchen towel, wring out excess moisture from cauliflower and place into food processor.
4. Add egg to food processor and sprinkle with Cheddar and salt. Pulse five times until mixture is mostly smooth.
5. Cut two pieces of parchment to fit air fryer basket. Separate mixture into six even scoops and place three on each piece of ungreased parchment, keeping at least 2" of space between each scoop. Press each into a hash brown shape, about ¼" thick.
6. Place one batch on parchment into air fryer basket. Adjust the temperature to 375°F and set the timer for 12 minutes, turning hash browns halfway through cooking. Hash browns will be golden brown when done. Repeat with second batch.
7. Allow 5 minutes to cool. Serve warm.

Mozzarella Rolls

Servings: 6
Cooking Time: 6 Minutes
Ingredients:
- 6 wonton wrappers
- 1 tablespoon keto tomato sauce
- ½ cup Mozzarella, shredded
- 1 ounce pepperoni, chopped
- 1 egg, beaten
- Cooking spray

Directions:
1. Before cooking, heat your air fryer to 400 degrees F/ 205 degrees C.
2. Spritz the cooking spray over an air fryer basket with cooking spray.
3. Mix the pepperoni, shredded Mozzarella cheese, and tomato sauce in a big bowl until homogenous.
4. Separate the mixture onto wonton wraps.
5. Roll the wraps into sticks.
6. Use the beaten eggs to brush the sticks.
7. Arrange evenly on the air fryer basket and cook in your air fryer for 6 minutes and flip the sticks halfway through cooking.

Pita And Pepperoni Pizza

Servings:1
Cooking Time: 6 Minutes
Ingredients:
- 1 teaspoon olive oil
- 1 tablespoon pizza sauce
- 1 pita bread
- 6 pepperoni slices
- ¼ cup grated Mozzarella cheese
- ¼ teaspoon garlic powder
- ¼ teaspoon dried oregano

Directions:
1. Preheat the air fryer to 350ºF (177ºC). Grease the air fryer basket with olive oil.
2. Spread the pizza sauce on top of the pita bread. Put the pepperoni slices over the sauce, followed by the Mozzarella cheese.
3. Season with garlic powder and oregano.
4. Put the pita pizza inside the air fryer and place a trivet on top.
5. Bake in the preheated air fryer for 6 minutes and serve.

Spinach And Mushroom Mini Quiche

Servings:4
Cooking Time: 15 Minutes
Ingredients:
- 1 teaspoon olive oil, plus more for spraying
- 1 cup coarsely chopped mushrooms
- 1 cup fresh baby spinach, shredded
- 4 eggs, beaten
- ½ cup shredded Cheddar cheese
- ½ cup shredded mozzarella cheese
- ¼ teaspoon salt
- ¼ teaspoon black pepper

Directions:
1. Spray 4 silicone baking cups with olive oil and set aside.
2. In a medium sauté pan over medium heat, warm 1 teaspoon of olive oil. Add the mushrooms and sauté until soft, 3 to 4 minutes.
3. Add the spinach and cook until wilted, 1 to 2 minutes. Set aside.
4. In a medium bowl, whisk together the eggs, Cheddar cheese, mozzarella cheese, salt, and pepper.
5. Gently fold the mushrooms and spinach into the egg mixture.
6. Pour ¼ of the mixture into each silicone baking cup.
7. Place the baking cups into the fryer basket and air fry for 5 minutes. Stir the mixture in each ramekin slightly and air fry until the egg has set, an additional 3 to 5 minutes.

Chapter 4: Appetizers And Snacks Recipes

Home-style Buffalo Chicken Wings
Servings: 4
Cooking Time: 35 Minutes
Ingredients:
- 2 lb chicken wing portions
- 6 tbsp chili sauce
- 1 tsp dried oregano
- 1 tsp smoked paprika
- 1tsp garlic powder
- ½ tsp salt
- ¼ cup crumbled blue cheese
- 1/3 cup low-fat yogurt
- ½ tbsp lemon juice
- ½ tbsp white wine vinegar
- 2 celery stalks, cut into sticks
- 2 carrots, cut into sticks

Directions:
1. Add chicken with 1 tbsp of chili sauce, oregano, garlic, paprika, and salt to a large bowl. Toss to coat well, then set aside. In a small bowl, mash blue cheese and yogurt with a fork. Stir lemon juice and vinegar until smooth and blended. Refrigerate covered until it is time to serve.
2. Preheat air fryer to 300°F. Place the chicken in the greased frying basket and Air Fry for 22 minutes, flipping the chicken once until crispy and browned. Set aside in a clean bowl. Coat with the remaining tbsp of chili sauce. Serve with celery, carrot sticks and the blue cheese dip.

Thyme Sweet Potato Chips
Servings: 2
Cooking Time: 20 Minutes
Ingredients:
- 1 tbsp olive oil
- 1 sweet potato, sliced
- ¼ tsp dried thyme
- Salt to taste

Directions:
1. Preheat air fryer to 390°F. Spread the sweet potato slices in the greased basket and brush with olive oil. Air Fry for 6 minutes. Remove the basket, shake, and sprinkle with thyme and salt. Cook for 6 more minutes or until lightly browned. Serve warm and enjoy!

Beef Steak Sliders
Servings: 8
Cooking Time: 22 Minutes
Ingredients:
- 1 pound top sirloin steaks, about ¾-inch thick
- salt and pepper
- 2 large onions, thinly sliced
- 1 tablespoon extra-light olive oil
- 8 slider buns
- Horseradish Mayonnaise
- 1 cup light mayonnaise
- 4 teaspoons prepared horseradish
- 2 teaspoons Worcestershire sauce
- 1 teaspoon coarse brown mustard

Directions:
1. Place steak in air fryer basket and cook at 390°F for 6minutes. Turn and cook 6 more minutes for medium rare. If you prefer your steak medium, continue cooking for 3 minutes.
2. While the steak is cooking, prepare the Horseradish Mayonnaise by mixing all ingredients together.
3. When steak is cooked, remove from air fryer, sprinkle with salt and pepper to taste, and set aside to rest.
4. Toss the onion slices with the oil and place in air fryer basket. Cook at 390°F for 7 minutes, until onion rings are soft and browned.
5. Slice steak into very thin slices.
6. Spread slider buns with the horseradish mayo and pile on the meat and onions. Serve with remaining horseradish dressing for dipping.

Crispy Paprika Chips
Servings: 4
Cooking Time: 5 Minutes
Ingredients:
- 8 ounces' cheddar cheese, shredded
- 1 teaspoon sweet paprika

Directions:
1. Divide the cheese in small heaps in a suitable pan.
2. After sprinkling the paprika on top, arrange the cheeses to the air fryer and cook at 400 degrees F/ 205 degrees C for 5 minutes.
3. Cool the chips down before serving them.

Stuffed Baby Bella Caps
Servings: 16
Cooking Time: 12 Minutes
Ingredients:
- 16 fresh, small Baby Bella mushrooms
- 2 green onions
- 4 ounces mozzarella cheese
- ½ cup diced ham
- 2 tablespoons breadcrumbs
- ½ teaspoon garlic powder
- ¼ teaspoon ground oregano
- ¼ teaspoon ground black pepper
- 1 to 2 teaspoons olive oil

Directions:
1. Remove stems and wash mushroom caps.
2. Cut green onions and cheese in small pieces and place in food processor.
3. Add ham, breadcrumbs, garlic powder, oregano, and pepper and mince ingredients.
4. With food processor running, dribble in just enough olive oil to make a thick paste.
5. Divide stuffing among mushroom caps and pack down lightly.
6. Place stuffed mushrooms in air fryer basket in single layer and cook at 390°F for 12minutes or until tops are golden brown and mushrooms are tender.
7. Repeat step 6 to cook remaining mushrooms.

Glazed Chicken Wings

Servings: 4
Cooking Time: 25 Minutes
Ingredients:
- 8 chicken wings
- 3 tablespoons honey
- 1 tablespoons lemon juice
- 1 tablespoon low sodium chicken stock
- 2 cloves garlic, minced
- ¼ cup thinly sliced green onion
- ¾ cup low sodium barbecue sauce
- 4 stalks celery, cut into pieces

Directions:
1. Pat the chicken wings dry. Cut off the small end piece and discard or freeze it to make chicken stock later.
2. Put the wings into the air fryer basket. Air fry for 20 minutes, shaking the basket twice while cooking.
3. Meanwhile, combine the honey, lemon juice, chicken stock, and garlic, and whisk until combined.
4. Remove the wings from the air fryer and put into a 6" x 2" pan. Pour the sauce over the wings and toss gently to coat.
5. Return the pan to the air fryer and air fry for another 4 to 5 minutes or until the wings are glazed and a food thermometer registers 165°F. Sprinkle with the green onion and serve the wings with the barbecue sauce and celery.

Peppery Chicken Meatballs

Servings: 16
Cooking Time: 13 To 20 Minutes
Ingredients:
- 2 teaspoons olive oil
- ¼ cup minced onion
- ¼ cup minced red bell pepper
- 2 vanilla wafers, crushed
- 1 egg white
- ½ teaspoon dried thyme
- ½ pound (227 g) ground chicken breast

Directions:
1. Preheat the air fryer to 370°F (188°C).
2. In a baking pan, mix the olive oil, onion, and red bell pepper. Put the pan in the air fryer. Air fry for 3 to 5 minutes, or until the vegetables are tender.
3. In a medium bowl, mix the cooked vegetables, crushed wafers, egg white, and thyme until well combined
4. Mix in the chicken, gently but thoroughly, until everything is combined.
5. Form the mixture into 16 meatballs and place them in the air fryer basket. Air fry for 10 to 15 minutes, or until the meatballs reach an internal temperature of 165°F (74°C) on a meat thermometer.
6. Serve immediately.

Potato Chips

Servings: 2
Cooking Time: 15 Minutes
Ingredients:
- 2 medium potatoes
- 2 teaspoons extra-light olive oil
- oil for misting or cooking spray
- salt and pepper

Directions:
1. Peel the potatoes.
2. Using a mandoline or paring knife, shave potatoes into thin slices, dropping them into a bowl of water as you cut them.
3. Dry potatoes as thoroughly as possible with paper towels or a clean dish towel. Toss potato slices with the oil to coat completely.
4. Spray air fryer basket with cooking spray and add potato slices.
5. Stir and separate with a fork.
6. Cook 390°F for 5minutes. Stir and separate potato slices. Cook 5 more minutes. Stir and separate potatoes again. Cook another 5 minutes.
7. Season to taste.

Buffalo Cauliflower Wings

Servings: 4
Cooking Time: 14 Minutes
Ingredients:
- 1 cauliflower head, cut into florets
- 1 tbsp butter, melted
- 1/2 cup buffalo sauce
- Pepper
- Salt

Directions:
1. Spray air fryer basket with cooking spray.
2. In a bowl, mix together buffalo sauce, butter, pepper, and salt.
3. Add cauliflower florets into the air fryer basket and cook at 400 °F for 7 minutes.
4. Transfer cauliflower florets into the buffalo sauce mixture and toss well.
5. Again, add cauliflower florets into the air fryer basket and cook for 7 minutes more at 400 °F.
6. Serve and enjoy.

Stuffed Jalapeno Poppers

Servings: 5
Cooking Time: 5 Minutes
Ingredients:
- 10 Fresh jalapeno peppers, cut in ½ and remove seeds
- 2 bacon slices, cooked and crumbled
- ¼ cup cheddar cheese, shredded
- 6 ounces cream cheese, softened

Directions:
1. In a suitable bowl, combine together bacon, cream cheese, and cheddar cheese.
2. Stuff each jalapeno ½ with bacon cheese mixture.
3. Grease its air fryer basket with cooking spray.

Air Fryer Cookbook for Beginners

4. Place stuffed jalapeno halved in air fryer basket and cook at almost 370 degrees F/ 185 degrees C for 5 minutes.
5. Serve and enjoy.

Spiced Sweet Potato Fries

Servings:2
Cooking Time: 15 Minutes
Ingredients:
- 2 tablespoons olive oil
- 1½ teaspoons smoked paprika
- 1½ teaspoons kosher salt, plus more as needed
- 1 teaspoon chili powder
- ½ teaspoon ground cumin
- ½ teaspoon ground turmeric
- ½ teaspoon mustard powder
- ¼ teaspoon cayenne pepper
- 2 medium sweet potatoes (about 10 ounces / 284 g each), cut into wedges, ½ inch thick and 3 inches long
- Freshly ground black pepper, to taste
- ⅔ cup sour cream
- 1 garlic clove, grated

Directions:
1. Preheat the air fryer to 400ºF (204ºC).
2. In a large bowl, combine the olive oil, paprika, salt, chili powder, cumin, turmeric, mustard powder, and cayenne. Add the sweet potatoes, season with black pepper, and toss to evenly coat.
3. Transfer the sweet potatoes to the air fryer (save the bowl with the leftover oil and spices) and air fry for 15 minutes, shaking the basket halfway through, or until golden brown and crisp. Return the potato wedges to the reserved bowl and toss again while they are hot.
4. Meanwhile, in a small bowl, stir together the sour cream and garlic. Season with salt and black pepper and transfer to a serving dish.
5. Serve the potato wedges hot with the garlic sour cream.

Zucchini Chips

Servings: 3
Cooking Time: 17 Minutes
Ingredients:
- 1½ small Zucchini, washed but not peeled, and cut into ¼-inch-thick rounds
- Olive oil spray
- ¼ teaspoon Table salt

Directions:
1. Preheat the air fryer to 375°F.
2. Lay some paper towels on your work surface. Set the zucchini rounds on top, then set more paper towels over the rounds. Press gently to remove some of the moisture. Remove the top layer of paper towels and lightly coat the rounds with olive oil spray on both sides.
3. When the machine is at temperature, set the rounds in the basket, overlapping them a bit as needed. Air-fry for 15 minutes, tossing and rearranging the rounds at the 5- and 10-minute marks, until browned, soft, yet crisp at the edges.
4. Gently pour the contents of the basket onto a wire rack. Cool for at least 10 minutes or up to 2 hours before serving.

Crispy Fried Pickle Chips

Servings: 4
Cooking Time: 10 Minutes
Ingredients:
- 1 pound whole dill pickles
- 2 eggs
- ⅓ cup all-purpose flour
- ⅓ cup bread crumbs
- Cooking oil

Directions:
1. Cut the pickles crosswise into ½-inch-thick slices. Dry the slices completely using a paper towel.
2. In a small bowl, beat the eggs. In another small bowl, add the flour. Place the bread crumbs in a third small bowl.
3. Spray the air fryer basket with cooking oil.
4. Dip the pickle slices in the flour, then the egg, and then the bread crumbs.
5. Place the breaded pickle slices in the air fryer. It is okay to stack them. Spray them with cooking oil. Cook for 6 minutes.
6. Open the air fryer and flip the pickles. Cook for an additional 2 to 3 minutes, or until the pickles are crisp.

Ranch Broccoli With Cheddar

Servings: 6
Cooking Time: 35 Minutes
Ingredients:
- 4 cups broccoli florets
- ¼ cup ranch dressing
- ½ cup sharp cheddar cheese, shredded
- ¼ cup heavy whipping cream
- Kosher black pepper and salt to taste

Directions:
1. At 375 degrees F/ 190 degrees C preheat your air fryer.
2. In a suitable bowl, combine all of the recipe ingredients until the broccoli is well-covered.
3. In a casserole dish, spread out the broccoli mixture.
4. Air fry for 30 minutes.
5. Take out of your fryer and mix.
6. If the florets are not tender, Air fry for another 5 minutes until tender.
7. Serve!

Roasted Jalapeño Salsa Verde

Servings:4
Cooking Time: 20 Minutes
Ingredients:
- ¾ lb fresh tomatillos, husked
- 1 jalapeño, stem removed
- 4 green onions, sliced
- 3 garlic cloves, peeled

- ½ tsp salt
- 1 tsp lime juice
- ¼ tsp apple cider vinegar
- ¼ cup cilantro leaves

Directions:
1. Preheat air fryer to 400°F. Add tomatillos and jalapeño to the frying basket and Bake for 5 minutes. Put in green onions and garlic and Bake for 5 more minutes. Transfer it into a food processor along with salt, lime juice, vinegar and cilantro and blend until the sauce is finely chopped. Pour it into a small sealable container and refrigerate it until ready to use up to five days.

Garlicky Radish Chips

Servings: 1
Cooking Time: 10 Minutes
Ingredients:
- 2 cups water
- 1 pound radishes
- ½ teaspoon garlic powder
- ¼ teaspoon onion powder
- 2 tablespoons coconut oil, melted

Directions:
1. Boil the water over the stove.
2. Slice off the radish's tops and bottoms and, using a mandolin, shave into thin slices of equal size.
3. Put the radish chips in the pot of boiling water and allow to cook for 5 minutes, ensuring they become translucent.
4. Take care when removing from the water and place them on a paper towel to dry.
5. Add the radish chips, garlic powder, onion powder, and melted coconut oil into a bowl and toss to coat.
6. Cook at almost 320 degrees F/ 160 degrees C for 5 minutes.
7. Serve.

Salmon Bites With Coconut

Servings: 12
Cooking Time: 10 Minutes
Ingredients:
- 2 avocados, peeled, pitted and mashed
- 4 ounces smoked salmon, skinless, boneless and chopped
- 2 tablespoons coconut cream
- 1 teaspoon avocado oil
- 1 teaspoon dill, chopped
- A pinch of salt and black pepper

Directions:
1. Mix the avocados, smoked salmon, coconut cream, avocado oil, the chopped dill, salt, and black pepper well in a clean bowl.
2. Shape medium balls out of this mix.
3. Place the balls in the basket of your air fryer.
4. Cook at 350 degrees F/ 175 degrees C for 10 minutes.
5. Serve as an appetizer.

Cheesy Green Dip

Servings: 6
Cooking Time: 30 Minutes
Ingredients:
- ½ cup canned artichoke hearts, chopped
- ½ cup cream cheese, softened
- 2 tbsp grated Romano cheese
- ¼ cup grated mozzarella
- ½ cup spinach, chopped
- ½ cup milk
- Salt and pepper to taste

Directions:
1. Preheat air fryer to 350°F. Whisk the milk, cream cheese, Romano cheese, spinach, artichoke hearts, salt, and pepper in a mixing bowl. Pour the mixture into a greased baking pan, and sprinkle the grated mozzarella cheese over the top. Bake in the air fryer for 20 minutes. Serve.

Herby Breaded Artichoke Hearts

Servings: 6
Cooking Time: 25 Minutes
Ingredients:
- 12 canned artichoke hearts
- 2 eggs
- ½ cup all-purpose flour
- 1/3 cup panko bread crumbs
- ½ tsp dried thyme
- ½ tsp dried parsley

Directions:
1. Preheat air fryer to 380°F. Set out three small bowls. In the first, add flour. In the second, beat the eggs. In the third, mix the crumbs, thyme, and parsley.
2. Dip the artichoke in the flour, then dredge in the egg, then in the bread crumb. Place the breaded artichokes in the greased frying basket and Air Fry for 8 minutes, flipping them once until just browned and crisp. Allow to cool slightly and serve.

Uncle´s Potato Wedges

Servings: 4
Cooking Time: 65 Minutes
Ingredients:
- 2 russet potatoes, cut into wedges
- 1 head garlic
- 3 tbsp olive oil
- ¼ cup mayonnaise
- ½ tbsp lemon juice
- ½ tsp Worcestershire sauce
- ⅛ tsp cayenne pepper
- Salt and pepper to taste
- ½ tsp chili powder
- ¼ tsp ground cumin
- 1 tbsp dried Italian herbs
- ½ cup Parmesan cheese

Directions:

Air Fryer Cookbook for Beginners

1. Preheat air fryer to 400°F. Cut off garlic head top and drizzle with olive oil. Wrap loosely in foil and transfer to the frying basket. Cook for 30 minutes. Remove from air fryer and open the foil. Cool the garlic for 10 minutes, then squeeze the cloves out of their place in the head. Chop and transfer all but ½ teaspoon to a small bowl. Stir in mayonnaise, lemon juice, Worcestershire, and cayenne pepper. Cover and refrigerate.
2. Toss potatoes with the rest of the olive oil as well as salt, black pepper, Italian herbs, Parmesan cheese, chili powder, cumin, and the remaining chopped garlic. When coated, place the wedges in the frying basket in a single layer. Air Fry for 10 minutes, then shake the basket. Air Fry for another 8-10 minutes until potatoes are tender. Bring out the garlic aioli. Place the potato wedges on a serving dish along with the aioli for dipping. Serve warm.

Mustard Pork Meatballs

Servings: 8
Cooking Time: 17 Minutes
Ingredients:
- 1 ½ pounds ground pork
- 2 small onions, chopped
- 4 garlic cloves, minced
- 2 tablespoons brie cheese, grated
- 1 ½ teaspoon mustard
- 1 teaspoon cayenne pepper
- Black pepper, to taste
- Salt, to taste

Directions:
1. Add all the recipe ingredients into the bowl and mix until well combined.
2. Make small balls from meat mixture and place into the air fryer basket.
3. Cook at almost 375 degrees F/ 190 degrees C for 17 minutes.
4. Serve and enjoy.

Crab Cake Bites

Servings: 6
Cooking Time: 20 Minutes
Ingredients:
- 8 oz lump crab meat
- 1 diced red bell pepper
- 1 spring onion, diced
- 1 garlic clove, minced
- 1 tbsp capers, minced
- 1 tbsp cream cheese
- 1 egg, beaten
- ¼ cup bread crumbs
- ¼ tsp salt
- 1 tbsp olive oil
- 1 lemon, cut into wedges

Directions:
1. Preheat air fryer to 360°F. Combine the crab, bell pepper, spring onion, garlic, and capers in a bowl until combined. Stir in the cream cheese and egg. Mix in the bread crumbs and salt. Divide this mixture into 6 equal portions and pat out into patties. Put the crab cakes into the frying basket in a single layer. Drizzle the tops of each patty with a bit of olive oil and Bake for 10 minutes. Serve with lemon wedges on the side. Enjoy!

Fried Dill Pickle Chips

Servings: 4
Cooking Time: 12 Minutes
Ingredients:
- 1 cup All-purpose flour or tapioca flour
- 1 Large egg white(s)
- 1 tablespoon Brine from a jar of dill pickles
- 1 cup Seasoned Italian-style dried bread crumbs (gluten-free, if a concern)
- 2 Large dill pickle(s), cut into ½-inch-thick rounds
- Vegetable oil spray

Directions:
1. Preheat the air fryer to 400°F.
2. Set up and fill three shallow soup plates or small pie plates on your counter: one for the flour, one for the egg white(s) whisked with the pickle brine, and one for the bread crumbs.
3. Set a pickle round in the flour and turn it to coat all sides, even the edge. Gently shake off the excess flour, then dip the round into the egg-white mixture and turn to coat both sides and the edge. Let any excess egg white mixture slip back into the rest, then set the round in the bread crumbs and turn it to coat both sides as well as the edge. Set aside on a cutting board and soldier on, dipping and coating the remaining rounds. Lightly coat the coated rounds on both sides with vegetable oil spray.
4. Set the pickle rounds in the basket in one layer. Air-fry undisturbed for 7 minutes, or until golden brown and crunchy. Cool in the basket for a few minutes before using kitchen tongs to transfer the rounds to a serving platter.

Shrimp Pirogues

Servings: 8
Cooking Time: 5 Minutes
Ingredients:
- 12 ounces small, peeled, and deveined raw shrimp
- 3 ounces cream cheese, room temperature
- 2 tablespoons plain yogurt
- 1 teaspoon lemon juice
- 1 teaspoon dried dill weed, crushed
- salt
- 4 small hothouse cucumbers, each approximately 6 inches long

Directions:
1. Pour 4 tablespoons water in bottom of air fryer drawer.
2. Place shrimp in air fryer basket in single layer and cook at 390°F for 5 minutes, just until done. Watch carefully because shrimp cooks quickly, and overcooking makes it tough.

3. Chop shrimp into small pieces, no larger than ½ inch. Refrigerate while mixing the remaining ingredients.
4. With a fork, mash and whip the cream cheese until smooth.
5. Stir in the yogurt and beat until smooth. Stir in lemon juice, dill weed, and chopped shrimp.
6. Taste for seasoning. If needed, add ¼ to ½ teaspoon salt to suit your taste.
7. Store in refrigerator until serving time.
8. When ready to serve, wash and dry cucumbers and split them lengthwise. Scoop out the seeds and turn cucumbers upside down on paper towels to drain for 10 minutes.
9. Just before filling, wipe centers of cucumbers dry. Spoon the shrimp mixture into the pirogues and cut in half crosswise. Serve immediately.

Middle Eastern Roasted Chickpeas

Servings: 3
Cooking Time: 30 Minutes
Ingredients:
- 2 tsp olive oil
- 1 can chickpeas
- Salt to taste
- 1 tsp za'atar seasoning
- 1 tsp ground sumac
- ¼ tsp garlic powder
- 1 tbsp cilantro, chopped

Directions:
1. Combine salt, za´atar, sumac, and garlic powder in a bowl. Preheat air fryer to 375°F. Put half of the chickpeas in the greased frying basket. Bake for 12 minutes, shaking every 5 minutes until crunchy and golden brown. Transfer the chickpeas to a bowl. Lightly coat them with olive oil, then toss them with half of the spice mix while they are still hot. Serve topped with cilantro.

Bacon Tater Tots

Servings: 4
Cooking Time: 17 Minutes
Ingredients:
- 24 frozen tater tots
- 6 slices precooked bacon
- 2 tablespoons maple syrup
- 1 cup shredded Cheddar cheese

Directions:
1. Put the tater tots in the air fryer basket. Air-fry for 10 minutes, shaking the basket halfway through the cooking time.
2. Meanwhile, cut the bacon into 1-inch pieces and shred the cheese.
3. Remove the tater tots from the air fryer basket and put into a 6-by-6-by-2-inch pan. Top with the bacon and drizzle with the maple syrup. Air-fry for 5 minutes or until the tots and bacon are crisp.
4. Top with the cheese and air-fry for 2 minutes or until the cheese is melted.

Bacon-y Cauliflower Skewers

Servings: 4
Cooking Time: 12 Minutes
Ingredients:
- 4 slices sugar-free bacon, cut into thirds
- ¼ medium yellow onion, peeled and cut into 1" pieces
- 4 ounces cauliflower florets
- 1½ tablespoons olive oil
- ¼ teaspoon salt
- ¼ teaspoon garlic powder

Directions:
1. Place 1 piece bacon and 2 pieces onion on a 6" skewer. Add a second piece bacon, and 2 cauliflower florets, followed by another piece of bacon onto skewer. Repeat with remaining ingredients and three additional skewers to make four total skewers.
2. Drizzle skewers with olive oil, then sprinkle with salt and garlic powder. Place skewers into ungreased air fryer basket. Adjust the temperature to 375°F and set the timer for 12 minutes, turning the skewers halfway through cooking. When done, vegetables will be tender and bacon will be crispy. Serve warm.

Bbq Chips

Servings: 2
Cooking Time: 30 Minutes
Ingredients:
- 1 scrubbed russet potato, sliced
- ½ tsp smoked paprika
- ¼ tsp chili powder
- ¼ tsp garlic powder
- 1/8 tsp onion powder
- ¼ tbsp smoked paprika
- 1/8 tsp light brown sugar
- Salt and pepper to taste
- 2 tsp olive oil

Directions:
1. Preheat air fryer at 400ºF. Combine all seasoning in a bowl. Set aside. In another bowl, mix potato chips, olive oil, black pepper, and salt until coated. Place potato chips in the frying basket and Air Fry for 17 minutes, shaking 3 times. Transfer it into a bowl. Sprinkle with the bbq mixture and let sit for 15 minutes. Serve immediately.

Salmon Nachos

Servings: 6
Cooking Time: 9 To 12 Minutes
Ingredients:
- 2 ounces (about 36) baked no-salt corn tortilla chips (see Tip)
- 1 (5-ounce) baked salmon fillet, flaked
- ½ cup canned low-sodium black beans, rinsed and drained
- 1 red bell pepper, chopped
- ½ cup grated carrot
- 1 jalapeño pepper, minced

Air Fryer Cookbook for Beginners

- ⅓ cup shredded low-sodium low-fat Swiss cheese
- 1 tomato, chopped

Directions:
1. In a 6-by-2-inch pan, layer the tortilla chips. Top with the salmon, black beans, red bell pepper, carrot, jalapeño, and Swiss cheese.
2. Bake in the air fryer for 9 to 12 minutes, or until the cheese is melted and starts to brown.
3. Top with the tomato and serve.

Lemony Pear Chips

Servings: 4
Cooking Time: 9 To 13 Minutes
Ingredients:
- 2 firm Bosc pears, cut crosswise into ⅛-inch-thick slices
- 1 tablespoon freshly squeezed lemon juice
- ½ teaspoon ground cinnamon
- ⅛ teaspoon ground cardamom

Directions:
1. Preheat the air fryer to 380ºF (193ºC).
2. Separate the smaller stem-end pear rounds from the larger rounds with seeds. Remove the core and seeds from the larger slices. Sprinkle all slices with lemon juice, cinnamon, and cardamom.
3. Put the smaller chips into the air fryer basket. Air fry for 3 to 5 minutes, or until light golden brown, shaking the basket once during cooking. Remove from the air fryer.
4. Repeat with the larger slices, air frying for 6 to 8 minutes, or until light golden brown, shaking the basket once during cooking.
5. Remove the chips from the air fryer. Cool and serve or store in an airtight container at room temperature up for to 2 days.

Popcorn Chicken Bites

Servings: 2
Cooking Time: 8 Minutes
Ingredients:
- 1 pound chicken breasts, cutlets or tenders
- 1 cup buttermilk
- 3 to 6 dashes hot sauce (optional)
- 8 cups cornflakes (or 2 cups cornflake crumbs)
- ½ teaspoon salt
- 1 tablespoon butter, melted
- 2 tablespoons chopped fresh parsley

Directions:
1. Cut the chicken into bite-sized pieces (about 1-inch) and place them in a bowl with the buttermilk and hot sauce (if using). Cover and let the chicken marinate in the buttermilk for 1 to 3 hours in the refrigerator.
2. Preheat the air fryer to 380°F.
3. Crush the cornflakes into fine crumbs by either crushing them with your hands in a bowl, rolling them with a rolling pin in a plastic bag or processing them in a food processor. Place the crumbs in a bowl, add the salt, melted butter and parsley and mix well. Working in batches, remove the chicken from the buttermilk marinade, letting any excess drip off and transfer the chicken to the cornflakes. Toss the chicken pieces in the cornflake mixture to coat evenly, pressing the crumbs onto the chicken.
4. Air-fry the chicken in two batches for 8 minutes per batch, shaking the basket halfway through the cooking process. Re-heat the first batch with the second batch for a couple of minutes if desired.
5. Serve the popcorn chicken bites warm with BBQ sauce or honey mustard for dipping.

Bacon With Chocolate Coating

Servings: 4
Cooking Time: 10 Minutes
Ingredients:
- 4 bacon slices, halved
- 1 cup dark chocolate, melted A pinch of pink salt

Directions:
1. Make each bacon slice be coated some chocolate and then sprinkle pink salt over them.
2. Arrange them in the cooking tray of your air fryer.
3. Cook at 350 degrees F/ 175 degrees C for 10 minutes.
4. When cooked, serve as a snack.

Fried String Beans With Greek Sauce

Servings: 4
Cooking Time: 10 Minutes
Ingredients:
- 1 egg
- 1 tbsp flour
- ¼ tsp paprika
- ½ tsp garlic powder
- Salt to taste
- ¼ cup bread crumbs
- ¼ lemon zest
- ½ lb whole string beans
- ½ cup Greek yogurt
- 1 tbsp lemon juice
- ⅛ tsp cayenne pepper

Directions:
1. Preheat air fryer to 380°F. Whisk the egg and 2 tbsp of water in a bowl until frothy. Sift the flour, paprika, garlic powder, and salt in another bowl, then stir in the bread crumbs. Dip each string bean into the egg mixture, then roll into the bread crumb mixture. Put the string beans in a single layer in the greased frying basket. Air Fry them for 5 minutes until the breading is golden brown. Stir the yogurt, lemon juice and zest, salt, and cayenne in a small bowl. Serve the bean fries with lemon-yogurt sauce.

Fried Ranch Pickles

Servings: 4
Cooking Time: 10 Minutes
Ingredients:
- 4 dill pickle spears, halved lengthwise
- ¼ cup ranch dressing

- ½ cup blanched finely ground almond flour
- ½ cup grated Parmesan cheese
- 2 tablespoons dry ranch seasoning

Directions:
1. Wrap spears in a kitchen towel 30 minutes to soak up excess pickle juice.
2. Pour ranch dressing into a medium bowl and add pickle spears. In a separate medium bowl, mix flour, Parmesan, and ranch seasoning.
3. Remove each spear from ranch dressing and shake off excess. Press gently into dry mixture to coat all sides. Place spears into ungreased air fryer basket. Adjust the temperature to 400°F and set the timer for 10 minutes, turning spears three times during cooking. Serve warm.

Thick-crust Pepperoni Pizza

Servings: 2
Cooking Time: 10 Minutes
Ingredients:
- 10 ounces Purchased fresh pizza dough (not a prebaked crust)
- Olive oil spray
- ¼ cup Purchased pizza sauce
- 10 slices Sliced pepperoni
- ⅓ cup Purchased shredded Italian 3- or 4-cheese blend

Directions:
1. Preheat the air fryer to 400°F.
2. Generously coat the inside of a 6-inch round cake pan for a small air fryer, a 7-inch round cake pan for a medium air fryer, or an 8-inch round cake pan for a large model with olive oil spray.
3. Set the dough in the pan and press it to fill the bottom in an even, thick layer. Spread the sauce over the dough, then top with the pepperoni and cheese.
4. When the machine is at temperature, set the pan in the basket and air-fry undisturbed for 10 minutes, or until puffed, brown, and bubbling.
5. Use kitchen tongs to transfer the cake pan to a wire rack. Cool for only a minute or so. Use a spatula to loosen the pizza from the pan and lift it out and onto the rack. Continue cooling for a few minutes before cutting into wedges to serve.

Barbecue Chicken Nachos

Servings: 3
Cooking Time: 5 Minutes
Ingredients:
- 3 heaping cups (a little more than 3 ounces) Corn tortilla chips (gluten-free, if a concern)
- ¾ cup Shredded deboned and skinned rotisserie chicken meat (gluten-free, if a concern)
- 3 tablespoons Canned black beans, drained and rinsed
- 9 rings Pickled jalapeño slices
- 4 Small pickled cocktail onions, halved
- 3 tablespoons Barbecue sauce (any sort)
- ¾ cup (about 3 ounces) Shredded Cheddar cheese

Directions:
1. Preheat the air fryer to 400°F.
2. Cut a circle of parchment paper to line a 6-inch round cake pan for a small air fryer, a 7-inch round cake pan for a medium air fryer, or an 8-inch round cake pan for a large machine.
3. Fill the pan with an even layer of about two-thirds of the chips. Sprinkle the chicken evenly over the chips. Set the pan in the basket and air-fry undisturbed for 2 minutes.
4. Remove the basket from the machine. Scatter the beans, jalapeño rings, and pickled onion halves over the chicken. Drizzle the barbecue sauce over everything, then sprinkle the cheese on top.
5. Return the basket to the machine and air-fry undisturbed for 3 minutes, or until the cheese has melted and is bubbly. Remove the pan from the machine and cool for a couple of minutes before serving.

Cucumber Sushi

Servings: 10
Cooking Time: 10 Minutes
Ingredients:
- 10 bacon slices
- 2 tablespoons cream cheese
- 1 cucumber

Directions:
1. Place the bacon slices in the air fryer in one layer and cook for 10 minutes at 400°F. Meanwhile, cut the cucumber into small wedges. When the bacon is cooked, cool it to the room temperature and spread with cream cheese. Then place the cucumber wedges over the cream cheese and roll the bacon into the sushi.

Caponata Salsa

Servings: 6
Cooking Time: 16 Minutes
Ingredients:
- 4 cups (one 1-pound eggplant) Purple Italian eggplant(s), stemmed and diced (no need to peel)
- Olive oil spray
- 1½ cups Celery, thinly sliced
- 16 (about ½ pound) Cherry or grape tomatoes, halved
- 1 tablespoon Drained and rinsed capers, chopped
- Up to 1 tablespoon Minced fresh rosemary leaves
- 1½ tablespoons Red wine vinegar
- 1½ teaspoons Granulated white sugar
- ¾ teaspoon Table salt
- ¾ teaspoon Ground black pepper

Directions:
1. Preheat the air fryer to 350°F.
2. Put the eggplant pieces in a bowl and generously coat them with olive oil spray. Toss and stir, spray again, and toss some more, until the pieces are glistening.
3. When the machine is at temperature, pour the eggplant pieces into the basket and spread them out into

an even layer. Air-fry for 8 minutes, tossing and rearranging the pieces twice.
4. Meanwhile, put the celery and tomatoes in the same bowl the eggplant pieces had been in. Generously coat them with olive oil spray; then toss well, spray again, and toss some more, until the vegetables are well coated.
5. When the eggplant has cooked for 8 minutes, pour the celery and tomatoes on top in the basket. Air-fry undisturbed for 8 minutes more, until the tomatoes have begun to soften.
6. Pour the contents of the basket back into the same bowl. Add the capers, rosemary, vinegar, sugar, salt, and pepper. Toss well to blend, breaking up the tomatoes a bit to create more moisture in the mixture.
7. Cover and refrigerate for 2 hours to blend the flavors. Serve chilled or at room temperature. The caponata salsa can stay in its covered bowl in the fridge for up to 2 days before the vegetables weep too much moisture and the dish becomes too wet.

Prosciutto Mozzarella Bites

Servings: 8
Cooking Time: 6 Minutes
Ingredients:
- 8 pieces full-fat mozzarella string cheese
- 8 thin slices prosciutto
- 16 basil leaves

Directions:
1. Preheat the air fryer to 360°F.
2. Cut the string cheese in half across the center, not lengthwise. Do the same with the prosciutto.
3. Place a piece of prosciutto onto a clean workspace. Top the prosciutto with a basil leaf and then a piece of string cheese. Roll up the string cheese inside the prosciutto and secure with a wooden toothpick. Repeat with the remaining cheese sticks.
4. Place the prosciutto mozzarella bites into the air fryer basket and cook for 6 minutes, checking for doneness at 4 minutes.

Sweet Plantain Chips

Servings: 4
Cooking Time: 11 Minutes
Ingredients:
- 2 Very ripe plantain(s), peeled and sliced into 1-inch pieces
- Vegetable oil spray
- 3 tablespoons Maple syrup
- For garnishing Coarse sea salt or kosher salt

Directions:
1. Pour about ½ cup water into the bottom of your air fryer basket or into a metal tray on a lower rack in some models. Preheat the air fryer to 400°F.
2. Put the plantain pieces in a bowl, coat them with vegetable oil spray, and toss gently, spraying at least one more time and tossing repeatedly, until the pieces are well coated.
3. When the machine is at temperature, arrange the plantain pieces in the basket in one layer. Air-fry undisturbed for 5 minutes.
4. Remove the basket from the machine and spray the back of a metal spatula with vegetable oil spray. Use the spatula to press down on the plantain pieces, spraying it again as needed, to flatten the pieces to about half their original height. Brush the plantain pieces with maple syrup, then return the basket to the machine and continue air-frying undisturbed for 6 minutes, or until the plantain pieces are soft and caramelized.
5. Use kitchen tongs to transfer the pieces to a serving platter. Sprinkle the pieces with salt and cool for a couple of minutes before serving. Or cool to room temperature before serving, about 1 hour.

Cheesy Hash Brown Bruschetta

Servings: 4
Cooking Time: 6 To 8 Minutes
Ingredients:
- 4 frozen hash brown patties
- 1 tablespoon olive oil
- ⅓ cup chopped cherry tomatoes
- 3 tablespoons diced fresh Mozzarella
- 2 tablespoons grated Parmesan cheese
- 1 tablespoon balsamic vinegar
- 1 tablespoon minced fresh basil

Directions:
1. Preheat the air fryer to 400°F (204°C).
2. Place the hash brown patties in the air fryer in a single layer. Air fry for 6 to 8 minutes, or until the potatoes are crisp, hot, and golden brown.
3. Meanwhile, combine the olive oil, tomatoes, Mozzarella, Parmesan, vinegar, and basil in a small bowl.
4. When the potatoes are done, carefully remove from the basket and arrange on a serving plate. Top with the tomato mixture and serve.

Savory Sausage Balls

Servings: 10
Cooking Time: 8 Minutes
Ingredients:
- 2 cups all-purpose flour
- 1 tablespoon baking powder
- ½ teaspoon garlic powder
- ¼ teaspoon onion powder
- ½ teaspoon salt
- 3 tablespoons milk
- 2½ cups grated pepper jack cheese
- 1 pound fresh sausage, casing removed

Directions:
1. Preheat the air fryer to 370°F.
2. In a large bowl, whisk together the flour, baking powder, garlic powder, onion powder, and salt. Add in the milk, grated cheese, and sausage.
3. Using a tablespoon, scoop out the sausage and roll it between your hands to form a rounded ball. You should end up with approximately 32 balls. Place them in the air

fryer basket in a single layer and working in batches as necessary.
4. Cook for 8 minutes, or until the outer coating turns light brown.
5. Carefully remove, repeating with the remaining sausage balls.

Spicy Cocktail Wieners
Servings: 4
Cooking Time: 15 Minutes
Ingredients:
- 1 lb. pork cocktail sausages
- For the Sauce:
- ¼ cup mayonnaise
- ¼ cup cream cheese
- 1 whole grain mustard
- ¼- ½ teaspoon balsamic vinegar
- 1 garlic clove, finely minced
- ¼ teaspoon chili powder

Directions:
1. Pork the sausages a few times with a fork, them place them on the cooking pan of your air fryer.
2. Cook the sausages at 390 degrees F/ 200 degrees C for 15 minutes;
3. After 8 minutes of cooking, turn the sausages over and resume cooking.
4. Check for doneness and take the sausages out of the machine.
5. At the same time, thoroughly combine all the ingredients for the sauce.
6. Serve with warm sausages and enjoy!

Ham And Cheese Sliders
Servings:3
Cooking Time: 10 Minutes
Ingredients:
- 6 Hawaiian sweet rolls
- 12 slices thinly sliced Black Forest ham
- 6 slices sharp Cheddar cheese
- ⅓ cup salted butter, melted
- 1 ½ teaspoons minced garlic

Directions:
1. Preheat the air fryer to 350°F.
2. For each slider, slice horizontally through the center of a roll without fully separating the two halves. Place 2 slices ham and 2 slices cheese inside roll and close. Repeat with remaining rolls, ham, and cheese.
3. In a small bowl, mix butter and garlic and brush over all sides of rolls.
4. Place in the air fryer and cook 10 minutes until rolls are golden on top and cheese is melted. Serve warm.

Crispy Curried Sweet Potato Fries
Servings: 4
Cooking Time: 20 Minutes
Ingredients:
- ½ cup sour cream
- ½ cup peach chutney
- 3 tsp curry powder
- 2 sweet potatoes, julienned
- 1 tbsp olive oil
- Salt and pepper to taste

Directions:
1. Preheat air fryer to 390°F. Mix together sour cream, peach chutney, and 1 ½ tsp curry powder in a small bowl. Set aside. In a medium bowl, add sweet potatoes, olive oil, the rest of the curry powder, salt, and pepper. Toss to coat. Place the potatoes in the frying basket. Bake for about 6 minutes, then shake the basket once. Cook for an additional 4 -6 minutes or until the potatoes are golden and crispy. Serve the fries hot in a basket along with the chutney sauce for dipping.

Garlic Spinach Dip
Servings: 8
Cooking Time: 20 Minutes
Ingredients:
- 8 ounces cream cheese, softened
- ¼ teaspoon garlic powder
- ½ cup onion, minced
- ⅓ cup water chestnuts, drained and chopped
- 1 cup mayonnaise
- 1 cup parmesan cheese, grated
- 1 cup frozen spinach, thawed and squeeze out all liquid
- ½ teaspoon black pepper

Directions:
1. Grease its air fryer basket with cooking spray.
2. Add all the recipe ingredients into the bowl and mix until well combined.
3. Transfer bowl mixture into the prepared baking dish and place dish in air fryer basket.
4. Cook at almost 300 degrees F/ 150 degrees C for 35-40 minutes. After 20 minutes of cooking stir dip.
5. Serve and enjoy.

Cheesy Jalapeño Poppers
Servings:4
Cooking Time: 10 Minutes
Ingredients:
- 8 jalapeño peppers
- ½ cup whipped cream cheese
- ¼ cup shredded Cheddar cheese

Directions:
1. Preheat the air fryer to 360ºF (182ºC).
2. Use a paring knife to carefully cut off the jalapeño tops, then scoop out the ribs and seeds. Set aside.
3. In a medium bowl, combine the whipped cream cheese and shredded Cheddar cheese. Place the mixture in a sealable plastic bag, and using a pair of scissors, cut off one corner from the bag. Gently squeeze some cream cheese mixture into each pepper until almost full.
4. Place a piece of parchment paper on the bottom of the air fryer basket and place the poppers on top, distributing evenly. Air fry for 10 minutes.
5. Allow the poppers to cool for 5 to 10 minutes before serving.

Indian Cauliflower Tikka Bites

Servings: 6
Cooking Time: 20 Minutes
Ingredients:
- 1 cup plain Greek yogurt
- 1 teaspoon fresh ginger
- 1 teaspoon minced garlic
- 1 teaspoon vindaloo
- ½ teaspoon cardamom
- ½ teaspoon paprika
- ½ teaspoon turmeric powder
- ½ teaspoon cumin powder
- 1 large head of cauliflower, washed and cut into medium-size florets
- ½ cup panko breadcrumbs
- 1 lemon, quartered

Directions:
1. Preheat the air fryer to 350°F.
2. In a large bowl, mix the yogurt, ginger, garlic, vindaloo, cardamom, paprika, turmeric, and cumin. Add the cauliflower florets to the bowl, and coat them with the yogurt.
3. Remove the cauliflower florets from the bowl and place them on a baking sheet. Sprinkle the panko breadcrumbs over the top. Place the cauliflower bites into the air fryer basket, leaving space between the florets. Depending on the size of your air fryer, you may need to make more than one batch.
4. Cook the cauliflower for 10 minutes, shake the basket, and continue cooking another 10 minutes (or until the florets are lightly browned).
5. Remove from the air fryer and keep warm. Continue to cook until all the florets are done.
6. Before serving, lightly squeeze lemon over the top. Serve warm.

Chives Meatballs

Servings: 6
Cooking Time: 20 Minutes
Ingredients:
- 1 pound beef meat, ground
- 1 teaspoon onion powder
- 1 teaspoon garlic powder
- A pinch of salt and black pepper
- 2 tablespoons chives, chopped
- Cooking spray

Directions:
1. In a bowl, mix all the ingredients except the cooking spray, stir well and shape medium meatballs out of this mix. Pace them in your lined air fryer's basket, grease with cooking spray and cook at 360°F for 20 minutes. Serve as an appetizer.

Spicy Turkey Meatballs

Servings:18
Cooking Time: 15 Minutes
Ingredients:
- 1 pound 85/15 ground turkey
- 1 large egg, whisked
- ¼ cup sriracha hot chili sauce
- ½ teaspoon salt
- ½ teaspoon paprika
- ¼ teaspoon ground black pepper

Directions:
1. Combine all ingredients in a large bowl. Roll mixture into eighteen meatballs, about 3 tablespoons each.
2. Place meatballs into ungreased air fryer basket. Adjust the temperature to 375°F and set the timer for 15 minutes, shaking the basket three times during cooking. Meatballs will be done when browned and internal temperature is at least 165°F. Serve warm.

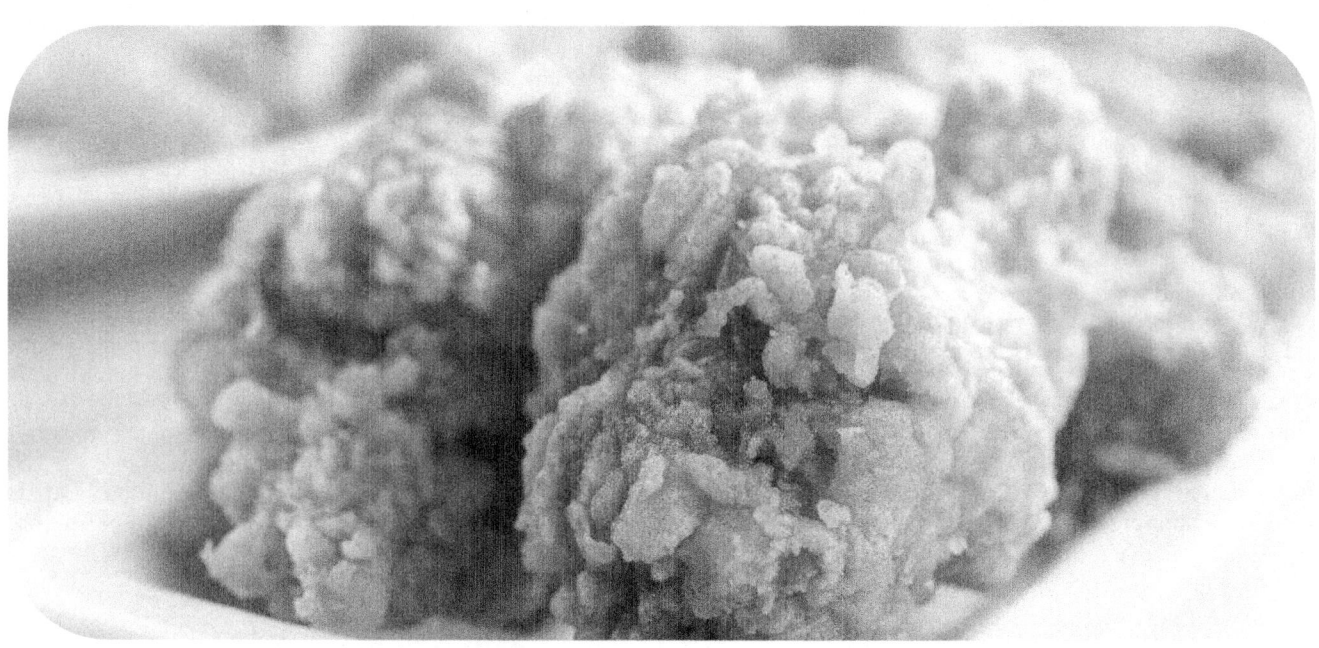

Chapter 5: Vegetarians Recipes

Easy Cheese & Spinach Lasagna

Servings: 6
Cooking Time: 50 Minutes
Ingredients:
- 1 zucchini, cut into strips
- 1 tbsp butter
- 4 garlic cloves, minced
- ½ yellow onion, diced
- 1 tsp dried oregano
- ¼ tsp red pepper flakes
- 1 can diced tomatoes
- 4 oz ricotta
- 3 tbsp grated mozzarella
- ½ cup grated cheddar
- 3 tsp grated Parmesan cheese
- ⅛ cup chopped basil
- 2 tbsp chopped parsley
- Salt and pepper to taste
- ¼ tsp ground nutmeg

Directions:
1. Preheat air fryer to 375°F. Melt butter in a medium skillet over medium heat. Stir in half of the garlic and onion and cook for 2 minutes. Stir in oregano and red pepper flakes and cook for 1 minute. Reduce the heat to medium-low and pour in crushed tomatoes and their juices. Cover the skillet and simmer for 5 minutes.
2. Mix ricotta, mozzarella, cheddar cheese, rest of the garlic, basil, black pepper, and nutmeg in a large bowl. Arrange a layer of zucchini strips in the baking dish. Scoop 1/3 of the cheese mixture and spread evenly over the zucchini. Spread 1/3 of the tomato sauce over the cheese. Repeat the steps two more times, then top the lasagna with Parmesan cheese. Bake in the frying basket for 25 minutes until the mixture is bubbling and the mozzarella is melted. Allow sitting for 10 minutes before cutting. Serve warm sprinkled with parsley and enjoy!

Eggplant Parmesan

Servings: 4
Cooking Time: 8 Minutes Per Batch
Ingredients:
- 1 medium eggplant, 6–8 inches long
- salt
- 1 large egg
- 1 tablespoon water
- ⅔ cup panko breadcrumbs
- ⅓ cup grated Parmesan cheese, plus more for serving
- 1 tablespoon Italian seasoning
- ¾ teaspoon oregano
- oil for misting or cooking spray
- 1 24-ounce jar marinara sauce
- 8 ounces spaghetti, cooked
- pepper

Directions:
1. Preheat air fryer to 390°F.
2. Leaving peel intact, cut eggplant into 8 round slices about ¾-inch thick. Salt to taste.
3. Beat egg and water in a shallow dish.
4. In another shallow dish, combine panko, Parmesan, Italian seasoning, and oregano.
5. Dip eggplant slices in egg wash and then crumbs, pressing lightly to coat.
6. Mist slices with oil or cooking spray.
7. Place 4 eggplant slices in air fryer basket and cook for 8 minutes, until brown and crispy.
8. While eggplant is cooking, heat marinara sauce.
9. Repeat step 7 to cook remaining eggplant slices.
10. To serve, place cooked spaghetti on plates and top with marinara and eggplant slices. At the table, pass extra Parmesan cheese and freshly ground black pepper.

Parmesan Portobello Mushroom Caps

Servings: 2
Cooking Time: 14 Minutes
Ingredients:
- ¼ cup flour*
- 1 egg, lightly beaten
- 1 cup seasoned breadcrumbs*
- 2 large portobello mushroom caps, stems and gills removed
- olive oil, in a spray bottle
- ½ cup tomato sauce
- ¾ cup grated mozzarella cheese
- 1 tablespoon grated Parmesan cheese
- 1 tablespoon chopped fresh basil or parsley

Directions:
1. Set up a dredging station with three shallow dishes. Place the flour in the first shallow dish, egg in the second dish and breadcrumbs in the last dish. Dredge the mushrooms in flour, then dip them into the egg and finally press them into the breadcrumbs to coat on all sides. Spray both sides of the coated mushrooms with olive oil.
2. Preheat the air fryer to 400°F.
3. Air-fry the mushrooms at 400°F for 10 minutes, turning them over halfway through the cooking process.
4. Fill the underside of the mushrooms with the tomato sauce and then top the sauce with the mozzarella and Parmesan cheeses. Reset the air fryer temperature to 350°F and air-fry for an additional 4 minutes, until the cheese has melted and is slightly browned.
5. Serve the mushrooms with pasta tossed with tomato sauce and garnish with some chopped fresh basil or parsley.

Mushroom, Zucchini And Black Bean Burgers

Servings: 4
Cooking Time: 18 Minutes
Ingredients:
- 1 cup diced zucchini, (about ½ medium zucchini)
- 1 tablespoon olive oil
- salt and freshly ground black pepper

- 1 cup chopped brown mushrooms (about 3 ounces)
- 1 small clove garlic
- 1 (15-ounce) can black beans, drained and rinsed
- 1 teaspoon lemon zest
- 1 tablespoon chopped fresh cilantro
- ½ cup plain breadcrumbs
- 1 egg, beaten
- ½ teaspoon salt
- freshly ground black pepper
- whole-wheat pita bread, burger buns or brioche buns
- mayonnaise, tomato, avocado and lettuce, for serving

Directions:
1. Preheat the air fryer to 400°F.
2. Toss the zucchini with the olive oil, season with salt and freshly ground black pepper and air-fry for 6 minutes, shaking the basket once or twice while it cooks.
3. Transfer the zucchini to a food processor with the mushrooms, garlic and black beans and process until still a little chunky but broken down and pasty. Transfer the mixture to a bowl. Add the lemon zest, cilantro, breadcrumbs and egg and mix well. Season again with salt and freshly ground black pepper. Shape the mixture into four burger patties and refrigerate for at least 15 minutes.
4. Preheat the air fryer to 370°F. Transfer two of the veggie burgers to the air fryer basket and air-fry for 12 minutes, flipping the burgers gently halfway through the cooking time. Keep the burgers warm by loosely tenting them with foil while you cook the remaining two burgers. Return the first batch of burgers back into the air fryer with the second batch for the last two minutes of cooking to re-heat.
5. Serve on toasted whole-wheat pita bread, burger buns or brioche buns with some mayonnaise, tomato, avocado and lettuce.

Tofu & Spinach Lasagna
Servings: 4
Cooking Time: 30 Minutes
Ingredients:
- 8 oz cooked lasagne noodles
- 1 tbsp olive oil
- 2 cups crumbled tofu
- 2 cups fresh spinach
- 2 tbsp cornstarch
- 1 tsp onion powder
- Salt and pepper to taste
- 2 garlic cloves, minced
- 2 cups marinara sauce
- ½ cup shredded mozzarella

Directions:
1. Warm the olive oil in a large pan over medium heat. Add the tofu and spinach and stir-fry for a minute. Add the cornstarch, onion powder, salt, pepper, and garlic. Stir until the spinach wilts. Remove from heat.
2. Preheat air fryer to 390°F. Pour a thin layer of pasta sauce in a baking pan. Layer 2-3 lasagne noodles on top of the marinara sauce. Top with a little more sauce and some of the tofu mix. Add another 2-3 noodles on top, then another layer of sauce, then another layer of tofu. Finish with a layer of noodles and a final layer of sauce. Sprinkle with mozzarella cheese on top. Place the pan in the air fryer and Bake for 15 minutes or until the noodle edges are browned and the cheese is melted. Cut and serve.

Spiced Vegetable Galette
Servings: 4
Cooking Time: 30 Minutes
Ingredients:
- ¼ cup cooked eggplant, chopped
- ¼ cup cooked zucchini, chopped
- 1 refrigerated pie crust
- 2 eggs
- ¼ cup milk
- Salt and pepper to taste
- 1 red chili, finely sliced
- ¼ cup tomato, chopped
- ½ cup shredded mozzarella cheese

Directions:
1. Preheat air fryer to 360°F. In a baking dish, add the crust and press firmly. Trim off any excess edges. Poke a few holes. Beat the eggs in a bowl. Stir in the milk, half of the cheese, eggplant, zucchini, tomato, red chili, salt, and pepper. Mix well. Transfer the mixture to the baking dish and place in the air fryer. Bake for 15 minutes or until firm and almost crusty. Slide the basket out and top with the remaining cheese. Cook further for 5 minutes, or until golden brown. Let cool slightly and serve.

Mushroom And Fried Onion Quesadilla
Servings: 2
Cooking Time: 33 Minutes
Ingredients:
- 1 onion, sliced
- 2 tablespoons butter, melted
- 10 ounces button mushrooms, sliced
- 2 tablespoons Worcestershire sauce
- salt and freshly ground black pepper
- 4 (8-inch) flour tortillas
- 2 cups grated Fontina cheese
- vegetable or olive oil

Directions:
1. Preheat the air fryer to 400°F.
2. Toss the onion slices with the melted butter and transfer them to the air fryer basket. Air-fry at 400°F for 15 minutes, shaking the basket several times during the cooking process. Add the mushrooms and Worcestershire sauce to the onions and stir to combine. Air-fry at 400°F for an additional 10 minutes. Season with salt and freshly ground black pepper.
3. Lay two of the tortillas on a cutting board. Top each tortilla with ½ cup of the grated cheese, half of the onion and mushroom mixture and then finally another ½ cup of

the cheese. Place the remaining tortillas on top of the cheese and press down firmly.
4. Brush the air fryer basket with a little oil. Place a quesadilla in the basket and brush the top with a little oil. Secure the top tortilla to the bottom with three toothpicks and air-fry at 400°F for 5 minutes. Flip the quesadilla over by inverting it onto a plate and sliding it back into the basket. Remove the toothpicks and brush the other side with oil. Air-fry for an additional 3 minutes.
5. Invert the quesadilla onto a cutting board and cut it into 4 or 6 triangles. Serve immediately.

Golden Breaded Mushrooms
Servings: 2
Cooking Time: 20 Minutes
Ingredients:
- 2 cups crispy rice cereal
- 1 tsp nutritional yeast
- 2 tsp garlic powder
- 1tsp dried oregano
- 1 tsp dried basil
- Salt to taste
- 1 tbsp Dijon mustard
- 1 tbsp mayonnaise
- ¼ cup milk
- 8 oz whole mushrooms
- 4 tbsp chili sauce
- 3 tbsp mayonnaise

Directions:
1. Preheat air fryer at 350ºF. Blend rice cereal, garlic powder, oregano, basil, nutritional yeast, and salt in a food processor until it gets a breadcrumb consistency. Set aside in a bowl. Mix the mustard, mayonnaise, and milk in a bowl. Dip mushrooms in the mustard mixture; shake off any excess. Then, dredge them in the breadcrumbs; shake off any excess. Places mushrooms in the greased frying basket and Air Fry for 7 minutes, shaking once. Mix the mayonnaise with chili sauce in a small bowl. Serve the mushrooms with the dipping sauce on the side.

Savory Herb Cloud Eggs
Servings:2
Cooking Time: 8 Minutes
Ingredients:
- 2 large eggs, whites and yolks separated
- ¼ teaspoon salt
- ¼ teaspoon dried oregano
- 2 tablespoons chopped fresh chives
- 2 teaspoons salted butter, melted

Directions:
1. In a large bowl, whip egg whites until stiff peaks form, about 3 minutes. Place egg whites evenly into two ungreased 4" ramekins. Sprinkle evenly with salt, oregano, and chives. Place 1 whole egg yolk in center of each ramekin and drizzle with butter.

2. Place ramekins into air fryer basket. Adjust the temperature to 350°F and set the timer for 8 minutes. Egg whites will be fluffy and browned when done. Serve warm.

Caramelized Carrots
Servings:3
Cooking Time:15 Minutes
Ingredients:
- 1 small bag baby carrots
- ½ cup butter, melted
- ½ cup brown sugar

Directions:
1. Preheat the Air fryer to 400°F and grease an Air fryer basket.
2. Mix the butter and brown sugar in a bowl.
3. Add the carrots and toss to coat well.
4. Arrange the carrots in the Air fryer basket and cook for about 15 minutes.
5. Dish out and serve warm.

Stuffed Mushrooms
Servings:4
Cooking Time: 10 Minutes
Ingredients:
- 12 baby bella mushrooms, stems removed
- 4 ounces full-fat cream cheese, softened
- ¼ cup grated vegetarian Parmesan cheese
- ¼ cup Italian bread crumbs
- 1 teaspoon crushed red pepper flakes

Directions:
1. Preheat the air fryer to 400°F.
2. Use a spoon to hollow out mushroom caps.
3. In a medium bowl, combine cream cheese, Parmesan, bread crumbs, and red pepper flakes. Scoop approximately 1 tablespoon mixture into each mushroom cap.
4. Place stuffed mushrooms in the air fryer basket and cook 10 minutes until stuffing is brown. Let cool 5 minutes before serving.

Gourmet Wasabi Popcorn
Servings: 2
Cooking Time: 30 Minutes
Ingredients:
- 1/2 teaspoon brown sugar
- 1 teaspoon salt
- 1/2 teaspoon wasabi powder, sifted
- 1 tablespoon avocado oil
- 3 tablespoons popcorn kernels

Directions:
1. Add the dried corn kernels to the Air Fryer basket; toss with the remaining ingredients.
2. Cook at 395°F for 15 minutes, shaking the basket every 5 minutes. Work in two batches.
3. Taste, adjust the seasonings and serve immediately. Bon appétit!

Brussels Sprouts With Balsamic Oil

Servings: 4
Cooking Time: 15 Minutes
Ingredients:
- ¼ teaspoon salt
- 1 tablespoon balsamic vinegar
- 2 cups Brussels sprouts, halved
- 2 tablespoons olive oil

Directions:
1. Preheat the air fryer for 5 minutes.
2. Mix all ingredients in a bowl until the zucchini fries are well coated.
3. Place in the air fryer basket.
4. Close and cook for 15 minutes for 350°F.

Cauliflower Pizza Crust

Servings: 2
Cooking Time: 7 Minutes
Ingredients:
- 1 steamer bag cauliflower, cooked according to package instructions
- ½ cup shredded sharp Cheddar cheese
- 1 large egg
- 2 tablespoons blanched finely ground almond flour
- 1 teaspoon Italian seasoning

Directions:
1. Let cooked cauliflower cool for 10 minutes. Using a kitchen towel, wring out excess moisture from cauliflower and place into food processor.
2. Add Cheddar, egg, flour, and Italian seasoning to processor and pulse ten times until cauliflower is smooth and all ingredients are combined.
3. Cut two pieces of parchment paper to fit air fryer basket. Divide cauliflower mixture into two equal portions and press each into a 6" round on ungreased parchment.
4. Place crusts on parchment into air fryer basket. Adjust the temperature to 360°F and set the timer for 7 minutes, gently turning crusts halfway through cooking.
5. Store crusts in refrigerator in an airtight container up to 4 days or freeze between sheets of parchment in a sealable storage bag for up to 2 months.

Breadcrumbs Stuffed Mushrooms

Servings: 4
Cooking Time: 10 Minutes
Ingredients:
- 1½ spelt bread slices
- 1 tablespoon flat-leaf parsley, finely chopped
- 16 small button mushrooms, stemmed and gills removed
- 1½ tablespoons olive oil
- 1 garlic clove, crushed
- Salt and black pepper, to taste

Directions:
1. Preheat the Air fryer to 390°F and grease an Air fryer basket.
2. Put the bread slices in a food processor and pulse until fine crumbs form.
3. Transfer the crumbs into a bowl and stir in the olive oil, garlic, parsley, salt, and black pepper.
4. Stuff the breadcrumbs mixture in each mushroom cap and arrange the mushrooms in the Air fryer basket.
5. Cook for about 10 minutes and dish out in a bowl to serve warm.

Roasted Vegetable, Brown Rice And Black Bean Burrito

Servings: 2
Cooking Time: 20 Minutes
Ingredients:
- ½ zucchini, sliced ¼-inch thick
- ½ red onion, sliced
- 1 yellow bell pepper, sliced
- 2 teaspoons olive oil
- salt and freshly ground black pepper
- 2 burrito size flour tortillas
- 1 cup grated pepper jack cheese
- ½ cup cooked brown rice
- ½ cup canned black beans, drained and rinsed
- ¼ teaspoon ground cumin
- 1 tablespoon chopped fresh cilantro
- fresh salsa, guacamole and sour cream, for serving

Directions:
1. Preheat the air fryer to 400°F.
2. Toss the vegetables in a bowl with the olive oil, salt and freshly ground black pepper. Air-fry at 400°F for 12 to 15 minutes, shaking the basket a few times during the cooking process. The vegetables are done when they are cooked to your liking.
3. In the meantime, start building the burritos. Lay the tortillas out on the counter. Sprinkle half of the cheese in the center of the tortillas. Combine the rice, beans, cumin and cilantro in a bowl, season to taste with salt and freshly ground black pepper and then divide the mixture between the two tortillas. When the vegetables have finished cooking, transfer them to the two tortillas, placing the vegetables on top of the rice and beans. Sprinkle the remaining cheese on top and then roll the burritos up, tucking in the sides of the tortillas as you roll. Brush or spray the outside of the burritos with olive oil and transfer them to the air fryer.
4. Air-fry at 360°F for 8 minutes, turning them over when there are about 2 minutes left. The burritos will have slightly brown spots, but will still be pliable.
5. Serve with some fresh salsa, guacamole and sour cream.

Bengali Samosa With Mango Chutney

Servings: 4
Cooking Time: 65 Minutes
Ingredients:
- ¼ tsp ground fenugreek seeds
- 1 cup diced mango
- 1 tbsp minced red onion

- 2 tsp honey
- 1 tsp minced ginger
- 1 tsp apple cider vinegar
- 1 phyllo dough sheet
- 2 tbsp olive oil
- 1 potato, mashed
- ½ tsp garam masala
- ¼ tsp ground turmeric
- ⅛ tsp chili powder
- ¼ tsp ground cumin
- ½ cup green peas
- 2 scallions, chopped

Directions:
1. Mash mango in a small bowl until chunky. Stir in onion, ginger, honey, and vinegar. Save in the fridge until ready to use. Place the mashed potato in a bowl. Add half of the olive oil, garam masala, turmeric, chili powder, ground fenugreek seeds, cumin, and salt and stir until mostly smooth. Stir in peas and scallions.
2. Preheat air fryer to 425°F. Lightly flour a flat work surface and transfer the phyllo dough. Cut into 8 equal portions and roll each portion to ¼-inch thick rounds. Divide the potato filling between the dough rounds. Fold in three sides and pinch at the meeting point, almost like a pyramid. Arrange the samosas in the frying basket and brush with the remaining olive oil. Bake for 10 minutes, then flip the samosas. Bake for another 4-6 minutes until the crust is crisp and golden. Serve with mango chutney.

Kale & Lentils With Crispy Onions
Servings: 4
Cooking Time: 40 Minutes
Ingredients:
- 2 cups cooked red lentils
- 1 onion, cut into rings
- ½ cup kale, steamed
- 3 garlic cloves, minced
- ½ lemon, juiced and zested
- 2 tsp cornstarch
- 1 tsp dried oregano
- Salt and pepper to taste

Directions:
1. Preheat air fryer to 390°F. Put the onion rings in the greased frying basket; do not overlap. Spray with oil and season with salt. Air Fry for 14-16 minutes, stirring twice until crispy and crunchy. Place the kale and lentils into a pan over medium heat and stir until heated through. Remove and add the garlic, lemon juice, cornstarch, salt, zest, oregano and black pepper. Stir well and pour in bowls. Top with the crisp onion rings and serve.

Zucchini Tamale Pie
Servings: 4
Cooking Time: 45 Minutes
Ingredients:
- 1 cup canned diced tomatoes with juice
- 1 zucchini, diced
- 3 tbsp safflower oil
- 1 cup cooked pinto beans
- 3 garlic cloves, minced
- 1 tbsp corn masa flour
- 1 tsp dried oregano
- ½ tsp ground cumin
- 1 tsp onion powder
- Salt to taste
- ½ tsp red chili flakes
- ½ cup ground cornmeal
- 1 tsp nutritional yeast
- 2 tbsp chopped cilantro
- ½ tsp lime zest

Directions:
1. Warm 2 tbsp of the oil in a skillet over medium heat and sauté the zucchini for 3 minutes or until they begin to brown. Add the beans, tomatoes, garlic, flour, oregano, cumin, onion powder, salt, and chili flakes. Cook over medium heat, stirring often, about 5 minutes until the mix is thick and no liquid remains. Remove from heat. Spray a baking pan with oil and pour the mix inside. Smooth out the top and set aside.
2. In a pot over high heat, add the cornmeal, 1 ½ cups of water, and salt. Whisk constantly as the mix begins to boil. Once it boils, reduce the heat to low. Add the yeast and oil and continue to cook, stirring often, for 10 minutes or until the mix is thick and hard to stir. Remove. Preheat air fryer to 325°F. Add the cilantro and lime zest into the cornmeal mix and thoroughly combine. Using a rubber spatula, spread it evenly over the filling in the baking pan to form a crust topping. Put in the frying basket and Bake for 20 minutes or until the top is golden. Let it cool for 5 to 10 minutes, then cut and serve.

Green Bean Sautée
Servings: 4
Cooking Time: 25 Minutes
Ingredients:
- 1 ½ lb green beans, trimmed
- 1 tbsp olive oil
- ½ tsp garlic powder
- Salt and pepper to taste
- 4 garlic cloves, thinly sliced
- 1 tbsp fresh basil, chopped

Directions:
1. Preheat the air fryer to 375°F. Toss the beans with the olive oil, garlic powder, salt, and pepper in a bowl, then add to the frying basket. Air Fry for 6 minutes, shaking the basket halfway through the cooking time. Add garlic to the air fryer and cook for 3-6 minutes or until the green beans are tender and the garlic slices start to brown. Sprinkle with basil and serve warm.

Bell Pepper & Lentil Tacos

Servings: 2
Cooking Time: 40 Minutes
Ingredients:
- 2 corn tortilla shells
- ½ cup cooked lentils
- ½ white onion, sliced
- ½ red pepper, sliced
- ½ green pepper, sliced
- ½ yellow pepper, sliced
- ½ cup shredded mozzarella
- ½ tsp Tabasco sauce

Directions:
1. Preheat air fryer to 320°F. Sprinkle half of the mozzarella cheese over one of the tortillas, then top with lentils, Tabasco sauce, onion, and peppers. Scatter the remaining mozzarella cheese, cover with the other tortilla and place in the frying basket. Bake for 6 minutes, flipping halfway through cooking. Serve and enjoy!

Rice & Bean Burritos

Servings: 4
Cooking Time: 20 Minutes
Ingredients:
- 1 bell pepper, sliced
- ½ red onion, thinly sliced
- 2 garlic cloves, peeled
- 1 tbsp olive oil
- 1 cup cooked brown rice
- 1 can pinto beans
- ½ tsp salt
- ¼ tsp chili powder
- ¼ tsp ground cumin
- ¼ tsp smoked paprika
- 1 tbsp lime juice
- 4 tortillas
- 2 tsp grated Parmesan cheese
- 1 avocado, diced
- 4 tbsp salsa
- 2 tbsp chopped cilantro

Directions:
1. Preheat air fryer to 400°F. Combine bell pepper, onion, garlic, and olive oil. Place in the frying basket and Roast for 5 minutes. Shake and roast for another 5 minutes.
2. Remove the garlic from the basket and mince finely. Add to a large bowl along with brown rice, pinto beans, salt, chili powder, cumin, paprika, and lime juice. Divide the roasted vegetable mixture between the tortillas. Top with rice mixture, Parmesan, avocado, cilantro, and salsa. Fold in the sides, then roll the tortillas over the filling. Serve.

Vegetable Burgers

Servings: 4
Cooking Time: 12 Minutes
Ingredients:
- 8 ounces cremini mushrooms
- 2 large egg yolks
- ½ medium zucchini, trimmed and chopped
- ¼ cup peeled and chopped yellow onion
- 1 clove garlic, peeled and finely minced
- ½ teaspoon salt
- ¼ teaspoon ground black pepper

Directions:
1. Place all ingredients into a food processor and pulse twenty times until finely chopped and combined.
2. Separate mixture into four equal sections and press each into a burger shape. Place burgers into ungreased air fryer basket. Adjust the temperature to 375°F and set the timer for 12 minutes, turning burgers halfway through cooking. Burgers will be browned and firm when done.
3. Place burgers on a large plate and let cool 5 minutes before serving.

Mushroom Lasagna

Servings: 4
Cooking Time: 40 Minutes
Ingredients:
- 2 tbsp olive oil
- 1 zucchini, diced
- ½ cup diced mushrooms
- ¼ cup diced onion
- 1 cup marinara sauce
- 1 cup ricotta cheese
- 1/3 cup grated Parmesan
- 1 egg
- 2 tsp Italian seasoning
- 2 tbsp fresh basil, chopped
- ½ tsp thyme
- 1 tbsp red pepper flakes
- ½ tsp salt
- 5 lasagna noodle sheets
- 1 cup grated mozzarella

Directions:
1. Heat the oil in a skillet over medium heat. Add zucchini, mushrooms, 1 tbsp of basil, thyme, red pepper flakes and onion and cook for 4 minutes until the veggies are tender. Toss in marinara sauce, and bring it to a bowl. Then, low the heat and simmer for 3 minutes.
2. Preheat air fryer at 375°F. Combine ricotta cheese, Parmesan cheese, egg, Italian seasoning, and salt in a bowl. Spoon ¼ of the veggie mixture into a cake pan. Add a layer of lasagna noodles on top, breaking apart noodles first to fit pan. Then, top with 1/3 of ricotta mixture and ¼ of mozzarella cheese. Repeat the layer 2 more times, finishing with mozzarella cheese on top. Cover cake pan with aluminum foil.
3. Place cake pan in the frying basket and Bake for 12 minutes. Remove the foil and cook for 3 more minutes. Let rest for 10 minutes before slicing. Serve immediately sprinkled with the remaining fresh basil.

Layered Ravioli Bake

Servings: 4
Cooking Time: 20 Minutes
Ingredients:
- 2 cups marinara sauce, divided
- 2 packages fresh cheese ravioli
- 12 slices provolone cheese
- ½ cup Italian bread crumbs
- ½ cup grated vegetarian Parmesan cheese

Directions:
1. Preheat the air fryer to 350°F.
2. In the bottom of a 3-quart baking pan, spread ⅓ cup marinara. Place 6 ravioli on top of the sauce, then add 3 slices provolone on top, then another layer of ⅓ cup marinara. Repeat these layers three times to use up remaining ravioli, provolone, and sauce.
3. In a small bowl, mix bread crumbs and Parmesan. Sprinkle over the top of dish.
4. Cover pan with foil, being sure to tuck foil under the bottom of the pan to ensure the air fryer fan does not blow it off. Place pan in the air fryer basket and cook 15 minutes.
5. Remove foil and cook an additional 5 minutes until the top is brown and bubbling. Serve warm.

Italian-style Fried Cauliflower

Servings: 4
Cooking Time: 35 Minutes
Ingredients:
- 2 eggs
- 1/3 cup all-purpose flour
- ½ tsp Italian seasoning
- ½ cup bread crumbs
- 1 tsp garlic powder
- 3 tsp grated Parmesan cheese
- Salt and pepper to taste
- 1 head cauliflower, cut into florets
- ½ tsp ground coriander

Directions:
1. Preheat air fryer to 370°F. Set out 3 small bowls. In the first, mix the flour with Italian seasoning. In the second, beat the eggs. In the third bowl, combine the crumbs, garlic, Parmesan, ground coriander, salt, and pepper.
2. Dip the cauliflower in the flour, then dredge in egg, and finally in the bread crumb mixture. Place a batch of cauliflower in the greased frying basket and spray with cooking oil. Bake for 10-12 minutes, shaking once until golden. Serve warm and enjoy!

Pizza Dough

Servings: 4
Cooking Time: 1 Hour 10 Minutes, Plus 10 Minutes For Additional Batches
Ingredients:
- 2 cups all-purpose flour
- 1 tablespoon granulated sugar
- 1 tablespoon quick-rise yeast
- 4 tablespoons olive oil, divided
- ¾ cup warm water

Directions:
1. In a large bowl, mix flour, sugar, and yeast until combined. Add 2 tablespoons oil and warm water and mix until dough becomes smooth.
2. On a lightly floured surface, knead dough 10 minutes, then form into a smooth ball. Drizzle with remaining 2 tablespoons oil, then cover with plastic. Let dough rise 1 hour until doubled in size.
3. Preheat the air fryer to 320°F.
4. Separate dough into four pieces and press each into a 6" pan or air fryer pizza tray that has been spritzed with cooking oil.
5. Add any desired toppings. Place in the air fryer basket, working in batches as necessary, and cook 10 minutes until crust is brown at the edges and toppings are heated through. Serve warm.

Falafels

Servings: 12
Cooking Time: 10 Minutes
Ingredients:
- 1 pouch falafel mix
- 2–3 tablespoons plain breadcrumbs
- oil for misting or cooking spray

Directions:
1. Prepare falafel mix according to package directions.
2. Preheat air fryer to 390°F.
3. Place breadcrumbs in shallow dish or on wax paper.
4. Shape falafel mixture into 12 balls and flatten slightly. Roll in breadcrumbs to coat all sides and mist with oil or cooking spray.
5. Place falafels in air fryer basket in single layer and cook for 5 minutes. Shake basket, and continue cooking for 5 minutes, until they brown and are crispy.

Chewy Glazed Parsnips

Servings: 6
Cooking Time: 44 Minutes
Ingredients:
- 2 pounds parsnips, peeled and cut into 1-inch chunks
- 1 tablespoon butter, melted
- 2 tablespoons maple syrup
- 1 tablespoon dried parsley flakes, crushed
- ¼ teaspoon red pepper flakes, crushed

Directions:
1. Preheat the Air fryer to 355°F and grease an Air fryer basket.
2. Mix parsnips and butter in a bowl and toss to coat well.
3. Arrange the parsnips in the Air fryer basket and cook for about 40 minutes.
4. Meanwhile, mix remaining ingredients in a large bowl.
5. Transfer this mixture into the Air fryer basket and cook for about 4 more minutes.
6. Dish out and serve warm.

Crustless Spinach And Cheese Frittata

Servings: 4
Cooking Time: 20 Minutes
Ingredients:
- 6 large eggs
- ½ cup heavy whipping cream
- 1 cup frozen chopped spinach, drained
- 1 cup shredded sharp Cheddar cheese
- ¼ cup peeled and diced yellow onion
- ½ teaspoon salt
- ¼ teaspoon ground black pepper

Directions:
1. In a large bowl, whisk eggs and cream together. Whisk in spinach, Cheddar, onion, salt, and pepper.
2. Pour mixture into an ungreased 6" round nonstick baking dish. Place dish into air fryer basket. Adjust the temperature to 320°F and set the timer for 20 minutes. Eggs will be firm and slightly browned when done. Serve immediately.

Two-cheese Grilled Sandwiches

Servings: 2
Cooking Time: 30 Minutes
Ingredients:
- 4 sourdough bread slices
- 2 cheddar cheese slices
- 2 Swiss cheese slices
- 1 tbsp butter
- 2 dill pickles, sliced

Directions:
1. Preheat air fryer to 360°F. Smear both sides of the sourdough bread with butter and place them in the frying basket. Toast the bread for 6 minutes, flipping once.
2. Divide the cheddar cheese between 2 of the bread slices. Cover the remaining 2 bread slices with Swiss cheese slices. Bake for 10 more minutes until the cheeses have melted and lightly bubbled and the bread has golden brown. Set the cheddar-covered bread slices on a serving plate, cover with pickles, and top each with the Swiss-covered slices. Serve and enjoy!

Vegan Buddha Bowls(1)

Servings: 2
Cooking Time: 45 Minutes
Ingredients:
- ½ cup quinoa
- 1 cup sweet potato cubes
- 12 oz broccoli florets
- ¾ cup bread crumbs
- ¼ cup chickpea flour
- ¼ cup hot sauce
- 16 oz super-firm tofu, cubed
- 1 tsp lemon juice
- 2 tsp olive oil
- Salt to taste
- 2 scallions, thinly sliced
- 1 tbsp sesame seeds

Directions:
1. Preheat air fryer to 400°F. Add quinoa and 1 cup of boiling water in a baking pan, cover it with aluminum foil, and Air Fry for 10 minutes. Set aside covered. Put the sweet potatoes in the basket and Air Fry for 2 minutes. Add in broccoli and Air Fry for 5 more minutes. Shake up and cook for another 3 minutes. Set the veggies aside.
2. On a plate, put the breadcrumbs. In a bowl, whisk chickpea flour and hot sauce. Toss in tofu cubes until coated and dip them in the breadcrumbs. Air Fry for 10 minutes until crispy. Share quinoa and fried veggies into 2 bowls. Top with crispy tofu and drizzle with lemon juice, olive oil and salt to taste. Scatter with scallions and sesame seeds before serving.

Zucchini & Bell Pepper Stir-fry

Servings: 4
Cooking Time: 25 Minutes
Ingredients:
- 1 zucchini, cut into rounds
- 1 red bell pepper, sliced
- 3 garlic cloves, sliced
- 2 tbsp olive oil
- 1/3 cup vegetable broth
- 1 tbsp lemon juice
- 2 tsp cornstarch
- 1 tsp dried basil
- Salt and pepper to taste

Directions:
1. Preheat the air fryer to 400°F. Combine the veggies, garlic, and olive oil in a bowl. Put the bowl in the frying basket and Air Fry the zucchini mixture for 5 minutes, stirring once; drain. While the veggies are cooking, whisk the broth, lemon juice, cornstarch, basil, salt, and pepper in a bowl. Pour the broth into the bowl along with the veggies and stir. Air Fry for 5-9 more minutes until the veggies are tender and the sauce is thick. Serve and enjoy!

Curried Potato, Cauliflower And Pea Turnovers

Servings: 4
Cooking Time: 40 Minutes
Ingredients:
- Dough:
- 2 cups all-purpose flour
- ½ teaspoon baking powder
- 1 teaspoon salt
- freshly ground black pepper
- ¼ teaspoon dried thyme
- ¼ cup canola oil
- ½ to ⅔ cup water
- Turnover Filling:
- 1 tablespoon canola or vegetable oil
- 1 onion, finely chopped
- 1 clove garlic, minced

Air Fryer Cookbook for Beginners

- 1 tablespoon grated fresh ginger
- ½ teaspoon cumin seeds
- ½ teaspoon fennel seeds
- 1 teaspoon curry powder
- 2 russet potatoes, diced
- 2 cups cauliflower florets
- ½ cup frozen peas
- 2 tablespoons chopped fresh cilantro
- salt and freshly ground black pepper
- 2 tablespoons butter, melted
- mango chutney, for serving

Directions:
1. Start by making the dough. Combine the flour, baking powder, salt, pepper and dried thyme in a mixing bowl or the bowl of a stand mixer. Drizzle in the canola oil and pinch it together with your fingers to turn the flour into a crumby mixture. Stir in the water (enough to bring the dough together). Knead the dough for 5 minutes or so until it is smooth. Add a little more water or flour as needed. Let the dough rest while you make the turnover filling.
2. Preheat a large skillet on the stovetop over medium-high heat. Add the oil and sauté the onion until it starts to become tender – about 4 minutes. Add the garlic and ginger and continue to cook for another minute. Add the dried spices and toss everything to coat. Add the potatoes and cauliflower to the skillet and pour in 1½ cups of water. Simmer everything together for 20 to 25 minutes, or until the potatoes are soft and most of the water has evaporated. If the water has evaporated and the vegetables still need more time, just add a little water and continue to simmer until everything is tender. Stir well, crushing the potatoes and cauliflower a little as you do so. Stir in the peas and cilantro, season to taste with salt and freshly ground black pepper and set aside to cool.
3. Divide the dough into 4 balls. Roll the dough balls out into ¼-inch thick circles. Divide the cooled potato filling between the dough circles, placing a mound of the filling on one side of each piece of dough, leaving an empty border around the edge of the dough. Brush the edges of the dough with a little water and fold one edge of circle over the filling to meet the other edge of the circle, creating a half moon. Pinch the edges together with your fingers and then press the edge with the tines of a fork to decorate and seal.
4. Preheat the air fryer to 380°F.
5. Spray or brush the air fryer basket with oil. Brush the turnovers with the melted butter and place 2 turnovers into the air fryer basket. Air-fry for 15 minutes. Flip the turnovers over and air-fry for another 5 minutes. Repeat with the remaining 2 turnovers.
6. These will be very hot when they come out of the air fryer. Let them cool for at least 20 minutes before serving warm with mango chutney.

Portobello Mini Pizzas

Servings: 4
Cooking Time: 10 Minutes

Ingredients:
- 4 large portobello mushrooms, stems removed
- 2 cups shredded mozzarella cheese, divided
- ½ cup full-fat ricotta cheese
- 1 teaspoon salt, divided
- ½ teaspoon ground black pepper
- 1 teaspoon Italian seasoning
- 1 cup pizza sauce

Directions:
1. Preheat the air fryer to 350°F.
2. Use a spoon to hollow out mushroom caps. Spritz mushrooms with cooking spray. Place ¼ cup mozzarella into each mushroom cap.
3. In a small bowl, mix ricotta, ½ teaspoon salt, pepper, and Italian seasoning. Divide mixture evenly and spoon into mushroom caps.
4. Pour ¼ cup pizza sauce into each mushroom cap, then top each with ¼ cup mozzarella. Sprinkle tops of pizzas with remaining salt.
5. Place mushrooms in the air fryer basket and cook 10 minutes until cheese is brown and bubbling. Serve warm.

Chapter 6: Beef, pork & Lamb Recipes

Italian Sausage Rolls

Servings: 4
Cooking Time: 20 Minutes
Ingredients:
- 1 red bell pepper, cut into strips
- 4 Italian sausages
- 1 zucchini, cut into strips
- ½ onion, cut into strips
- 1 tsp dried oregano
- ½ tsp garlic powder
- 5 Italian rolls

Directions:
1. Preheat air fryer to 360°F. Place all sausages in the air fryer. Bake for 10 minutes. While the sausages are cooking, season the bell pepper, zucchini and onion with oregano and garlic powder. When the time is up, flip the sausages, then add the peppers and onions. Cook for another 5 minutes or until the vegetables are soft and the sausages are cooked through. Put the sausage on Italian rolls, then top with peppers and onions. Serve.

Moroccan-style Steak With Salad

Servings: 4
Cooking Time: 20 Minutes
Ingredients:
- 2 lbs. flank steak
- ¼ cup soy sauce
- 1 cup dry red wine
- Salt, to taste
- ½-teaspoon ground black pepper
- 2 parsnips, peeled and sliced lengthways
- 1 tablespoon paprika
- ½ teaspoon onion powder
- ½ teaspoon garlic powder
- ½-teaspoon ground coriander
- ¼-teaspoon ground allspice
- 1 tablespoon olive oil
- ½ tablespoon lime juice
- 1 teaspoon honey
- 1 cup lettuce leaves, shredded
- ½ cup pomegranate seeds

Directions:
1. In a suitable bowl, add the soy sauce, wine, salt, black pepper and flank steak, then refrigerate the mixture for 2 hours to marinate the steak completely.
2. Spray the cooking basket with cooking spray and then transfer the marinated steak on it.
3. Sprinkle the parsnips on the top, add the paprika, onion powder, garlic powder, coriander, and allspice.
4. Cook at 400 degrees F/ 205 degrees C for 7 minutes, then turn the steak over and cook for 5 minutes more.
5. To make the dressing, mix up the olive oil, lime juice and honey. In a salad bowl, add the lettuce leaves and roasted parsnip, then toss with the dressing.
6. When the steak cook, slice and place on top of the salad.
7. Sprinkle over the pomegranate seeds and serve. Enjoy!

Pork Tenderloins

Servings: 3
Cooking Time: 30 Minutes
Ingredients:
- 1 teaspoon salt
- ½ teaspoon pepper
- 1 lb. pork tenderloin
- 2 tablespoons minced fresh rosemary
- 2 tablespoons olive oil, divided
- 1 garlic cloves, minced
- Apricot Glaze Ingredients:
- 1 cup apricot preserves
- 3 garlic cloves, minced
- 4 tablespoons lemon juice

Directions:
1. After mixing the pepper, salt, garlic, oil, and rosemary well, brush the pork with them on all sides.
2. If needed, you can cut pork crosswise in half.
3. Arrange the pork to the sprayed cooking pan and cook at 390 degrees F/ 200 degrees C for 3 minutes on each side.
4. While cooking the pork, mix all of the glaze ingredients well.
5. Baste the pork every 5 minutes.
6. Cook at 330 degrees F/ 165 degrees C and cook for 20 minutes more.
7. When done, serve and enjoy.

Sriracha Pork Strips With Rice

Servings: 4
Cooking Time: 30 Minutes + Chilling Time
Ingredients:
- ½ cup lemon juice
- 2 tbsp lemon marmalade
- 1 tbsp avocado oil
- 1 tbsp tamari
- 2 tsp sriracha
- 1 tsp yellow mustard
- 1 lb pork shoulder strips
- 4 cups cooked white rice
- ¼ cup chopped cilantro
- 1 tsp black pepper

Directions:
1. Whisk the lemon juice, lemon marmalade, avocado oil, tamari, sriracha, and mustard in a bowl. Reserve half of the marinade. Toss pork strips with half of the marinade and let marinate covered in the fridge for 30 minutes.
2. Preheat air fryer at 350ºF. Place pork strips in the frying basket and Air Fry for 17 minutes, tossing twice. Transfer them to a bowl and stir in the remaining marinade. Serve over cooked rice and scatter with cilantro and pepper.

Kochukaru Pork Lettuce Cups

Servings: 4
Cooking Time: 25 Minutes
Ingredients:
- 1 tsp kochukaru (chili pepper flakes)
- 12 baby romaine lettuce leaves
- 1 lb pork tenderloin, sliced
- Salt and pepper to taste
- 3 scallions, chopped
- 3 garlic cloves, crushed
- ¼ cup soy sauce
- 2 tbsp gochujang
- ½ tbsp light brown sugar
- ½ tbsp honey
- 1 tbsp grated fresh ginger
- 2 tbsp rice vinegar
- 1 tsp toasted sesame oil
- 2 ¼ cups cooked brown rice
- ½ tbsp sesame seeds
- 2 spring onions, sliced

Directions:
1. Mix the scallions, garlic, soy sauce, kochukaru, honey, brown sugar, and ginger in a small bowl. Mix well. Place the pork in a large bowl. Season with salt and pepper. Pour the marinade over the pork, tossing the meat in the marinade until coated. Cover the bowl with plastic wrap and allow to marinate overnight. When ready to cook,
2. Preheat air fryer to 400°F. Remove the pork from the bowl and discard the marinade. Place the pork in the greased frying basket and Air Fry for 10 minutes, flipping once until browned and cooked through. Meanwhile, prepare the gochujang sauce. Mix the gochujang, rice vinegar, and sesame oil until smooth. To make the cup, add 3 tbsp of brown rice on the lettuce leaf. Place a slice of pork on top, drizzle a tsp of gochujang sauce and sprinkle with some sesame seeds and spring onions. Wrap the lettuce over the mixture similar to a burrito. Serve warm.

Garlic Beef Cubes

Servings: 4
Cooking Time: 20 Minutes
Ingredients:
- 1 lb. beef sirloin steak, cut into cubes
- ⅓ cup sesame oil
- ½ teaspoon salt
- ¼ cup soy sauce
- ½ teaspoon pepper
- ½ teaspoon garlic powder
- ¼ teaspoon ground cumin
- ¼ cup fresh lemon juice
- 1 teaspoon dried basil
- 1 tablespoon dried parsley
- 2 carrots, sliced
- 1 large onion, sliced
- 2 Russet potatoes, peeled and sliced
- 1 ½ tablespoon fresh coriander, finely chopped

Directions:
1. In a large bowl, put the sesame oil, lemon juice, salt, pepper, garlic powder, soy sauce, cumin, basil, and parsley, then add the beef cubes to coat well.
2. Refrigerate the coated beef cubes for 2 hours.
3. Cook the marinated beef cubes in your air fryer at 360 degrees F/ 180 degrees C for 20 minutes.
4. Once cooked, serve immediately.

Rib Eye Steak Seasoned With Italian Herb

Servings: 4
Cooking Time: 45 Minutes
Ingredients:
- 1 packet Italian herb mix
- 1 tablespoon olive oil
- 2 pounds bone-in rib eye steak
- Salt and pepper to taste

Directions:
1. Preheat the air fryer to 390°F.
2. Place the grill pan accessory in the air fryer.
3. Season the steak with salt, pepper, Italian herb mix, and olive oil. Cover top with foil.
4. Grill for 45 minutes and flip the steak halfway through the cooking time.

Garlic Fillets

Servings: 4
Cooking Time: 15 Minutes
Ingredients:
- 1-pound beef filet mignon
- 1 teaspoon minced garlic
- 1 tablespoon peanut oil
- ½ teaspoon salt
- 1 teaspoon dried oregano

Directions:
1. Chop the beef into the medium size pieces and sprinkle with salt and dried oregano. Then add minced garlic and peanut oil and mix up the meat well. Place the bowl with meat in the fridge for 10 minutes to marinate. Meanwhile, preheat the air fryer to 400°F. Put the marinated beef pieces in the air fryer and cook them for 10 minutes Then flip the beef on another side and cook for 5 minutes more.

Beef & Mushrooms

Servings: 1
Cooking Time: 3 Hours 15 Minutes
Ingredients:
- 6 oz. beef
- ¼ onion, diced
- ½ cup mushroom slices
- 2 tbsp. favorite marinade [preferably bulgogi]

Directions:
1. Slice or cube the beef and put it in a bowl.

2. Cover the meat with the marinade, place a layer of aluminum foil or saran wrap over the bowl, and place the bowl in the refrigerator for 3 hours.
3. Put the meat in a baking dish along with the onion and mushrooms
4. Air Fry at 350°F for 10 minutes. Serve hot.

Spinach And Provolone Steak Rolls
Servings:8
Cooking Time: 12 Minutes
Ingredients:
- 1 flank steak, butterflied
- 8 deli slices provolone cheese
- 1 cup fresh spinach leaves
- ½ teaspoon salt
- ¼ teaspoon ground black pepper

Directions:
1. Place steak on a large plate. Place provolone slices to cover steak, leaving 1" at the edges. Lay spinach leaves over cheese. Gently roll steak and tie with kitchen twine or secure with toothpicks. Carefully slice into eight pieces. Sprinkle each with salt and pepper.
2. Place rolls into ungreased air fryer basket, cut side up. Adjust the temperature to 400°F and set the timer for 12 minutes. Steak rolls will be browned and cheese will be melted when done and have an internal temperature of at least 150°F for medium steak and 180°F for well-done steak. Serve warm.

Beef Loin With Thyme And Parsley
Servings:4
Cooking Time: 15 Minutes
Ingredients:
- 1 tablespoon butter, melted
- ¼ dried thyme
- 1 teaspoon garlic salt
- ¼ teaspoon dried parsley
- 1 pound (454 g) beef loin

Directions:
1. In a bowl, combine the melted butter, thyme, garlic salt, and parsley.
2. Cut the beef loin into slices and generously apply the seasoned butter using a brush.
3. Preheat the air fryer to 400ºF (204ºC) and place a rack inside.
4. Air fry the beef on the rack for 15 minutes.
5. Take care when removing it and serve hot.

Beef And Mushroom Meatballs
Servings:6
Cooking Time: 15 Minutes
Ingredients:
- Olive oil
- 2 pounds lean ground beef
- ⅔ cups finely chopped mushrooms
- 4 tablespoons chopped parsley
- 2 eggs, beaten
- 2 teaspoons salt
- 1 teaspoon freshly ground black pepper
- 1 cup whole-wheat bread crumbs

Directions:
1. Spray a fryer basket lightly with olive oil.
2. In a large bowl, mix together the beef, mushrooms, and parsley. Add the eggs, salt, and pepper and mix gently. Add the bread crumbs and mix until the bread crumbs are no longer dry. Be careful not to overmix.
3. Using a small cookie scoop, form 24 meatballs.
4. Place the meatballs in the fryer basket in a single layer and spray lightly with olive oil. You may need to cook the meatballs in batches.
5. Air fry until the internal temperature reaches at least 160°F, 10 to 15 minutes, shaking the basket every 5 minutes for even cooking.

Mediterranean-style Beef Steak
Servings: 4
Cooking Time: 12 Minutes
Ingredients:
- 1 ½ pounds beef steak
- 1-pound zucchini
- 1 teaspoon dried rosemary
- 1 teaspoon dried basil
- 1 teaspoon dried oregano
- 2 tablespoons extra-virgin olive oil
- 2 tablespoons fresh chives, chopped

Directions:
1. At 400 degrees F/ 205 degrees C, preheat your Air Fryer.
2. Toss the steak and zucchini with the spices and olive oil.
3. Transfer to the cooking basket and cook for 6 minutes.
4. Now, shale the basket and cook another 6 minutes.
5. Serve immediately garnished with fresh chives.
6. Enjoy!

Cheeseburger-stuffed Bell Peppers
Servings:4
Cooking Time: 20 Minutes
Ingredients:
- Olive oil
- 4 large red bell peppers
- 1 pound lean ground beef
- 1 cup diced onion
- Salt
- Freshly ground black pepper
- 1 cup cooked brown rice
- ½ cup shredded reduced-fat Cheddar cheese
- ½ cup tomato sauce
- 2 tablespoons dill pickle relish
- 2 tablespoons ketchup
- 1 tablespoon Worcestershire sauce
- 1 tablespoon mustard
- ½ cup shredded lettuce
- ½ cup diced tomatoes

Directions:

1. Spray a fryer basket lightly with olive oil.
2. Cut about ½ inch off the tops of the peppers. Remove any seeds from the insides. Set aside.
3. In a large skillet over medium-high heat, cook the ground beef and onion until browned, about 5 minutes. Season with salt and pepper.
4. In a large bowl, mix together the ground beef mixture, rice, Cheddar cheese, tomato sauce, relish, ketchup, Worcestershire sauce, and mustard.
5. Spoon the meat and rice mixture equally into the peppers.
6. Place the stuffed peppers into the fryer basket. Air fry until golden brown on top, 10 to 15 minutes.
7. Top each pepper with the shredded lettuce and diced tomatoes and serve.

Tender Pork Ribs With Bbq Sauce

Servings: 4
Cooking Time: 25 Minutes
Ingredients:
- 1 lb. baby back ribs
- 3 tablespoons olive oil
- ½ teaspoon pepper
- ½ teaspoon smoked salt
- 1 tablespoon Dijon mustard
- ⅓ cup soy sauce
- 2 cloves garlic, minced
- ½ cup BBQ sauce

Directions:
1. Cut the ribs in half after removing their back membrane.
2. To marinate the ribs completely, prepare a large dish, add the olive oil, pepper, salt, Dijon mustard, soy sauce, garlic and ribs, then cover and refrigerate for 2 hours.
3. When ready, cook the pork ribs in your air fryer at 370 degrees F/ 185 degrees C for 25 minutes.
4. With the BBQ sauce on the top, serve and enjoy!

Crumbed Golden Filet Mignon

Servings: 4
Cooking Time: 12 Minutes
Ingredients:
- ½ pound (227 g) filet mignon
- Sea salt and ground black pepper, to taste
- ½ teaspoon cayenne pepper
- 1 teaspoon dried basil
- 1 teaspoon dried rosemary
- 1 teaspoon dried thyme
- 1 tablespoon sesame oil
- 1 small egg, whisked
- ½ cup bread crumbs

Directions:
1. Preheat the air fryer to 360°F (182°C).
2. Cover the filet mignon with the salt, black pepper, cayenne pepper, basil, rosemary, and thyme. Coat with sesame oil.
3. Put the egg in a shallow plate.
4. Pour the bread crumbs in another plate.
5. Dip the filet mignon into the egg. Roll it into the crumbs.
6. Transfer the steak to the air fryer and air fry for 12 minutes or until it turns golden.
7. Serve immediately.

Balsamic Marinated Rib Eye Steak With Balsamic Fried Cipollini Onions

Servings: 2
Cooking Time: 22-26 Minutes
Ingredients:
- 3 tablespoons balsamic vinegar
- 2 cloves garlic, sliced
- 1 tablespoon Dijon mustard
- 1 teaspoon fresh thyme leaves
- 1 (16-ounce) boneless rib eye steak
- coarsely ground black pepper
- salt
- 1 (8-ounce) bag cipollini onions, peeled
- 1 teaspoon balsamic vinegar

Directions:
1. Combine the 3 tablespoons of balsamic vinegar, garlic, Dijon mustard and thyme in a small bowl. Pour this marinade over the steak. Pierce the steak several times with a paring knife or
2. a needle-style meat tenderizer and season it generously with coarsely ground black pepper. Flip the steak over and pierce the other side in a similar fashion, seasoning again with the coarsely ground black pepper. Marinate the steak for 2 to 24 hours in the refrigerator. When you are ready to cook, remove the steak from the refrigerator and let it sit at room temperature for 30 minutes.
3. Preheat the air fryer to 400°F.
4. Season the steak with salt and air-fry at 400°F for 12 minutes (medium-rare), 14 minutes (medium), or 16 minutes (well-done), flipping the steak once half way through the cooking time.
5. While the steak is air-frying, toss the onions with 1 teaspoon of balsamic vinegar and season with salt.
6. Remove the steak from the air fryer and let it rest while you fry the onions. Transfer the onions to the air fryer basket and air-fry for 10 minutes, adding a few more minutes if your onions are very large. Then, slice the steak on the bias and serve with the fried onions on top.

Beef Chuck With Brussels Sprouts

Servings: 4
Cooking Time: 15 Minutes
Ingredients:
- 1 pound (454 g) beef chuck shoulder steak
- 2 tablespoons vegetable oil
- 1 tablespoon red wine vinegar
- 1 teaspoon fine sea salt
- ½ teaspoon ground black pepper
- 1 teaspoon smoked paprika
- 1 teaspoon onion powder

- ½ teaspoon garlic powder
- ½ pound (227 g) Brussels sprouts, cleaned and halved
- ½ teaspoon fennel seeds
- 1 teaspoon dried basil
- 1 teaspoon dried sage

Directions:
1. Massage the beef with the vegetable oil, wine vinegar, salt, black pepper, paprika, onion powder, and garlic powder, coating it well.
2. Allow to marinate for a minimum of 3 hours.
3. Preheat the air fryer to 390ºF (199ºC).
4. Remove the beef from the marinade and put in the preheated air fryer. Air fry for 10 minutes. Flip the beef halfway through.
5. Put the prepared Brussels sprouts in the air fryer along with the fennel seeds, basil, and sage.
6. Lower the heat to 380ºF (193ºC) and air fry everything for another 5 minutes.
7. Give them a good stir. Air fry for an additional 10 minutes.
8. Serve immediately.

Lemon-garlic Strip Steak

Servings: 2
Cooking Time: 15 Minutes
Ingredients:
- 3 cloves garlic, minced
- 1 tbsp lemon juice
- 1 tbsp olive oil
- Salt and pepper to taste
- 1 tbsp chopped parsley
- ½ tsp chopped rosemary
- ½ tsp chopped sage
- 1 strip steak

Directions:
1. In a small bowl, whisk all ingredients. Brush mixture over strip steak and let marinate covered in the fridge for 30 minutes. Preheat air fryer at 400ºF. Place strip steak in the greased frying basket and Bake for 8 minutes until rare, turning once. Let rest onto a cutting board for 5 minutes before serving.

Crispy Lamb Shoulder Chops

Servings: 3
Cooking Time: 28 Minutes
Ingredients:
- ¾ cup All-purpose flour or gluten-free all-purpose flour
- 2 teaspoons Mild paprika
- 2 teaspoons Table salt
- 1½ teaspoons Garlic powder
- 1½ teaspoons Dried sage leaves
- 3 6-ounce bone-in lamb shoulder chops, any excess fat trimmed
- Olive oil spray

Directions:
1. Whisk the flour, paprika, salt, garlic powder, and sage in a large bowl until the mixture is of a uniform color. Add the chops and toss well to coat. Transfer them to a cutting board.
2. Preheat the air fryer to 375°F .
3. When the machine is at temperature, again dredge the chops one by one in the flour mixture. Lightly coat both sides of each chop with olive oil spray before putting it in the basket. Continue on with the remaining chop(s), leaving air space between them in the basket.
4. Air-fry, turning once, for 25 minutes, or until the chops are well browned and tender when pierced with the point of a paring knife. If the machine is at 360°F, you may need to add up to 3 minutes to the cooking time.
5. Use kitchen tongs to transfer the chops to a wire rack. Cool for 5 minutes before serving.

Delectable Beef With Kale Pieces

Servings: 4
Cooking Time: 15-20 Minutes
Ingredients:
- 1 cup kale, make pieces and wilted
- 1 tomato, chopped
- ¼ teaspoon brown sugar
- ½ pound leftover beef, coarsely chopped
- 2 garlic cloves, pressed
- 4 eggs, beaten
- 4 tablespoons heavy cream
- ½ teaspoon turmeric powder
- Salt and ground black pepper, as needed
- ⅛ teaspoon ground allspice

Directions:
1. Make 4 ramekins and lightly oil them.
2. Divide the remaining ingredients among the ramekins.
3. Coat the cooking basket of your air fryer with cooking oil or spray.
4. Place the ramekins on the basket and then arrange the basket to the air fryer.
5. Cook the ramekins at 360 degrees F/ 180 degrees C for 15 minutes.
6. When done, serve warm!

Baharat Lamb Kebab With Mint Sauce

Servings: 6
Cooking Time: 50 Minutes
Ingredients:
- 1 lb ground lamb
- ¼ cup parsley, chopped
- 3 garlic cloves, minced
- 1 shallot, diced
- Salt and pepper to taste
- 1 tsp ground cumin
- ¼ tsp ground cinnamon
- ¼ tsp baharat seasoning
- ¼ tsp chili powder
- ¼ tsp ground ginger

- 3 tbsp olive oil
- 1 cup Greek yogurt
- ½ cup mint, chopped
- 2 tbsp lemon juice
- ¼ tsp hot paprika

Directions:
1. Preheat air fryer to 360°F. Mix the ground lamb, parsley, 2 garlic cloves, shallot, 2 tbsp olive oil, salt, black pepper, cumin, cinnamon, baharat seasoning, chili powder, and ginger in a bowl. Divide the mixture into 4 equal quantities, and roll each into a long oval. Drizzle with the remaining olive oil, place them in a single layer in the frying basket and Air Fry for 10 minutes. While the kofta is cooking, mix together the Greek yogurt, mint, remaining garlic, lemon juice, hot paprika, salt, and pepper in a bowl. Serve the kofta with mint sauce.

Tacos Norteños

Servings: 4
Cooking Time: 25 Minutes
Ingredients:
- ½ cup minced purple onions
- 5 radishes, julienned
- 2 tbsp white wine vinegar
- ½ tsp granulated sugar
- Salt and pepper to taste
- ¼ cup olive oil
- ½ tsp ground cumin
- 1 flank steak
- 10 mini flour tortillas
- 1 cup shredded red cabbage
- ½ cup cucumber slices
- ½ cup fresh radish slices

Directions:
1. Combine the radishes, vinegar, sugar, and salt in a bowl. Let sit covered in the fridge until ready to use. Whisk the olive oil, salt, black pepper and cumin in a bowl. Toss in flank steak and let marinate in the fridge for 30 minutes.
2. Preheat air fryer at 325ºF. Place flank steak in the frying basket and Bake for 18-20 minutes, tossing once. Let rest onto a cutting board for 5 minutes before slicing thinly against the grain. Add steak slices to flour tortillas along with red cabbage, chopped purple onions, cucumber slices, radish slices and fresh radish slices. Serve warm.

Chinese-style Lamb Chops

Servings: 4
Cooking Time: 25 Minutes
Ingredients:
- 8 lamb chops, trimmed
- 2 tbsp scallions, sliced
- ¼ tsp Chinese five-spice
- 3 garlic cloves, crushed
- ½ tsp ginger powder
- ¼ cup dark soy sauce
- 2 tsp orange juice
- 3 tbsp honey
- ½ tbsp light brown sugar
- ¼ tsp red pepper flakes

Directions:
1. Season the chops with garlic, ginger, soy sauce, five-spice powder, orange juice, and honey in a bowl. Toss to coat. Cover the bowl with plastic wrap and marinate for 2 hours and up to overnight.
2. Preheat air fryer to 400°F. Remove the chops from the bowl but reserve the marinade. Place the chops in the greased frying basket and Bake for 5 minutes. Using tongs, flip the chops. Brush the lamb with the reserved marinade, then sprinkle with brown sugar and pepper flakes. Cook for another 4 minutes until brown and caramelized medium-rare. Serve with scallions on top.

Cheese Beef Roll

Servings: 4
Cooking Time: 15 Minutes
Ingredients:
- Black pepper and salt to taste
- 3 tablespoons pesto
- 6 slices cheese
- ¾ cup spinach, chopped
- 3 oz. bell pepper, deseeded and sliced

Directions:
1. At 400 degrees F/ 205 degrees C, preheat your air fryer.
2. Top the steak slices with pesto, cheese, spinach, bell pepper.
3. Roll up the steak slices and secure using a toothpick.
4. Season with black pepper and salt accordingly.
5. Place the prepared slices in your air fryer's cooking basket and cook for almost 15 minutes.
6. Serve and enjoy!

Stress-free Beef Patties

Servings: 2
Cooking Time: 30 Minutes
Ingredients:
- ½ lb ground beef
- 1 ½ tbsp ketchup
- 1 ½ tbsp tamari
- ½ tsp jalapeño powder
- ½ tsp mustard powder
- Salt and pepper to taste

Directions:
1. Preheat air fryer to 350°F. Add the beef, ketchup, tamari, jalapeño, mustard salt, and pepper in a bowl and mix until evenly combined. Shape into 2 patties, then place them on the greased frying basket. Air Fry for 18-20 minutes, turning once. Serve and enjoy!

Mushroom And Beef Meatloaf

Servings: 4
Cooking Time: 25 Minutes
Ingredients:
- 1 pound (454 g) ground beef

Air Fryer Cookbook for Beginners

- 1 egg, beaten
- 1 mushrooms, sliced
- 1 tablespoon thyme
- 1 small onion, chopped
- 3 tablespoons bread crumbs
- Ground black pepper, to taste

Directions:
1. Preheat the air fryer to 400ºF (204ºC).
2. Put all the ingredients into a large bowl and combine entirely.
3. Transfer the meatloaf mixture into the loaf pan and move it to the air fryer basket.
4. Bake for 25 minutes. Slice up before serving.

Sun-dried Tomato Crusted Chops

Servings: 4
Cooking Time: 10 Minutes
Ingredients:
- ½ cup oil-packed sun-dried tomatoes
- ½ cup toasted almonds
- ¼ cup grated Parmesan cheese
- ½ cup olive oil, plus more for brushing the air fryer basket
- 2 tablespoons water
- ½ teaspoon salt
- Freshly ground black pepper, to taste
- 4 center-cut boneless pork chops (about 1¼ pounds / 567 g)

Directions:
1. Put the sun-dried tomatoes into a food processor and pulse them until they are coarsely chopped. Add the almonds, Parmesan cheese, olive oil, water, salt and pepper. Process into a smooth paste. Spread most of the paste (leave a little in reserve) onto both sides of the pork chops and then pierce the meat several times with a needle-style meat tenderizer or a fork. Let the pork chops sit and marinate for at least 1 hour (refrigerate if marinating for longer than 1 hour).
2. Preheat the air fryer to 370ºF (188ºC).
3. Brush more olive oil on the bottom of the air fryer basket. Transfer the pork chops into the air fryer basket, spooning a little more of the sun-dried tomato paste onto the pork chops if there are any gaps where the paste may have been rubbed off. Air fry the pork chops for 10 minutes, turning the chops over halfway through.
4. When the pork chops have finished cooking, transfer them to a serving plate and serve.

Indian Fry Bread Tacos

Servings: 4
Cooking Time: 20 Minutes
Ingredients:
- 1 cup all-purpose flour
- 1½ teaspoons salt, divided
- 1½ teaspoons baking powder
- ¼ cup milk
- ¼ cup warm water
- ½ pound lean ground beef
- One 14.5-ounce can pinto beans, drained and rinsed
- 1 tablespoon taco seasoning
- ½ cup shredded cheddar cheese
- 2 cups shredded lettuce
- ¼ cup black olives, chopped
- 1 Roma tomato, diced
- 1 avocado, diced
- 1 lime

Directions:
1. In a large bowl, whisk together the flour, 1 teaspoon of the salt, and baking powder. Make a well in the center and add in the milk and water. Form a ball and gently knead the dough four times. Cover the bowl with a damp towel, and set aside.
2. Preheat the air fryer to 380°F.
3. In a medium bowl, mix together the ground beef, beans, and taco seasoning. Crumble the meat mixture into the air fryer basket and cook for 5 minutes; toss the meat and cook an additional 2 to 3 minutes, or until cooked fully. Place the cooked meat in a bowl for taco assembly; season with the remaining ½ teaspoon salt as desired.
4. On a floured surface, place the dough. Cut the dough into 4 equal parts. Using a rolling pin, roll out each piece of dough to 5 inches in diameter. Spray the dough with cooking spray and place in the air fryer basket, working in batches as needed. Cook for 3 minutes, flip over, spray with cooking spray, and cook for an additional 1 to 3 minutes, until golden and puffy.
5. To assemble, place the fry breads on a serving platter. Equally divide the meat and bean mixture on top of the fry bread. Divide the cheese, lettuce, olives, tomatoes, and avocado among the four tacos. Squeeze lime over the top prior to serving.

Air-fried Pork With Wine Sauce

Servings: 4
Cooking Time: 20 Minutes
Ingredients:
- For the Ribs:
- ½ teaspoon cracked black peppercorns
- ½ teaspoon Hickory-smoked salt
- 1 pound pork ribs
- 2 tablespoons olive oil
- 1 tablespoon Dijon honey mustard
- ¼ cup soy sauce
- 1 clove garlic, minced
- For the Sauce:
- 1 teaspoon brown sugar
- 1 teaspoon balsamic vinegar
- 1½ cups beef stock
- 1 cup red wine
- ¼ teaspoon salt

Directions:
1. To marinate, prepare a large dish, add the ingredients and seal and refrigerate for 3-4 hours or overnight.

2. Coat the cooking basket of your air fryer with cooking oil or spray.
3. Place the ribs on the basket and then arrange the basket to the air fryer.
4. Cook the ribs at 320 degrees F/ 160 degrees C for 10 minutes.
5. Add the stock in a deep saucepan and boil over medium flame until half reduces it.
6. Add the remaining sauce ingredients. Cook for 10 minutes over high heat or until the sauce is reduced by half.
7. Serve the air fried pork ribs with the wine sauce.

Jerk Pork Butt Pieces
Servings: 4
Cooking Time: 20 Minutes
Ingredients:
- 1 ½ pounds pork butt, chopped into pieces
- 3 tablespoons jerk paste

Directions:
1. Add meat and jerk paste into the bowl and coat well. Place in the fridge for overnight.
2. Grease its air fryer basket with cooking spray.
3. At 390 degrees F/ 200 degrees C, preheat your air fryer.
4. Add marinated meat into the air fryer and cook for 20 minutes. Turn halfway through the cooking time.
5. Serve and enjoy.

Potato And Prosciutto Salad
Servings: 8
Cooking Time: 7 Minutes
Ingredients:
- Salad:
- 4 pounds (1.8 kg) potatoes, boiled and cubed
- 15 slices prosciutto, diced
- 2 cups shredded Cheddar cheese
- Dressing:
- 15 ounces (425 g) sour cream
- 2 tablespoons mayonnaise
- 1 teaspoon salt
- 1 teaspoon black pepper
- 1 teaspoon dried basil

Directions:
1. Preheat the air fryer to 350ºF (177ºC).
2. Put the potatoes, prosciutto, and Cheddar in a baking dish. Put it in the air fryer and air fry for 7 minutes.
3. In a separate bowl, mix the sour cream, mayonnaise, salt, pepper, and basil using a whisk.
4. Coat the salad with the dressing and serve.

Greek-style Pork Stuffed Jalapeño Poppers
Servings: 6
Cooking Time: 30 Minutes
Ingredients:
- 6 jalapeños, halved lengthwise
- 3 tbsp diced Kalamata olives
- 3 tbsp olive oil
- ¼ lb ground pork
- 2 tbsp feta cheese
- 1 oz cream cheese, softened
- ½ tsp dried mint
- ½ cup Greek yogurt

Directions:
1. Warm 2 tbsp of olive oil in a skillet over medium heat. Stir in ground pork and cook for 6 minutes until no longer pink. Preheat air fryer to 350ºF. Mix the cooked pork, olives, feta cheese, and cream cheese in a bowl. Divide the pork mixture between the peppers. Place them in the frying basket and Air Fry for 6 minutes. Mix the Greek yogurt with the remaining olive oil and mint in a small bowl. Serve with the poppers.

Spinach And Mushroom Steak Rolls
Servings: 4
Cooking Time: 19 Minutes
Ingredients:
- ½ medium yellow onion, peeled and chopped
- ½ cup chopped baby bella mushrooms
- 1 cup chopped fresh spinach
- 1 pound flank steak
- 8 slices provolone cheese
- 1 teaspoon salt
- ½ teaspoon ground black pepper
- Cooking spray

Directions:
1. In a medium skillet over medium heat, sauté onion 2 minutes until fragrant and beginning to soften. Add mushrooms and spinach and continue cooking 5 more minutes until spinach is wilted and mushrooms are soft.
2. Preheat the air fryer to 400°F.
3. Carefully butterfly steak, leaving the two halves connected. Place slices of cheese on top of steak, then top with cooked vegetables.
4. Place steak so that the grain runs horizontally. Tightly roll up steak and secure it closed with eight evenly placed toothpicks or eight sections of butcher's twine.
5. Slice steak into four rolls. Spritz with cooking spray, then sprinkle with salt and pepper. Place in the air fryer basket and cook 12 minutes until steak is brown on the edges and internal temperature reaches at least 160°F for well-done. Serve.

Montreal Steak
Servings: 2
Cooking Time: 7 Minutes
Ingredients:
- 12 oz. steak
- ½-teaspoon liquid smoke
- 1 tablespoon soy sauce
- ½-tablespoon cocoa powder
- 1 tablespoon Montreal steak seasoning
- Pepper
- Salt

Directions:
1. In a large zip-lock bag, coat the steak well with the liquid smoke, soy sauce, and steak seasonings, then refrigerate the mixture for overnight.

2. Coat the cooking basket of your air fryer with cooking spray.
3. Arrange the marinated steak to the air fryer and cook at 375 degrees F/ 190 degrees C for 7 minutes.
4. After that, turn the steak and cook another side for 5 minutes more.
5. Serve and enjoy.

Double Cheese & Beef Burgers
Servings: 4
Cooking Time: 30 Minutes
Ingredients:
- 4 toasted onion buns, split
- ¼ cup breadcrumbs
- 2 tbsp milk
- 1 tp smoked paprika
- 6 tbsp salsa
- 2 tsp cayenne pepper
- 2 tbsp grated Cotija cheese
- 1 ¼ lb ground beef
- 4 Colby Jack cheese slices
- ¼ cup sour cream

Directions:
1. Preheat the air fryer to 375°F. Combine the breadcrumbs, milk, paprika, 2 tbsp of salsa, cayenne, and Cotija cheese in a bowl and mix. Let stand for 5 minutes. Add the ground beef and mix with your hands. Form into 4 patties and lay them on wax paper. Place the patties into the greased frying basket and Air Fry for 11-14 minutes, flipping once during cooking until golden and crunchy on the outside. Put a slice of Colby jack on top of each and cook for another minute until the cheese melts. Combine the remaining salsa with sour cream. Spread the mix on the bun bottoms, lay the patties on top, and spoon the rest of the mix over. Add the top buns and serve.

Grilled Pork & Bell Pepper Salad
Servings: 4
Cooking Time: 25 Minutes
Ingredients:
- 1 cup sautéed button mushrooms, sliced
- 2 lb pork tenderloin, sliced
- 1 tsp olive oil
- 1 tsp dried marjoram
- 6 tomato wedges
- 6 green olives
- 6 cups mixed salad greens
- 1 red bell pepper, sliced
- 1/3 cup vinaigrette dressing

Directions:
1. Preheat air fryer to 400°F. Combine the pork and olive oil, making sure the pork is well-coated. Season with marjoram. Lay the pork in the air fryer. Grill for 4-6 minutes, turning once until the pork is cooked through.
2. While the pork is cooking, toss the salad greens, red bell pepper, tomatoes, olives, and mushrooms into a bowl. Lay the pork slices on top of the salad, season with vinaigrette, and toss. Serve while the pork is still warm.

Delectable Pork Chops
Servings: 2
Cooking Time: 12 Minutes
Ingredients:
- ½ lb. pork chops, boneless
- 4 tablespoons Swerve
- ½-teaspoon steak seasoning blend
- ½-tablespoon mustard

Directions:
1. Mix up the Swerve, steak seasoning blend and mustard in a small bowl, then rub the steak with the spice mixture.
2. Transfer the coated steak to the cooking basket in the air fryer and cook at 350 degrees F/ 175 degrees C for 12 minutes. flipping halfway through.
3. When done, serve and enjoy.

Simple Pork Chops
Servings: 4
Cooking Time: 20 Minutes
Ingredients:
- 4 pork chops, boneless
- 1 1/2 tbsp Mr. Dash seasoning
- Pepper
- Salt

Directions:
1. Coat pork chops with Mr. dash seasoning, pepper, and salt.
2. Place pork chops in the air fryer and cook at 360°F for 10 minutes.
3. Turn pork chops to another side and cook for 10 minutes more.
4. Serve and enjoy.

Breaded Pork Cutlets
Servings:4
Cooking Time: 15 Minutes
Ingredients:
- Olive oil
- ½ cup whole wheat-panko bread crumbs
- ½ teaspoon garlic powder
- 2 eggs, beaten
- 4 (1-inch) boneless pork chops, fat trimmed
- Salt
- Freshly ground black pepper

Directions:
1. Spray a fryer basket lightly with olive oil.
2. In a shallow bowl, mix together the panko bread crumbs and garlic powder.
3. In another shallow bowl, whisk the eggs with 1 teaspoon of water.
4. Place the pork chops between two sheets of parchment paper or plastic wrap. Using a meat mallet or a rolling pin, pound the pork chops until they are ¼ inch thick. Season them with salt and pepper.
5. Coat the pork in the egg mixture and shake off any excess, then dredge them in the bread crumb mixture.
6. Place the pork in the fryer basket in a single layer. Lightly spray the pork cutlets with olive oil. You may need to cook them in batches.

7. Air fry for 8 minutes. Flip the pork cutlets and lightly spray with olive oil. Cook until the pork reaches an internal temperature of at least 145°F, an additional 4 to 7 minutes.

Cheeseburger Sliders With Pickle Sauce

Servings: 4
Cooking Time: 20 Minutes
Ingredients:
- 4 iceberg lettuce leaves, each halved lengthwise
- 2 red onion slices, rings separated
- ¼ cup shredded Swiss cheese
- 1 lb ground beef
- 1 tbsp Dijon mustard
- Salt and pepper to taste
- ¼ tsp shallot powder
- 2 tbsp mayonnaise
- 2 tsp ketchup
- ½ tsp mustard powder
- ½ tsp dill pickle juice
- ⅛ tsp onion powder
- ⅛ tsp garlic powder
- ⅛ tsp sweet paprika
- 8 tomato slices
- ½ cucumber, thinly sliced

Directions:
1. In a large bowl, use your hands to mix beef, Swiss cheese, mustard, salt, shallot, and black pepper. Do not overmix. Form 8 patties ½-inch thick. Mix together mayonnaise, ketchup, mustard powder, pickle juice, onion and garlic powder, and paprika in a medium bowl. Stir until smooth.
2. Preheat air fryer to 400°F. Place the sliders in the greased frying basket and Air Fry for about 8-10 minutes, flipping once until preferred doneness. Serve on top of lettuce halves with a slice of tomato, a slider, onion, a smear of special sauce, and cucumber.

Beef And Bean Chimichangas

Servings: 4
Cooking Time: 15 Minutes
Ingredients:
- Olive oil
- 1 pound lean ground beef
- 1 tablespoon taco seasoning
- ½ cup salsa
- 1 (16-ounce) can fat-free refried beans
- 4 large whole-wheat tortillas
- ½ cup shredded Cheddar cheese

Directions:
1. Spray fryer basket lightly with olive oil.
2. In a large skillet over medium heat, cook the ground beef until browned, about 5 minutes. Add the taco seasoning and salsa and stir to combine. Set aside.
3. Spread ½ cup of refried beans onto each tortilla, leaving a ½ inch border around the edge. Add ¼ of the ground beef mixture to each tortilla and sprinkle with 2 tablespoons of Cheddar cheese.

4. Fold the opposite sides of the tortilla in and roll up.
5. Place the chimichangas in the fryer basket, seam side down. Spray lightly with olive oil. You may need to cook the chimichangas in batches.
6. Air fry until golden brown, 5 to 10 minutes.

Air Fried Grilled Steak

Servings: 2
Cooking Time: 45 Minutes
Ingredients:
- 2 top sirloin steaks
- 3 tablespoons butter, melted
- 3 tablespoons olive oil
- Salt and pepper to taste

Directions:
1. Preheat the air fryer for 5 minutes.
2. Season the sirloin steaks with olive oil, salt and pepper.
3. Place the beef in the air fryer basket.
4. Cook for 45 minutes at 350°F.
5. Once cooked, serve with butter.

Flavorful Espresso-grilled Pork Tenderloin

Servings: 4
Cooking Time: 21 Minutes
Ingredients:
- 1 tablespoon packed brown sugar
- 2 teaspoons espresso powder
- 1 teaspoon ground paprika
- ½ teaspoon dried marjoram
- 1 tablespoon honey
- 1 tablespoon lemon juice
- 2 teaspoons olive oil
- 1 1-pound pork tenderloin

Directions:
1. In a suitable bowl, mix the brown sugar, espresso powder, paprika, and marjoram.
2. Add the olive oil, honey, and lemon juice in the bowl until well mixed.
3. Spread the honey mixture over the pork and let stand for almost 10 minutes at room temperature.
4. Roast the tenderloin in the air fryer basket for 9 to 11 minutes, or until the pork registers at least 145 degrees F/ 60 degrees C on a meat thermometer.
5. Slice the meat to serve.

Garlic Beef Meatloaf

Servings: 4
Cooking Time: 15 Minutes
Ingredients:
- 1 lb. ground beef
- ¼-teaspoon cinnamon
- tablespoon ginger, minced
- ¼ cup fresh cilantro, chopped
- 1 cup onion, diced
- 2 eggs, lightly beaten
- 1 teaspoon cayenne
- 1 teaspoon turmeric
- 1 teaspoon garam masala

Air Fryer Cookbook for Beginners

- 1 tablespoon garlic, minced
- 1 teaspoon salt

Directions:
1. Prepare a large bowl, mix up all of the ingredients.
2. Place the meat mixture in the cooking pan of your air fryer.
3. Arrange the pan to the air fryer and cook at 360 degrees F/ 180 degrees C for 15 minutes.
4. Slice before serving and enjoying.

Mustard Pork

Servings: 4
Cooking Time: 30 Minutes
Ingredients:
- 1 pound pork tenderloin, trimmed
- A pinch of salt and black pepper
- 2 tablespoons olive oil
- 3 tablespoons mustard
- 2 tablespoons balsamic vinegar

Directions:
1. In a bowl, mix the pork tenderloin with the rest of the ingredients and rub well. Put the roast in your air fryer's basket and cook at 380°F for 30 minutes. Slice the roast, divide between plates and serve.

Steak Fingers

Servings: 4
Cooking Time: 8 Minutes
Ingredients:
- 4 small beef cube steaks
- salt and pepper
- ½ cup flour
- oil for misting or cooking spray

Directions:
1. Cut cube steaks into 1-inch-wide strips.
2. Sprinkle lightly with salt and pepper to taste.
3. Roll in flour to coat all sides.
4. Spray air fryer basket with cooking spray or oil.
5. Place steak strips in air fryer basket in single layer, very close together but not touching. Spray top of steak strips with oil or cooking spray.
6. Cook at 390°F for 4minutes, turn strips over, and spray with oil or cooking spray.
7. Cook 4 more minutes and test with fork for doneness. Steak fingers should be crispy outside with no red juices inside. If needed, cook an additional 4 minutes or until well done.
8. Repeat steps 5 through 7 to cook remaining strips.

Pork Tenderloin With Apple Juice

Servings: 4
Cooking Time: 19 Minutes
Ingredients:
- 1 1-pound pork tenderloin, cut into 4 pieces
- 1 tablespoon apple butter
- 2 teaspoons olive oil
- 2 Granny Smith apples, sliced
- 3 celery stalks, sliced
- 1 onion, sliced
- ½ teaspoon dried marjoram
- ⅓ cup apple juice

Directions:
1. Rub each piece of pork with the apple butter and olive oil.
2. In a medium metal bowl, mix the pork, apples, celery, onion, marjoram, and apple juice.
3. Set the bowl into the air fryer and roast for 14 to 19 minutes.
4. Stir once during cooking.
5. Serve immediately.

Beef Chuck Cheeseburgers

Servings:4
Cooking Time: 15 Minutes
Ingredients:
- ¾ pound (340 g) ground beef chuck
- 1 envelope onion soup mix
- Kosher salt and freshly ground black pepper, to taste
- 1 teaspoon paprika
- 4 slices Monterey Jack cheese
- 4 ciabatta rolls

Directions:
1. In a bowl, stir together the ground chuck, onion soup mix, salt, black pepper, and paprika to combine well.
2. Preheat the air fryer to 385°F (196°C).
3. Take four equal portions of the mixture and mold each one into a patty. Transfer to the air fryer and air fry for 10 minutes.
4. Put the slices of cheese on the top of the burgers.
5. Air fry for another minute before serving on ciabatta rolls.

Sweet-and-sour Polish Sausage

Servings:4
Cooking Time: 10 To 15 Minutes
Ingredients:
- ¾ pound Polish sausage
- 1 red bell pepper, cut into 1-inch strips
- ½ cup minced onion
- 3 tablespoons brown sugar
- ⅓ cup ketchup
- 2 tablespoons mustard
- 2 tablespoons apple cider vinegar
- ½ cup chicken broth

Directions:
1. Cut the sausage into 1½-inch pieces and put into a 6-inch metal bowl. Add the pepper and minced onion.
2. In a small bowl, combine the brown sugar, ketchup, mustard, apple cider vinegar, and chicken broth, and mix well. Pour into the bowl.
3. Roast for 10 to 15 minutes or until the sausage is hot, the vegetables tender, and the sauce bubbling and slightly thickened.
4. Did You Know? Polish sausage is almost always fully cooked when it is sold; read the label carefully to make sure you buy a fully cooked type for this recipe. Uncooked sausages are too fatty and release too much grease to cook in this appliance.

Chapter 7: Poultry Recipes

Seasoned Chicken Breast

Servings: 4
Cooking Time: 20 Minutes
Ingredients:
- 1-pound chicken breast, skinless, boneless, and cut into chunks
- 2 cups broccoli florets
- 2 teaspoons hot sauce
- 2 teaspoons vinegar
- 1 teaspoon sesame oil
- 1 tablespoon soy sauce
- 1 tablespoon ginger, minced
- ½ teaspoon garlic powder
- 1 tablespoon olive oil
- ½ onion, sliced
- Black pepper
- Salt

Directions:
1. Add all the recipe ingredients into the suitable mixing bowl and toss well.
2. Grease its air fryer basket with cooking spray.
3. Transfer chicken and broccoli mixture into the air fryer basket.
4. Cook at almost 380 degrees F/ 195 degrees C for almost 15-20 minutes. Shake halfway through.
5. Serve and enjoy.

Hawaiian Pineapple Chicken Kebabs

Servings:6
Cooking Time: 20 Minutes
Ingredients:
- Olive oil
- 3 tablespoons soy sauce
- 1 (15-ounce) can pineapple chunks, 2 tablespoons of the juice reserved
- 1 tablespoon sesame oil
- ¼ teaspoon ground ginger
- ¼ teaspoon garlic powder
- 1½ pounds boneless, skinless chicken breasts, cut into 1-inch chunks
- 2 large bell peppers, cut into 1-inch chunks

Directions:
1. Spray a fryer basket lightly with olive oil.
2. In a large bowl, mix together the soy sauce, the reserved pineapple juice, sesame oil, ginger, and garlic powder. Add the chicken, bell peppers, and pineapple chunks and toss to coat.
3. Cover the bowl and refrigerate for at least 1 hour and up to 2 hours.
4. If using wooden skewers, soak the skewers in water for at least 30 minutes.
5. Thread the chicken, bell peppers, and pineapple onto the skewers, alternating with chicken, vegetable, and fruit. Place the skewers in the fryer basket in a single layer. Lightly spray the skewers with olive oil. You may need to cook the kebabs in batches.
6. Air fry for 10 minutes. Turn the skewers over, lightly spray with olive oil, and cook until the chicken is nicely browned and the veggies are starting to char on the edges, an additional 5 to 10 minutes.

Garlic Turkey With Tomato Mix

Servings: 4
Cooking Time: 25 Minutes
Ingredients:
- 1 pound turkey meat, cubed and browned
- A pinch of salt and black pepper
- 1 green bell pepper, chopped
- 3 garlic cloves, chopped
- 1 and ½ tsps. cumin, ground
- 12 ounces veggies stock
- 1 cup tomatoes, chopped

Directions:
1. Mix the turkey, salt, black pepper, green bell pepper, garlic cloves, ground cumin, veggies stock, and the chopped tomatoes together in a baking pan that fits in your air fryer.
2. Toss well to season.
3. Cook in your air fryer at 380 degrees F/ 195 degrees C for 25 minutes.
4. When the cooking time runs out, remove from the air fryer.
5. Serve hot on plates and enjoy!

Spinach And Feta Chicken Meatballs

Servings:6
Cooking Time: 18 Minutes
Ingredients:
- Olive oil
- 4 ounces fresh spinach, chopped
- ½ teaspoon salt, plus more as needed
- ½ cup whole-wheat panko bread crumbs
- ¼ teaspoon freshly ground black pepper
- ¼ teaspoon garlic powder
- 1 egg, beaten
- 1 pound lean ground chicken
- ⅓ cup crumbled feta cheese

Directions:
1. Spray a large skillet lightly with olive oil. Add the spinach, season lightly with salt, and cook over medium heat until the spinach has wilted, 2 to 3 minutes. Set aside.
2. In a large bowl, mix together the panko bread crumbs, ½ teaspoon of salt, pepper, and garlic powder. Add the egg, chicken, spinach, and feta and stir to gently combine.
3. Using a heaping tablespoon, form 24 meatballs.
4. Lightly spray a fryer basket with olive oil.
5. Place the meatballs in the fryer basket in a single layer. Spray the meatballs lightly with olive oil. You may need to cook them in batches.
6. Air fry for 7 minutes. Turn the meatballs over and cook until golden brown, an additional 5 to 8 minutes.

Chicken Wings With Lemon Pepper
Servings: 4
Cooking Time: 16 Minutes
Ingredients:
- 1-pound chicken wings
- 1 teaspoon lemon pepper
- 1 tablespoon olive oil
- 1 teaspoon salt

Directions:
1. Add chicken wings into the suitable mixing bowl.
2. Add the remaining ingredients over chicken and toss well to coat.
3. Place chicken wings in the air fryer basket.
4. Cook chicken wings for 8 minutes at 400 degrees F/ 205 degrees C.
5. Turn chicken wings to another side and cook for 8 minutes more.
6. Serve and enjoy.

Mushroom & Turkey Bread Pizza
Servings: 4
Cooking Time: 35 Minutes
Ingredients:
- 10 cooked turkey sausages, sliced
- 1 cup shredded mozzarella cheese
- 1 cup shredded Cheddar cheese
- 1 French loaf bread
- 2 tbsp butter, softened
- 1 tsp garlic powder
- 1 1/3 cups marinara sauce
- 1 tsp Italian seasoning
- 2 scallions, chopped
- 1 cup mushrooms, sliced

Directions:
1. Preheat the air fryer to 370°F. Cut the bread in half crosswise, then split each half horizontally. Combine butter and garlic powder, then spread on the cut sides of the bread. Bake the halves in the fryer for 3-5 minutes or until the leaves start to brown. Set the toasted bread on a work surface and spread marinara sauce over the top. Sprinkle the Italian seasoning, then top with sausages, scallions, mushrooms, and cheeses. Set the pizzas in the air fryer and Bake for 8-12 minutes or until the cheese is melted and starting to brown. Serve hot.

Mexican-inspired Chicken Breasts
Servings: 4
Cooking Time: 20 Minutes
Ingredients:
- ⅛ tsp crushed red pepper flakes
- 1 red pepper, deseeded and diced
- Salt to taste
- 4 chicken breasts
- ¾ tsp garlic powder
- ½ tsp onion powder
- ½ tsp ground cumin
- ½ tsp ancho chile powder
- ½ tsp sweet paprika
- ½ tsp Mexican oregano
- 1 tomato, chopped
- ½ diced red onion
- 3 tbsp fresh lime juice
- 10 ounces avocado, diced
- 1 tbsp chopped cilantro

Directions:
1. Preheat air fryer to 380°F. Stir together salt, garlic and onion powder, cumin, ancho chili powder, paprika, Mexican oregano, and pepper flakes in a bowl. Spray the chicken with cooking oil and rub with the spice mix. Air Fry the chicken for 10 minutes, flipping once until browned and fully cooked. Repeat for all of the chicken. Mix the onion and lime juice in a bowl. Fold in the avocado, cilantro, red pepper, salt, and tomato and coat gently. To serve, top the chicken with guacamole salsa.

Butter And Bacon Chicken
Servings: 6
Cooking Time: 65 Minutes
Ingredients:
- 1 whole chicken
- 2 tablespoons salted butter, softened
- 1 teaspoon dried thyme
- ½ teaspoon garlic powder
- 1 teaspoon salt
- ½ teaspoon ground black pepper
- 6 slices sugar-free bacon

Directions:
1. Pat chicken dry with a paper towel, then rub with butter on all sides. Sprinkle thyme, garlic powder, salt, and pepper over chicken.
2. Place chicken into ungreased air fryer basket, breast side up. Lay strips of bacon over chicken and secure with toothpicks.
3. Adjust the temperature to 350°F and set the timer for 65 minutes. Halfway through cooking, remove and set aside bacon and flip chicken over. Chicken will be done when the skin is golden and crispy and the internal temperature is at least 165°F. Serve warm with bacon.

Jerk Chicken Kebabs
Servings: 4
Cooking Time: 14 Minutes
Ingredients:
- 8 ounces boneless, skinless chicken thighs, cut into 1" cubes
- 2 tablespoons jerk seasoning
- 2 tablespoons coconut oil
- ½ medium red bell pepper, seeded and cut into 1" pieces
- ¼ medium red onion, peeled and cut into 1" pieces
- ½ teaspoon salt

Directions:
1. Place chicken in a medium bowl and sprinkle with jerk seasoning and coconut oil. Toss to coat on all sides.

Air Fryer Cookbook for Beginners

2. Using eight 6" skewers, build skewers by alternating chicken, pepper, and onion pieces, about three repetitions per skewer.
3. Sprinkle salt over skewers and place into ungreased air fryer basket. Adjust the temperature to 370°F and set the timer for 14 minutes, turning skewers halfway through cooking. Chicken will be golden and have an internal temperature of at least 165°F when done. Serve warm.

Cheddar Chicken Fajitas

Servings: 4
Cooking Time: 15 Minutes
Ingredients:
- 4 chicken breasts
- 1 onion, sliced
- 1 bell pepper, sliced
- 1 ½ tablespoons fajita seasoning
- 2 tablespoons olive oil
- ¾ cup cheddar cheese, shredded

Directions:
1. Before cooking, heat your air fryer to 380 degrees F/ 195 degrees C.
2. Brush oil over the chicken and toss together with seasoning.
3. Place the chicken in a baking dish that fits in your air fryer. Then add the onion and bell peppers on the top.
4. Sprinkle with shredded cheese and cook in the preheated air fryer for 1 to 2 minutes or until the cheese is melted.
5. When cooked, remove from the air fryer and serve.
6. Enjoy!

Buttermilk-fried Drumsticks

Servings: 2
Cooking Time: 25 Minutes
Ingredients:
- 1 egg
- ½ cup buttermilk
- ¾ cup self-rising flour
- ¾ cup seasoned panko breadcrumbs
- 1 teaspoon salt
- ¼ teaspoon ground black pepper (to mix into coating)
- 4 chicken drumsticks, skin on
- oil for misting or cooking spray

Directions:
1. Beat together egg and buttermilk in shallow dish.
2. In a second shallow dish, combine the flour, panko crumbs, salt, and pepper.
3. Sprinkle chicken legs with additional salt and pepper to taste.
4. Dip legs in buttermilk mixture, then roll in panko mixture, pressing in crumbs to make coating stick. Mist with oil or cooking spray.
5. Spray air fryer basket with cooking spray.
6. Cook drumsticks at 360°F for 10 minutes. Turn pieces over and cook an additional 10minutes.
7. Turn pieces to check for browning. If you have any white spots that haven't begun to brown, spritz them with oil or cooking spray. Continue cooking for 5 more minutes or until crust is golden brown and juices run clear. Larger, meatier drumsticks will take longer to cook than small ones.

Sage & Paprika Turkey Cutlets

Servings: 4
Cooking Time: 15 Minutes
Ingredients:
- ½ cup bread crumbs
- ¼ tsp paprika
- Salt and pepper to taste
- ⅛ tsp dried sage
- ⅛ tsp garlic powder
- ¼ tsp ground cumin
- 1 egg
- 4 turkey breast cutlets
- 2 tbsp chopped chervil

Directions:
1. Preheat air fryer to 380°F. Combine the bread crumbs, paprika, salt, black pepper, sage, cumin, and garlic powder in a bowl and mix well. Beat the egg in another bowl until frothy. Dip the turkey cutlets into the egg mixture, then coat them in the bread crumb mixture. Put the breaded turkey cutlets in the frying basket. Bake for 4 minutes. Turn the cutlets over, then Bake for 4 more minutes. Decorate with chervil and serve.

Spicy Pork Rind Fried Chicken

Servings:4
Cooking Time: 20 Minutes
Ingredients:
- ¼ cup buffalo sauce
- 4 boneless, skinless chicken breasts
- ½ teaspoon paprika
- ½ teaspoon garlic powder
- ¼ teaspoon ground black pepper
- 2 ounces plain pork rinds, finely crushed

Directions:
1. Pour buffalo sauce into a large sealable bowl or bag. Add chicken and toss to coat. Place sealed bowl or bag into refrigerator and let marinate at least 30 minutes up to overnight.
2. Remove chicken from marinade but do not shake excess sauce off chicken. Sprinkle both sides of thighs with paprika, garlic powder, and pepper.
3. Place pork rinds into a large bowl and press each chicken breast into pork rinds to coat evenly on both sides.
4. Place chicken into ungreased air fryer basket. Adjust the temperature to 400°F and set the timer for 20 minutes, turning chicken halfway through cooking. Chicken will be golden and have an internal temperature of at least 165°F when done. Serve warm.

Crunchy Chicken Strips

Servings: 4
Cooking Time: 40 Minutes
Ingredients:
- 1 chicken breast, sliced into strips
- 1 tbsp grated Parmesan cheese
- 1 cup breadcrumbs
- 1 tbsp chicken seasoning
- 2 eggs, beaten
- Salt and pepper to taste

Directions:
1. Preheat air fryer to 350°F. Mix the breadcrumbs, Parmesan cheese, chicken seasoning, salt, and pepper in a mixing bowl. Coat the chicken with the crumb mixture, then dip in the beaten eggs. Finally, coat again with the dry ingredients. Arrange the coated chicken pieces on the greased frying basket and Air Fry for 15 minutes. Turn over halfway through cooking and cook for another 15 minutes. Serve immediately.

Spicy Honey Mustard Chicken

Servings: 4
Cooking Time: 30 Minutes
Ingredients:
- 1/3 cup tomato sauce
- 2 tbsp yellow mustard
- 2 tbsp apple cider vinegar
- 1 tbsp honey
- 2 garlic cloves, minced
- 1 Fresno pepper, minced
- 1 tsp onion powder
- 4 chicken breasts

Directions:
1. Preheat air fryer to 370°F. Mix the tomato sauce, mustard, apple cider vinegar, honey, garlic, Fresno pepper, and onion powder in a bowl, then use a brush to rub the mix over the chicken breasts. Put the chicken in the air fryer and Grill for 10 minutes. Remove it, turn it, and rub with more sauce. Cook further for about 5 minutes. Remove the basket and flip the chicken. Add more sauce, return to the fryer, and cook for 3-5 more minutes or until the chicken is cooked through. Serve warm.

Gingery Turkey Meatballs

Servings: 4
Cooking Time: 25 Minutes
Ingredients:
- ¼ cup water chestnuts, chopped
- ¼ cup panko bread crumbs
- 1 lb ground turkey
- ½ tsp ground ginger
- 2 tbsp fish sauce
- 1 tbsp sesame oil
- 1 small onion, minced
- 1 egg, beaten

Directions:
1. Preheat air fryer to 400°F. Place the ground turkey, water chestnuts, ground ginger, fish sauce, onion, egg, and bread crumbs in a bowl and stir to combine. Form the turkey mixture into 1-inch meatballs. Arrange the meatballs in the baking pan. Drizzle with sesame oil. Bake until the meatballs are cooked through, 10-12 minutes, flipping once. Serve and enjoy!

Basic Chicken Breasts(2)

Servings: 4
Cooking Time: 15 Minutes
Ingredients:
- 2 tsp olive oil
- 2 chicken breasts
- Salt and pepper to taste
- ½ tsp garlic powder
- ½ tsp rosemary

Directions:
1. Preheat air fryer to 350°F. Rub the chicken breasts with olive oil over tops and bottom and sprinkle with garlic powder, rosemary, salt, and pepper. Place the chicken in the frying basket and Air Fry for 9 minutes, flipping once. Let rest onto a serving plate for 5 minutes before cutting into cubes. Serve and enjoy!

Buffalo Chicken Sandwiches

Servings: 4
Cooking Time: 20 Minutes
Ingredients:
- 4 boneless, skinless chicken thighs
- 1 packet dry ranch seasoning
- ¼ cup buffalo sauce
- 4 slices pepper jack cheese
- 4 sandwich buns

Directions:
1. Preheat the air fryer to 375°F.
2. Sprinkle each chicken thigh with ranch seasoning and spritz with cooking spray.
3. Place chicken in the air fryer basket and cook 20 minutes, turning chicken halfway through, until chicken is brown at the edges and internal temperature reaches at least 165°F.
4. Drizzle buffalo sauce over chicken, top with a slice of cheese, and place on buns to serve.

The Ultimate Chicken Bulgogi

Servings: 4
Cooking Time: 30 Minutes
Ingredients:
- 1 ½ lb boneless, skinless chicken thighs, cubed
- 1 cucumber, thinly sliced
- ¼ cup apple cider vinegar
- 4 garlic cloves, minced
- ¼ tsp ground ginger
- ⅛ tsp red pepper flakes
- 2 tsp honey
- ⅛ tsp salt
- 2 tbsp tamari
- 2 tsp sesame oil
- 2 tsp granular honey
- 2 tbsp lemon juice

Air Fryer Cookbook for Beginners

- ½ tsp lemon zest
- 3 scallions, chopped
- 2 cups cooked white rice
- 2 tsp roasted sesame seeds

Directions:
1. In a bowl, toss the cucumber, vinegar, half of the garlic, half of the ginger, pepper flakes, honey, and salt and store in the fridge covered. Combine the tamari, sesame oil, granular honey, lemon juice, remaining garlic, remaining ginger, and chicken in a large bowl. Toss to coat and marinate in the fridge for 10 minutes.
2. Preheat air fryer to 350°F. Place chicken in the frying basket, do not discard excess marinade. Air Fry for 11 minutes, shaking once and pouring excess marinade over. Place the chicken bulgogi over the cooked rice and scatter with scallion greens, pickled cucumbers, and sesame seeds. Serve and enjoy!

Spicy Coconut Chicken Wings

Servings: 4
Cooking Time: 20 Minutes
Ingredients:
- For the coconut chicken
- 16 chicken drumettes (party wings)
- ¼ cup full-fat coconut milk
- 1 tablespoon Sriracha
- 1 teaspoon onion powder
- 1 teaspoon garlic powder
- Salt
- Pepper
- ⅓ cup shredded unsweetened coconut
- ½ cup all-purpose flour
- Cooking oil
- For the mango salsa
- 1 cup mango sliced into ½ inch chunks
- ¼ cup cilantro, chopped
- ½ cup red onion, chopped
- 2 garlic cloves, minced
- Juice of ½ lime

Directions:
1. Place the drumettes in a sealable plastic bag.
2. In a small bowl, combine the coconut milk and Sriracha. Whisk until fully combined.
3. Drizzle the drumettes with the spicy coconut milk mixture. Season the drumettes with the onion powder, garlic powder, and salt and pepper to taste.
4. Seal the bag. Shake it thoroughly to combine the seasonings and coat the chicken. Marinate for at least 30 minutes, preferably overnight, in the refrigerator.
5. When the drumettes are almost done marinating, combine the shredded coconut and flour in a large bowl. Stir.
6. Spray the air fryer basket with cooking oil.
7. Dip the drumettes in the coconut and flour mixture. Place the drumettes in the air fryer. It is okay to stack them on top of each other. Spray the drumettes with cooking oil, being sure to cover the bottom layer. Cook for 5 minutes.
8. Remove the basket and shake it to ensure all of the pieces will cook fully.
9. Return the basket to the air fryer and continue to cook the chicken. Repeat shaking every 5 minutes until a total of 20 minutes has passed.
10. Cool before serving.

Sweet Marinated Chicken Wings

Servings: 6-8
Cooking Time: 12 Minutes
Ingredients:
- 16 chicken wings
- To make the marinade:
- 2 tablespoons honey
- 2 tablespoons light soya sauce
- ½ teaspoon sea salt
- ¼ teaspoon black pepper
- ¼ teaspoon white pepper, ground
- 2 tablespoons lemon juice

Directions:
1. To marinate, combine the marinade ingredients with the chicken wings in the zip-log bag. Then seal and refrigerate for 4 to 6 minutes.
2. On a flat kitchen surface, plug your air fryer and turn it on.
3. Before cooking, heat the air fryer to 355 degrees F/ 180 degrees C for 4 to 5 minutes.
4. Gently coat the air fryer basket with cooking oil or spray.
5. Place the chicken wings inside the air fryer basket. Cook in your air fryer for 5 to 6 minutes.
6. When cooked, remove the air fryer basket from the air fryer and serve warm with lemon wedges as you like.

Tuscan Stuffed Chicken

Servings: 4
Cooking Time: 30 Minutes
Ingredients:
- 1/3 cup ricotta cheese
- 1 cup Tuscan kale, chopped
- 4 chicken breasts
- 1 tbsp chicken seasoning
- Salt and pepper to taste
- 1 tsp paprika

Directions:
1. Preheat air fryer to 370°F. Soften the ricotta cheese in a microwave-safe bowl for 15 seconds. Combine in a bowl along with Tuscan kale. Set aside. Cut 4-5 slits in the top of each chicken breast about ¾ of the way down. Season with chicken seasoning, salt, and pepper.
2. Place the chicken with the slits facing up in the greased frying basket. Lightly spray the chicken with oil. Bake for 6-8 minutes. Slide-out and stuff the cream cheese mixture into the chicken slits. Sprinkle ½ tsp of paprika and cook for another 3 minutes. Serve and enjoy!

Chicken Wings With Sauce

Servings: 4
Cooking Time: 40 Minutes
Ingredients:
- 2 pounds' chicken wings
- For sauce:
- ¼ teaspoon Tabasco
- ¼ teaspoon Worcestershire sauce
- 6-tablespoon butter, melted
- 12 oz. hot sauce

Directions:
1. Grease its air fryer basket with cooking spray.
2. Add chicken wings in air fryer basket and cook for 25 minutes at 380 degrees F/ 195 degrees C. Shake basket after every 5 minutes.
3. After 25 minutes turn temperature to 400 degrees F/ 205 degrees C and cook for almost 10-15 minutes more.
4. Meanwhile, in a suitable bowl, mix together all sauce ingredients.
5. Add cooked chicken wings in a sauce bowl and toss well to coat.
6. Serve and enjoy.

Rich Turkey Burgers

Servings: 4
Cooking Time: 30 Minutes
Ingredients:
- 2 tbsp finely grated Emmental
- 1/3 cup minced onions
- ¼ cup grated carrots
- 2 garlic cloves, minced
- 2 tsp olive oil
- 1 tsp dried marjoram
- 1 egg
- 1 lb ground turkey

Directions:
1. Preheat air fryer to 400°F. Mix the onions, carrots, garlic, olive oil, marjoram, Emmental, and egg in a bowl, then add the ground turkey. Use your hands to mix the ingredients together. Form the mixture into 4 patties. Set them in the air fryer and Air Fry for 18-20 minutes, flipping once until cooked through and golden. Serve.

Asian Meatball Tacos

Servings: 4
Cooking Time: 10 Minutes
Ingredients:
- 1 pound lean ground turkey
- 3 tablespoons soy sauce
- 1 tablespoon brown sugar
- ½ teaspoon onion powder
- ½ teaspoon garlic powder
- 1 tablespoon sesame seeds
- 1 English cucumber
- 4 radishes
- 2 tablespoons white wine vinegar
- 1 lime, juiced and divided
- 1 tablespoon avocado oil
- Salt, to taste
- ½ cup Greek yogurt
- 1 to 3 teaspoons Sriracha, based on desired spiciness
- 1 cup shredded cabbage
- ¼ cup chopped cilantro
- Eight 6-inch flour tortillas

Directions:
1. Preheat the air fryer to 360°F.
2. In a large bowl, mix the ground turkey, soy sauce, brown sugar, onion powder, garlic powder, and sesame seeds. Form the meat into 1-inch meatballs and place in the air fryer basket. Cook for 5 minutes, shake the basket, and cook another 5 minutes. Using a food thermometer, make sure the internal temperature of the meatballs is 165°F.
3. Meanwhile, dice the cucumber and radishes and place in a medium bowl. Add the white wine vinegar, 1 teaspoon of the lime juice, and the avocado oil, and stir to coat. Season with salt to desired taste.
4. In a large bowl, mix the Greek yogurt, Sriracha, and the remaining lime juice, and stir. Add in the cabbage and cilantro; toss well to create a slaw.
5. In a heavy skillet, heat the tortillas over medium heat for 1 to 2 minutes on each side, or until warmed.
6. To serve, place a tortilla on a plate, top with 5 meatballs, then with cucumber and radish salad, and finish with 2 tablespoons of cabbage slaw.

Breaded Homestyle Chicken Strips

Servings: 4
Cooking Time: 20 Minutes
Ingredients:
- 1 tablespoon of olive oil, plus more for spraying
- 1 pound boneless, skinless chicken tenderloins
- 1 teaspoon salt
- ½ teaspoon freshly ground black pepper
- ½ teaspoon paprika
- ½ teaspoon garlic powder
- ½ cup whole-wheat seasoned bread crumbs
- 1 teaspoon dried parsley

Directions:
1. Spray a fryer basket lightly with olive oil.
2. In a medium bowl, toss the chicken with the salt, pepper, paprika, and garlic powder until evenly coated.
3. Add the olive oil and toss to coat the chicken evenly.
4. In a separate, shallow bowl, mix together the bread crumbs and parsley.
5. Coat each piece of chicken evenly in the bread crumb mixture.
6. Place the chicken in the fryer basket in a single layer and spray it lightly with olive oil. You may need to cook them in batches.
7. Air fry for 10 minutes. Flip the chicken over, lightly spray with olive oil, and cook until golden brown, an additional 8 to 10 minutes.

Grilled Chicken Pesto

Servings: 8
Cooking Time: 30 Minutes
Ingredients:
- 1 ¾ cup commercial pesto
- 8 chicken thighs
- Salt and pepper to taste

Directions:
1. Place all Ingredients in the Ziploc bag and allow to marinate in the fridge for at least 2 hours.
2. Preheat the air fryer to 390°F.
3. Place the grill pan accessory in the air fryer.
4. Grill the chicken for at least 30 minutes.
5. Make sure to flip the chicken every 10 minutes for even grilling.

Crispy Chicken Strips

Servings: 4
Cooking Time: 20 Minutes
Ingredients:
- 1 tablespoon olive oil
- 1 pound (454 g) boneless, skinless chicken tenderloins
- 1 teaspoon salt
- ½ teaspoon freshly ground black pepper
- ½ teaspoon paprika
- ½ teaspoon garlic powder
- ½ cup whole-wheat seasoned bread crumbs
- 1 teaspoon dried parsley
- Cooking spray

Directions:
1. Preheat the air fryer to 370ºF (188ºC). Spray the air fryer basket lightly with cooking spray.
2. In a medium bowl, toss the chicken with the salt, pepper, paprika, and garlic powder until evenly coated.
3. Add the olive oil and toss to coat the chicken evenly.
4. In a separate, shallow bowl, mix together the bread crumbs and parsley.
5. Coat each piece of chicken evenly in the bread crumb mixture.
6. Place the chicken in the air fryer basket in a single layer and spray it lightly with cooking spray. You may need to cook them in batches.
7. Air fry for 10 minutes. Flip the chicken over, lightly spray it with cooking spray, and air fry for an additional 8 to 10 minutes, until golden brown. Serve.

Breaded Chicken Patties

Servings: 4
Cooking Time: 15 Minutes
Ingredients:
- 1 pound ground chicken breast
- 1 cup shredded sharp Cheddar cheese
- ½ cup plain bread crumbs
- 1 teaspoon salt
- ½ teaspoon ground black pepper
- 2 tablespoons mayonnaise
- 1 cup panko bread crumbs
- Cooking spray

Directions:
1. Preheat the air fryer to 400°F.
2. In a large bowl, mix chicken, Cheddar, plain bread crumbs, salt, and pepper until well combined. Separate into four portions and form into patties ½" thick.
3. Brush each patty with mayonnaise, then press into panko bread crumbs to fully coat. Spritz with cooking spray.
4. Place in the air fryer basket and cook 15 minutes, turning halfway through cooking time, until patties are golden brown and internal temperature reaches at least 165°F. Serve warm.

Cheesy Chicken-avocado Paninis

Servings: 2
Cooking Time: 25 Minutes
Ingredients:
- 2 tbsp mayonnaise
- 4 tsp yellow mustard
- 4 sandwich bread slices
- 4 oz sliced deli chicken ham
- 2 oz sliced provolone cheese
- 2 oz sliced mozzarella
- 1 avocado, sliced
- 1 tomato, sliced
- Salt and pepper to taste
- 1 tsp sesame seeds
- 2 tbsp butter, melted

Directions:
1. Preheat air fryer at 350ºF. Rub mayonnaise and mustard on the inside of each bread slice. Top 2 bread slices with chicken ham, provolone and mozzarella cheese, avocado, sesame seeds, and tomato slices. Season with salt and pepper. Then, close sandwiches with the remaining bread slices. Brush the top and bottom of each sandwich lightly with melted butter. Place sandwiches in the frying basket and Bake for 6 minutes, flipping once. Serve.

Italian Chicken Parmesan

Servings: 4
Cooking Time: 20 Minutes
Ingredients:
- 2 (4-ounce) boneless, skinless chicken breasts
- 1 cup Italian bread crumbs
- ½ cup grated Parmesan cheese
- 2 teaspoons Italian seasoning
- Salt
- Pepper
- 2 egg whites
- Cooking oil
- ¾ cup marinara sauce
- ½ cup shredded mozzarella cheese

Directions:
1. With your knife blade parallel to the cutting board, slice the chicken breasts in half horizontally to create 4 thin cutlets.

2. On a solid surface, pound the cutlets to flatten them. You can use your hands, a rolling pin, a kitchen mallet, or a meat hammer.
3. In a bowl large enough to dip a chicken cutlet, combine the bread crumbs, Parmesan cheese, Italian seasoning, and salt and pepper to taste. Stir to combine.
4. Pour the egg whites into another bowl large enough to dip the chicken.
5. Spray the air fryer basket with cooking oil.
6. Dip each cutlet in the egg whites and then the bread crumb mixture.
7. Place 2 chicken cutlets in the air fryer basket. Spray the top of the chicken with cooking oil. Cook for 7 minutes.
8. Remove the cooked cutlets from the air fryer, then repeat step 7 with the remaining 2 cutlets.
9. Open the air fryer. Top the chicken cutlets with the marinara sauce and shredded mozzarella. If the chicken cutlets will fit in your air fryer without stacking, you can prepare all 4 at once. Otherwise, do this 2 cutlets at a time. Cook for an additional 3 minutes, or until the cheese has melted.
10. Cool before serving.

Crispy Chicken Nuggets With Turnip

Servings: 3
Cooking Time: 32 Minutes
Ingredients:
- 1 egg
- ½ teaspoon cayenne pepper
- ⅓ cup panko crumbs
- ¼ teaspoon Romano cheese, grated
- 2 teaspoons canola oil
- 1 pound chicken breast, cut into slices
- 1 medium-sized turnip, trimmed and sliced
- ½ teaspoon garlic powder
- Sea salt, to taste
- Ground black pepper, to taste

Directions:
1. Whisk the egg together with the cayenne pepper until frothy in a bowl.
2. Mix the cheese together with the panko crumbs in another shallow until well combined.
3. Dredge the chicken slices firstly in the egg mixture, then in the panko mixture until coat well.
4. Then using 1 teaspoon of canola oil brush the slices.
5. To season, add salt and pepper.
6. Before cooking, heat your air fryer to 380 degrees F/ 195 degrees C.
7. Cook the chicken slices in the air fryer for 12 minutes. Shake the basket halfway through cooking.
8. When done, the internal temperature of their thickest part should read 165 degrees F/ 75 degrees C.
9. Remove from the air fryer and reserve. Keep warm.
10. With the remaining canola oil, drizzle over the turnip slices.
11. To season, add salt, pepper, and garlic powder.
12. Cook the slices in your air fryer at 370 degrees F/ 185 degrees C for about 20 minutes.
13. Serve the parsnip slices with chicken nuggets. Enjoy!

Glazed Chicken Drumsticks With Herbs

Servings: 4
Cooking Time: 25 Minutes
Ingredients:
- ½ tablespoon fresh rosemary, minced
- 1 tablespoon fresh thyme, minced
- 4 6-ounces boneless chicken drumsticks
- ¼ cup Dijon mustard
- 1 tablespoon honey
- 2 tablespoons olive oil
- Black pepper and salt, to taste

Directions:
1. At 320 degrees F/ 160 degrees C, preheat your air fryer. and spray its air fryer basket.
2. Mix mustard, honey, oil, herbs, salt, and black pepper in a suitable bowl.
3. Rub the chicken drumsticks with marinade and refrigerate overnight.
4. Arrange the drumsticks into the air fryer basket in a single layer and cook for about 12 minutes.
5. Set the air fryer to 355 degrees F/ 180 degrees C and cook for 10 more minutes.
6. Dish out the chicken drumsticks onto a serving platter and serve hot.

Spiced Duck Legs

Servings: 2
Cooking Time: 30 Minutes
Ingredients:
- ½ tbsp. fresh thyme, chopped
- ½ tbsp. fresh parsley, chopped
- 2 duck legs
- 1 garlic clove, minced
- 1 tsp. five spice powder
- Salt and black pepper, as required

Directions:
1. Gently grease an air fryer basket.
2. Before cooking, heat your air fryer to 340 degrees F/ 170 degrees C.
3. In a bowl, combine together herbs, salt, black pepper, garlic, and five spice powder.
4. Rub the garlic mixture over the duck legs. Then transfer to the air fryer basket.
5. Cook in the preheated air fryer at 390 degrees F/ 200 degrees C for 25 minutes.
6. When the cooking time is up, cook for 5 more minutes if needed.
7. Remove from the air fryer and serve hot. Enjoy!

Crunchy Chicken And Ranch Wraps

Servings: 4
Cooking Time: 25 Minutes
Ingredients:

- 2 (4-ounce) boneless, skinless breasts
- ½ (1-ounce) packet Hidden Valley Ranch seasoning mix
- Chicken seasoning or rub
- 1 cup all-purpose flour
- 1 egg
- ½ cup bread crumbs
- Cooking oil
- 4 medium (8-inch) flour tortillas
- 1½ cups shredded lettuce
- 3 tablespoons ranch dressing

Directions:
1. With your knife blade parallel to the cutting board, slice the chicken breasts in half horizontally to create 4 thin cutlets.
2. Season the chicken cutlets with the ranch seasoning and chicken seasoning to taste.
3. In a bowl large enough to dip a chicken cutlet, beat the egg. In another bowl, place the flour. Put the bread crumbs in a third bowl.
4. Spray the air fryer basket with cooking oil.
5. Dip each chicken cutlet in the flour, then the egg, and then the bread crumbs.
6. Place the chicken in the air fryer. Do not stack. Cook in batches. Spray the chicken with cooking oil. Cook for 7 minutes.
7. Open the air fryer and flip the chicken. Cook for an additional 3 to 4 minutes, until crisp.
8. Remove the cooked chicken from the air fryer and allow to cool for 2 to 3 minutes.
9. Repeat steps 6 through 8 for the remaining chicken.
10. Cut the chicken into strips. Divide the chicken strips, shredded lettuce, and ranch dressing evenly among the tortillas and serve.

Mexican Sheet Pan Dinner
Servings: 4
Cooking Time: 15 Minutes
Ingredients:
- 1 pound boneless, skinless chicken tenderloins, cut into strips
- 3 bell peppers, any color, cut into chunks
- 1 onion, cut into chunks
- 1 tablespoon olive oil, plus more for spraying
- 1 tablespoon fajita seasoning mix

Directions:
1. In a large bowl, mix together the chicken, bell peppers, onion, 1 tablespoon of olive oil, and fajita seasoning mix until completely coated.
2. Spray a fryer basket lightly with olive oil.
3. Place the chicken and vegetables in the fryer basket and lightly spray with olive oil.
4. Air fry for 7 minutes. Shake the basket and cook until the chicken is cooked through and the veggies are starting to char, an additional 5 to 8 minutes.

Garlic Chicken
Servings: 4
Cooking Time: 30 Minutes
Ingredients:
- 4 bone-in skinless chicken thighs
- 1 tbsp olive oil
- 1 tbsp lemon juice
- 3 tbsp cornstarch
- 1 tsp dried sage
- Black pepper to taste
- 20 garlic cloves, unpeeled

Directions:
1. Preheat air fryer to 370°F. Brush the chicken with olive oil and lemon juice, then drizzle cornstarch, sage, and pepper. Put the chicken in the frying basket and scatter the garlic cloves on top. Roast for 25 minutes or until the garlic is soft, and the chicken is cooked through. Serve.

Kale & Rice Chicken Rolls
Servings: 4
Cooking Time: 35 Minutes
Ingredients:
- 4 boneless, skinless chicken thighs
- ½ tsp ground fenugreek seeds
- 1 cup cooked wild rice
- 2 sundried tomatoes, diced
- ½ cup chopped kale
- 2 garlic cloves, minced
- 1 tsp salt
- 1 lemon, juiced
- ½ cup crumbled feta
- 1 tbsp olive oil

Directions:
1. Preheat air fryer to 380°F. Put the chicken thighs between two pieces of plastic wrap, and using a meat mallet or a rolling pin, pound them out to about ¼-inch thick. Combine the rice, tomatoes, kale, garlic, salt, fenugreek seeds and lemon juice in a bowl and mix well.
2. Divide the rice mixture among the chicken thighs and sprinkle with feta. Fold the sides of the chicken thigh over the filling, and then gently place each of them seam-side down into the greased air frying basket. Drizzle the stuffed chicken thighs with olive oil. Roast the stuffed chicken thighs for 12 minutes, then turn them over and cook for an additional 10 minutes. Serve and enjoy!

Katsu Chicken Thighs
Servings: 4
Cooking Time: 35 Minutes
Ingredients:
- 1 ½ lb boneless, skinless chicken thighs
- 3 tbsp tamari sauce
- 3 tbsp lemon juice
- ½ tsp ground ginger
- Black pepper to taste
- 6 tbsp cornstarch
- 1 cup chicken stock
- 2 tbsp hoisin sauce

- 2 tbsp light brown sugar
- 2 tbsp sesame seeds

Directions:
1. Preheat the air fryer to 400°F. After cubing the chicken thighs, put them in a cake pan. Add a tbsp of tamari sauce, a tbsp of lemon juice, ginger, and black pepper. Mix and let marinate for 10 minutes. Remove the chicken and coat it in 4 tbsp of cornstarch; set aside. Add the rest of the marinade to the pan and add the stock, hoisin sauce, brown sugar, and the remaining tamari sauce, lemon juice, and cornstarch. Mix well. Put the pan in the frying basket and Air Fry for 5-8 minutes or until bubbling and thick, stirring once. Remove and set aside. Put the chicken in the frying basket and Fry for 15-18 minutes, shaking the basket once. Remove the chicken to the sauce in the pan and return to the fryer to reheat for 2 minutes. Sprinkle with the sesame seeds and serve.

Chicken Tenders With Veggies

Servings: 4
Cooking Time: 18 To 20 Minutes
Ingredients:
- 1 pound chicken tenders
- 1 tablespoon honey
- Pinch salt
- Freshly ground black pepper
- ½ cup soft fresh bread crumbs
- ½ teaspoon dried thyme
- 1 tablespoon olive oil
- 2 carrots, sliced
- 12 small red potatoes

Directions:
1. In a medium bowl, toss the chicken tenders with the honey, salt, and pepper.
2. In a shallow bowl, combine the bread crumbs, thyme, and olive oil, and mix.
3. Coat the tenders in the bread crumbs, pressing firmly onto the meat.
4. Place the carrots and potatoes in the air fryer basket and top with the chicken tenders.
5. Roast for 18 to 20 minutes or until the chicken is cooked to 165°F and the vegetables are tender, shaking the basket halfway during the cooking time.
6. Did You Know? Chicken tenders are cut from the chicken breast when this cut is sold boneless and skinless. The tender is a little muscle behind the breast.

Healthy Vegetable Patties

Servings: 6
Cooking Time: 10 Minutes
Ingredients:
- ¼ teaspoon black pepper
- ½ teaspoon paprika
- ¾ teaspoon salt
- 1 onion, chopped
- 1 teaspoon garlic powder
- 1 teaspoon onion powder
- 1-pound radish, peeled and grated
- 3 tablespoons coconut oil

Directions:
1. At 350 degrees F/ 175 degrees C, preheat your Air Fryer.
2. Place all the recipe ingredients in a suitable mixing bowl.
3. Form patties using your hands and place individual patties in the air fryer basket.
4. Spray with cooking spray before closing the air fryer.
5. Cook for 10 minutes at 350 degrees F/ 175 degrees C or until crispy.
6. When done, serve and enjoy.

Coconut Chicken With Apricot-ginger Sauce

Servings: 4
Cooking Time: 8 Minutes Per Batch
Ingredients:
- 1½ pounds boneless, skinless chicken tenders, cut in large chunks (about 1¼ inches)
- salt and pepper
- ½ cup cornstarch
- 2 eggs
- 1 tablespoon milk
- 3 cups shredded coconut (see below)
- oil for misting or cooking spray
- Apricot-Ginger Sauce
- ½ cup apricot preserves
- 2 tablespoons white vinegar
- ¼ teaspoon ground ginger
- ¼ teaspoon low-sodium soy sauce
- 2 teaspoons white or yellow onion, grated or finely minced

Directions:
1. Mix all ingredients for the Apricot-Ginger Sauce well and let sit for flavors to blend while you cook the chicken.
2. Season chicken chunks with salt and pepper to taste.
3. Place cornstarch in a shallow dish.
4. In another shallow dish, beat together eggs and milk.
5. Place coconut in a third shallow dish. (If also using panko breadcrumbs, as suggested below, stir them to mix well.)
6. Spray air fryer basket with oil or cooking spray.
7. Dip each chicken chunk into cornstarch, shake off excess, and dip in egg mixture.
8. Shake off egg mixture and roll lightly in coconut or coconut mixture. Spray with oil.
9. Place coated chicken chunks in air fryer basket in a single layer, close together but without sides touching.
10. Cook at 360°F for 4 minutes, stop, and turn chunks over.
11. Cook an additional 4 minutes or until chicken is done inside and coating is crispy brown.
12. Repeat steps 9 through 11 to cook remaining chicken chunks.

Parmesan-lemon Chicken

Servings: 4
Cooking Time: 20 Minutes
Ingredients:
- 1 egg
- 2 tablespoons lemon juice
- 2 teaspoons minced garlic
- ½ teaspoon salt
- ½ teaspoon freshly ground black pepper
- 4 boneless, skinless chicken breasts, thin cut
- Olive oil
- ½ cup whole-wheat bread crumbs
- ¼ cup grated Parmesan cheese

Directions:
1. In a medium bowl, whisk together the egg, lemon juice, garlic, salt, and pepper. Add the chicken breasts, cover, and refrigerate for up to 1 hour.
2. In a shallow bowl, combine the bread crumbs and Parmesan cheese.
3. Spray a fryer basket lightly with olive oil.
4. Remove the chicken breasts from the egg mixture, then dredge them in the bread crumb mixture, and place in the fryer basket in a single layer. Lightly spray the chicken breasts with olive oil. You may need to cook the chicken in batches.
5. Air fry for 8 minutes. Flip the chicken over, lightly spray with olive oil, and cook until the chicken reaches an internal temperature of 165°F, for an additional 7 to 12 minutes.

Garlic Chicken Popcorn

Servings: 1
Cooking Time: 15 Minutes
Ingredients:
- 1-pound skinless, boneless chicken breast
- 1 teaspoon chili flakes
- 1 teaspoon garlic powder
- ½ cup flour
- 1 tablespoon olive oil cooking spray

Directions:
1. Pre-heat your air fryer at 365 degrees F/ 185 degrees C. Spray with olive oil.
2. Cut the chicken breasts into cubes and place in a suitable bowl.
3. Toss with the chili flakes, garlic powder, and additional seasonings to taste.
4. Add the coconut flour and toss once more.
5. Cook the chicken in the air fryer for ten minutes almost.
6. Flip and continue cooking for 5 minutes before serving.

Fancy Chicken Piccata

Servings: 4
Cooking Time: 30 Minutes
Ingredients:
- 1 lb chicken breasts, cut into cutlets
- Salt and pepper to taste
- 2 egg whites
- 2/3 cup bread crumbs
- 1 tsp Italian seasoning
- 1 tbsp whipped butter
- ½ cup chicken broth
- ½ onion powder
- ¼ cup fino sherry
- Juice of 1 lemon
- 1 tbsp capers, drained
- 1 lemon, sliced
- 2 tbsp chopped parsley

Directions:
1. Preheat air fryer to 370°F. Place the cutlets between two sheets of parchment paper. Pound to a ¼-inch thickness and season with salt and pepper. Beat egg whites with 1 tsp of water in a bowl. Put the bread crumbs, Parmesan cheese, onion powder, and Italian seasoning in a second bowl. Dip the cutlet in the egg bowl, and then in the crumb mix. Put the cutlets in the greased frying basket. Air Fry for 6 minutes, flipping once until crispy and golden.
2. Melt butter in a skillet. Stir in broth, sherry, lemon juice, lemon halves, and black pepper. Bring to a boil over high heat until the sauce is reduced by half, 4 minutes. Remove from heat. Pick out the lemon rinds and discard them. Stir in capers. Plate a cutlet, spoon some sauce over and garnish with lemon sleeves and parsley to serve.

Easy Asian Turkey Meatballs

Servings: 4
Cooking Time: 11 To 14 Minutes
Ingredients:
- 2 tablespoons peanut oil, divided
- 1 small onion, minced
- ¼ cup water chestnuts, finely chopped
- ½ teaspoon ground ginger
- 2 tablespoons low-sodium soy sauce
- ¼ cup panko bread crumbs
- 1 egg, beaten
- 1 pound (454 g) ground turkey

Directions:
1. Preheat the air fryer to 400ºF (204ºC).
2. In a round metal pan, combine 1 tablespoon of peanut oil and onion. Air fry for 1 to 2 minutes or until crisp and tender. Transfer the onion to a medium bowl.
3. Add the water chestnuts, ground ginger, soy sauce, and bread crumbs to the onion and mix well. Add egg and stir well. Mix in the ground turkey until combined.
4. Form the mixture into 1-inch meatballs. Drizzle the remaining 1 tablespoon of oil over the meatballs.
5. Bake the meatballs in the pan in batches for 10 to 12 minutes or until they are 165ºF (74ºC) on a meat thermometer. Rest for 5 minutes before serving.

Herb-roasted Turkey Breast

Servings: 6
Cooking Time: 45 Minutes
Ingredients:
- 1 tablespoon olive oil, plus more for spraying
- 2 garlic cloves, minced
- 2 teaspoons Dijon mustard
- 1½ teaspoons rosemary
- 1½ teaspoons sage
- 1½ teaspoons thyme
- 1 teaspoon salt
- ½ teaspoon freshly ground black pepper
- 3 pounds turkey breast, thawed if frozen

Directions:
1. Spray a fryer basket lightly with olive oil.
2. In a small bowl, mix together the garlic, olive oil, Dijon mustard, rosemary, sage, thyme, salt, and pepper to make a paste. Smear the paste all over the turkey breast.
3. Place the turkey breast in the fryer basket.
4. Air fry for 20 minutes. Flip turkey breast over and baste it with any drippings that have collected in the bottom drawer of the air fryer. Air fry until the internal temperature of the meat reaches at least 170°F, 20 more minutes.
5. If desired, increase the temperature to 400°F, flip the turkey breast over one last time, and air fry for up to 5 minutes to get a crispy exterior.
6. Let the turkey rest for 10 minutes before slicing and serving.

Chipotle Drumsticks

Servings: 4
Cooking Time: 25 Minutes
Ingredients:
- 1 tablespoon tomato paste
- ½ teaspoon chipotle powder
- ¼ teaspoon apple cider vinegar
- ¼ teaspoon garlic powder
- 8 chicken drumsticks
- ½ teaspoon salt
- ⅛ teaspoon ground black pepper

Directions:
1. In a small bowl, combine tomato paste, chipotle powder, vinegar, and garlic powder.
2. Sprinkle drumsticks with salt and pepper, then place into a large bowl and pour in tomato paste mixture. Toss or stir to evenly coat all drumsticks in mixture.
3. Place drumsticks into ungreased air fryer basket. Adjust the temperature to 400°F and set the timer for 25 minutes, turning drumsticks halfway through cooking. Drumsticks will be dark red with an internal temperature of at least 165°F when done. Serve warm.

Creamy Chicken Tenders

Servings: 8
Cooking Time: 20 Minutes
Ingredients:
- 2 pounds chicken tenders
- 1 cup feta cheese
- 4 tablespoons olive oil
- 1 cup cream
- Salt and black pepper, to taste

Directions:
1. Preheat the Air fryer to 340°F and grease an Air fryer basket.
2. Season the chicken tenders with salt and black pepper.
3. Arrange the chicken tenderloins in the Air fryer basket and drizzle with olive oil.
4. Cook for about 15 minutes and set the Air fryer to 390°F.
5. Cook for about 5 more minutes and dish out to serve warm.
6. Repeat with the remaining mixture and dish out to serve hot.

Tempero Baiano Brazilian Chicken

Servings: 4
Cooking Time: 20 Minutes
Ingredients:
- 1 teaspoon cumin seeds
- 1 teaspoon dried oregano
- 1 teaspoon dried parsley
- 1 teaspoon ground turmeric
- ½ teaspoon coriander seeds
- 1 teaspoon kosher salt
- ½ teaspoon black peppercorns
- ½ teaspoon cayenne pepper
- ¼ cup fresh lime juice
- 2 tablespoons olive oil
- 1½ pounds (680 g) chicken drumsticks

Directions:
1. In a clean coffee grinder or spice mill, combine the cumin, oregano, parsley, turmeric, coriander seeds, salt, peppercorns, and cayenne. Process until finely ground.
2. In a small bowl, combine the ground spices with the lime juice and oil. Place the chicken in a resealable plastic bag. Add the marinade, seal, and massage until the chicken is well coated. Marinate at room temperature for 30 minutes or in the refrigerator for up to 24 hours.
3. Preheat the air fryer to 400°F (204°C).
4. Place the drumsticks skin-side up in the air fryer basket and air fry for 20 to 25 minutes, turning the drumsticks halfway through the cooking time. Use a meat thermometer to ensure that the chicken has reached an internal temperature of 165°F (74°C). Serve immediately.

Chapter 8: Fish And Seafood Recipes

Blackened Shrimp Tacos

Servings: 4
Cooking Time: 15 Minutes
Ingredients:
- 1 teaspoon olive oil, plus more for spraying
- 12 ounces medium shrimp, deveined, tails off
- 1 to 2 teaspoons blackened seasoning
- 8 corn tortillas, warmed
- 1 (14-ounce) bag coleslaw mix
- 2 limes, cut in half

Directions:
1. Spray a fryer basket lightly with olive oil.
2. Dry the shrimp with a paper towel to remove excess water.
3. In a medium bowl, toss the shrimp with 1 teaspoon of olive oil and blackened seasoning.
4. Place the shrimp in the fryer basket and cook for 5 minutes. Shake the basket, lightly spray with olive oil, and cook until the shrimp are cooked through and starting to brown, 5 to 10 more minutes.
5. Fill each tortilla with the coleslaw mix and top with the blackened shrimp. Squeeze fresh lime juice over top.

Easy Air Fried Salmon

Servings: 2
Cooking Time: 10 Minutes
Ingredients:
- 2 salmon fillets, skinless and boneless
- 1 teaspoon olive oil
- Black pepper
- Salt

Directions:
1. Coat boneless salmon fillets with olive oil and season with black pepper and salt.
2. Place salmon fillets in air fryer basket and Cook at almost 360 degrees F/ 180 degrees C for 8-10 minutes.
3. Serve and enjoy.

Crispy Cod Sticks

Servings: 5
Cooking Time: 12 Minutes
Ingredients:
- 1-pound cod
- 3 tablespoons milk
- 1 cup meal
- 2 cups bread crumbs
- 2 large eggs, beaten
- ½ teaspoon black pepper
- ¼ teaspoon salt

Directions:
1. Combine together the milk and eggs in a suitable bowl.
2. In a shallow dish, stir together bread crumbs, black pepper, and salt.
3. Pour the meal into a second shallow dish.
4. Coat the cod sticks with the meal before dipping each 1 in the egg and rolling in bread crumbs.
5. Put the prepared fish sticks in the air fryer basket.
6. Cook at almost 350 degrees F/ 175 degrees C for 12 minutes, shaking the basket halfway through cooking.
7. Serve.

Fish And Vegetable Tacos

Servings: 4
Cooking Time: 9 To 12 Minutes
Ingredients:
- 1 pound white fish fillets, such as sole or cod (see Tip)
- 2 teaspoons olive oil
- 3 tablespoons freshly squeezed lemon juice, divided
- 1½ cups chopped red cabbage
- 1 large carrot, grated
- ½ cup low-sodium salsa
- ⅓ cup low-fat Greek yogurt
- 4 soft low-sodium whole-wheat tortillas

Directions:
1. Brush the fish with the olive oil and sprinkle with 1 tablespoon of lemon juice. Air-fry in the air fryer basket for 9 to 12 minutes, or until the fish just flakes when tested with a fork.
2. Meanwhile, in a medium bowl, stir together the remaining 2 tablespoons of lemon juice, the red cabbage, carrot, salsa, and yogurt.
3. When the fish is cooked, remove it from the air fryer basket and break it up into large pieces.
4. Offer the fish, tortillas, and the cabbage mixture, and let each person assemble a taco.

Healthy Salmon With Cardamom

Servings: 2
Cooking Time: 12 Minutes
Ingredients:
- 2 salmon fillets
- 1 tablespoon olive oil
- ¼ teaspoon ground cardamom
- ½ teaspoon paprika
- Salt

Directions:
1. At 350 degrees F/ 175 degrees C, preheat your air fryer.
2. Coat salmon fillets with paprika, olive oil, cardamom, paprika, and salt and place into the air fryer basket.
3. Cook salmon for almost 10-12 minutes. Turn halfway through.
4. Serve and enjoy.

Mahi Mahi With Cilantro-chili Butter

Servings: 4
Cooking Time: 20 Minutes
Ingredients:
- Salt and pepper to taste
- 4 mahi-mahi fillets
- 2 tbsp butter, melted
- 2 garlic cloves, minced

- ¼ tsp chili powder
- ¼ tsp lemon zest
- 1 tsp ginger, minced
- 1 tsp Worcestershire sauce
- 1 tbsp lemon juice
- 1 tbsp chopped cilantro

Directions:
1. Preheat air fryer to 375°F. Combine butter, Worcestershire sauce, garlic, salt, lemon juice, ginger, pepper, lemon zest, and chili powder in a small bowl. Place the mahi-mahi on a large plate, then spread the seasoned butter on the top of each. Arrange the fish in a single layer in the parchment-lined frying basket. Bake for 6 minutes, then carefully flip the fish. Bake for another 6-7 minutes until the fish is flaky and cooked through. Serve immediately sprinkled with cilantro and enjoy.

Fish Tacos With Hot Coleslaw

Servings: 4
Cooking Time: 25 Minutes
Ingredients:
- 2 cups shredded green cabbage
- ½ red onion, thinly sliced
- 1 jalapeño, thinly sliced
- 1 tsp lemon juice
- 1 tbsp chives, chopped
- 3 tbsp mayonnaise
- 1 tbsp hot sauce
- 2 tbsp chopped cilantro
- 1 tbsp apple cider vinegar
- Salt to taste
- 1 large egg, beaten
- 1 cup crushed tortilla chips
- 1 lb cod fillets, cubed
- 8 corn tortillas

Directions:
1. Mix the lemon juice, chives, mayonnaise, and hot sauce in a bowl until blended. Add the cabbage to a large bowl. Then add onion, jalapeño, cilantro, vinegar and salt. Toss until well mixed. Put in the fridge until ready to serve.
2. Preheat air fryer to 360°F. In one shallow bowl, add the beaten egg. In another shallow bowl, add the crushed tortilla chips. Salt the cod, then dip into the egg mixture. Allow excess to drip off. Next, dip into the crumbs, gently pressing into the crumbs. Place the fish in the greased frying basket and Air Fry for 6 minutes, flipping once until crispy and completely cooked. Place 2 warm tortillas on each plate. Top with cod cubes, ¼ cup of slaw, and drizzle with spicy mayo. Serve and enjoy!

Lemon-roasted Salmon Fillets

Servings: 3
Cooking Time: 7 Minutes
Ingredients:
- 3 6-ounce skin-on salmon fillets
- Olive oil spray
- 9 Very thin lemon slices
- ¾ teaspoon Ground black pepper
- ¼ teaspoon Table salt

Directions:
1. Preheat the air fryer to 400°F.
2. Generously coat the skin of each of the fillets with olive oil spray. Set the fillets skin side down on your work surface. Place three overlapping lemon slices down the length of each salmon fillet. Sprinkle them with the pepper and salt. Coat lightly with olive oil spray.
3. Use a nonstick-safe spatula to transfer the fillets one by one to the basket, leaving as much air space between them as possible. Air-fry undisturbed for 7 minutes, or until cooked through.
4. Use a nonstick-safe spatula to transfer the fillets to serving plates. Cool for only a minute or two before serving.

Super Crunchy Flounder Fillets

Servings: 2
Cooking Time: 6 Minutes
Ingredients:
- ½ cup All-purpose flour or tapioca flour
- 1 Large egg white(s)
- 1 tablespoon Water
- ¾ teaspoon Table salt
- 1 cup Plain panko bread crumbs (gluten-free, if a concern)
- 2 4-ounce skinless flounder fillet(s)
- Vegetable oil spray

Directions:
1. Preheat the air fryer to 400°F.
2. Set up and fill three shallow soup plates or small pie plates on your counter: one for the flour; one for the egg white(s), beaten with the water and salt until foamy; and one for the bread crumbs.
3. Dip one fillet in the flour, turning it to coat both sides. Gently shake off any excess flour, then dip the fillet in the egg white mixture, turning it to coat. Let any excess egg white mixture slip back into the rest, then set the fish in the bread crumbs. Turn it several times, gently pressing it into the crumbs to create an even crust. Generously coat both sides of the fillet with vegetable oil spray. If necessary, set it aside and continue coating the remaining fillet(s) in the same way.
4. Set the fillet(s) in the basket. If working with more than one fillet, they should not touch, although they may be quite close together, depending on the basket's size. Air-fry undisturbed for 6 minutes, or until lightly browned and crunchy.
5. Use a nonstick-safe spatula to transfer the fillet(s) to a wire rack. Cool for only a minute or two before serving.

Cajun Flounder Fillets

Servings: 2
Cooking Time: 5 Minutes
Ingredients:
- 2 4-ounce skinless flounder fillet(s)
- 2 teaspoons Peanut oil
- 1 teaspoon Purchased or homemade Cajun dried seasoning blend

Directions:
1. Preheat the air fryer to 400°F.
2. Oil the fillet(s) by drizzling on the peanut oil, then gently rubbing in the oil with your clean, dry fingers. Sprinkle the seasoning blend evenly over both sides of the fillet(s).
3. When the machine is at temperature, set the fillet(s) in the basket. If working with more than one fillet, they should not touch, although they may be quite close together, depending on the basket's size. Air-fry undisturbed for 5 minutes, or until lightly browned and cooked through.
4. Use a nonstick-safe spatula to transfer the fillets to a serving platter or plate(s). Serve at once.

Snow Crab Legs

Servings: 6
Cooking Time: 15 Minutes Per Batch
Ingredients:
- 8 pounds fresh shell-on snow crab legs
- 2 tablespoons olive oil
- 2 teaspoons Old Bay Seasoning
- 4 tablespoons salted butter, melted
- 2 teaspoons lemon juice

Directions:
1. Preheat the air fryer to 400°F.
2. Drizzle crab legs with oil and sprinkle with Old Bay. Place in the air fryer basket, working in batches as necessary. Cook 15 minutes, turning halfway through cooking time, until crab turns a bright red-orange.
3. In a small bowl, whisk together butter and lemon juice. Serve as a dipping sauce with warm crab legs.

Garlic-lemon Steamer Clams

Servings: 2
Cooking Time: 30 Minutes
Ingredients:
- 25 Manila clams, scrubbed
- 2 tbsp butter, melted
- 1 garlic clove, minced
- 2 lemon wedges

Directions:
1. Add the clams to a large bowl filled with water and let sit for 10 minutes. Drain. Pour more water and let sit for 10 more minutes. Drain. Preheat air fryer to 350ºF. Place clams in the basket and Air Fry for 7 minutes. Discard any clams that don´t open. Remove clams from shells and place them into a large serving dish. Drizzle with melted butter and garlic and squeeze lemon on top. Serve.

Asian Steamed Tuna

Servings: 4
Cooking Time: 8 To 10 Minutes
Ingredients:
- 4 small tuna steaks
- 2 tablespoons low-sodium soy sauce
- 2 teaspoons sesame oil
- 2 teaspoons rice wine vinegar
- 1 teaspoon grated fresh ginger
- ⅛ teaspoon pepper
- 1 stalk lemongrass, bent in half
- 3 tablespoons lemon juice

Directions:
1. Place the tuna steaks on a plate.
2. In a small bowl, combine the soy sauce, sesame oil, rice wine vinegar, and ginger, and mix well. Pour this mixture over the tuna and marinate for 10 minutes. Rub the soy sauce mixture gently into both sides of the tuna. Sprinkle with the pepper.
3. Place the lemongrass on the air fryer basket and top with the steaks. Put the lemon juice and 1 tablespoon water in the pan below the basket.
4. Steam the fish for 8 to 10 minutes or until the tuna registers at least 145°F. Discard the lemongrass and serve the tuna.

Potato Chip-crusted Cod

Servings: 2
Cooking Time: 20 Minutes
Ingredients:
- ½ cup crushed potato chips
- 1 tsp chopped tarragon
- 1/8 tsp salt
- 1 tsp cayenne powder
- 1 tbsp Dijon mustard
- ¼ cup buttermilk
- 1 tsp lemon juice
- 1 tbsp butter, melted
- 2 cod fillets

Directions:
1. Preheat air fryer at 350ºF. Mix all ingredients in a bowl. Press potato chip mixture evenly across tops of cod. Place cod fillets in the greased frying basket and Air Fry for 10 minutes until the fish is opaque and flakes easily with a fork. Serve immediately.

Fish Sticks For Kids

Servings: 8
Cooking Time: 6 Minutes
Ingredients:
- 8 ounces fish fillets (pollock or cod)
- salt (optional)
- ½ cup plain breadcrumbs
- oil for misting or cooking spray

Directions:
1. Cut fish fillets into "fingers" about ½ x 3 inches. Sprinkle with salt to taste, if desired.

Air Fryer Cookbook for Beginners

2. Roll fish in breadcrumbs. Spray all sides with oil or cooking spray.
3. Place in air fryer basket in single layer and cook at 390°F for 6 minutes, until golden brown and crispy.

Crispy Sweet-and-sour Cod Fillets

Servings:3
Cooking Time: 12 Minutes
Ingredients:
- 1½ cups Plain panko bread crumbs (gluten-free, if a concern)
- 2 tablespoons Regular or low-fat mayonnaise (not fat-free; gluten-free, if a concern)
- ¼ cup Sweet pickle relish
- 3 4- to 5-ounce skinless cod fillets

Directions:
1. Preheat the air fryer to 400°F.
2. Pour the bread crumbs into a shallow soup plate or a small pie plate. Mix the mayonnaise and relish in a small bowl until well combined. Smear this mixture all over the cod fillets. Set them in the crumbs and turn until evenly coated on all sides, even on the ends.
3. Set the coated cod fillets in the basket with as much air space between them as possible. They should not touch. Air-fry undisturbed for 12 minutes, or until browned and crisp.
4. Use a nonstick-safe spatula to transfer the cod pieces to a wire rack. Cool for only a minute or two before serving hot.

Salmon On Bed Of Fennel And Carrot

Servings: 2
Cooking Time:13 To 14 Minutes
Ingredients:
- 1 fennel bulb, thinly sliced
- 1 large carrot, peeled and sliced
- 1 small onion, thinly sliced
- ¼ cup low-fat sour cream
- ¼ teaspoon coarsely ground pepper
- 2 (5 ounce) salmon fillets

Directions:
1. Combine the fennel, carrot, and onion in a bowl and toss.
2. Put the vegetable mixture into a 6-inch metal pan. Roast in the air fryer for 4 minutes or until the vegetables are crisp tender.
3. Remove the pan from the air fryer. Stir in the sour cream and sprinkle the vegetables with the pepper.
4. Top with the salmon fillets.
5. Return the pan to the air fryer. Roast for another 9 to 10 minutes or until the salmon just barely flakes when tested with a fork.

Tuna Wraps

Servings: 4
Cooking Time:4 To 7 Minutes
Ingredients:
- 1 pound fresh tuna steak, cut into 1-inch cubes
- 1 tablespoon grated fresh ginger
- 2 garlic cloves, minced
- ½ teaspoon toasted sesame oil
- 4 low-sodium whole-wheat tortillas
- ¼ cup low-fat mayonnaise
- 2 cups shredded romaine lettuce (see Tip)
- 1 red bell pepper, thinly sliced

Directions:
1. In a medium bowl, mix the tuna, ginger, garlic, and sesame oil. Let it stand for 10 minutes.
2. Grill the tuna in the air fryer for 4 to 7 minutes, or until done to your liking and lightly browned.
3. Make wraps with the tuna, tortillas, mayonnaise, lettuce, and bell pepper. Serve immediately.

Snapper Scampi

Servings:4
Cooking Time: 8 To 10 Minutes
Ingredients:
- 4 (6-ounce) skinless snapper or arctic char fillets
- 1 tablespoon olive oil
- 3 tablespoons lemon juice, divided
- ½ teaspoon dried basil
- Pinch salt
- Freshly ground black pepper
- 2 tablespoons butter
- 2 cloves garlic, minced

Directions:
1. Rub the fish fillets with olive oil and 1 tablespoon of the lemon juice. Sprinkle with the basil, salt, and pepper, and place in the air fryer basket.
2. Grill the fish for 7 to 8 minutes or until the fish just flakes when tested with a fork. Remove the fish from the basket and put on a serving plate. Cover to keep warm.
3. In a 6-by-6-by-2-inch pan, combine the butter, remaining 2 tablespoons lemon juice, and garlic. Cook in the air fryer for 1 to 2 minutes or until the garlic is sizzling. Pour this mixture over the fish and serve.
4. Did You Know? You can buy bottled lemon and lime juice at the supermarket, but for recipes such as this one, where the flavor is so important, squeeze the juice from a lemon yourself just before you make the recipe.

Mayonnaise Salmon With Spinach

Servings: 4
Cooking Time: 19 Minutes
Ingredients:
- 25 ounces salmon fillet
- 1 tablespoon green pesto
- 1 cup mayonnaise
- ½ ounce olive oil
- 1-pound fresh spinach
- 2 ounces parmesan cheese, grated
- Black pepper
- Salt

Directions:
1. At 370 degrees F/ 185 degrees C, preheat your air fryer.

2. Grease its air fryer basket with cooking spray.
3. Season salmon fillet with black pepper and salt and place into the air fryer basket.
4. In a suitable bowl, mix together mayonnaise, parmesan cheese, and pesto and spread over the salmon fillet.
5. Cook salmon for 14-16 minutes.
6. Meanwhile, in a pan, sauté spinach with olive oil until spinach is wilted, about 2-3 minutes. Season with black pepper and salt.
7. Transfer spinach in serving plate and top with cooked salmon.
8. Serve and enjoy.

Air Fried Cod With Basil Vinaigrette

Servings:4
Cooking Time: 15 Minutes
Ingredients:
- ¼ cup olive oil
- 4 cod fillets
- A bunch of basil, torn
- Juice from 1 lemon, freshly squeezed
- Salt and pepper to taste

Directions:
1. Preheat the air fryer for 5 minutes.
2. Season the cod fillets with salt and pepper to taste.
3. Place in the air fryer and cook for 15 minutes at 350°F.
4. Meanwhile, mix the rest of the ingredients in a bowl and toss to combine.
5. Serve the air fried cod with the basil vinaigrette.

Coconut Shrimp

Servings: 4
Cooking Time: 12 Minutes
Ingredients:
- 1 pound large shrimp (about 16 to 20), peeled and de-veined
- ½ cup flour
- salt and freshly ground black pepper
- 2 egg whites
- ½ cup fine breadcrumbs
- ½ cup shredded unsweetened coconut
- zest of one lime
- ½ teaspoon salt
- ⅛ to ¼ teaspoon ground cayenne pepper
- vegetable or canola oil
- sweet chili sauce or duck sauce (for serving)

Directions:
1. Set up a dredging station. Place the flour in a shallow dish and season well with salt and freshly ground black pepper. Whisk the egg whites in a second shallow dish. In a third shallow dish, combine the breadcrumbs, coconut, lime zest, salt and cayenne pepper.
2. Preheat the air fryer to 400°F.
3. Dredge each shrimp first in the flour, then dip it in the egg mixture, and finally press it into the breadcrumb-coconut mixture to coat all sides. Place the breaded shrimp on a plate or baking sheet and spray both sides with vegetable oil.
4. Air-fry the shrimp in two batches, being sure not to over-crowd the basket. Air-fry for 5 minutes, turning the shrimp over for the last minute or two. Repeat with the second batch of shrimp.
5. Lower the temperature of the air fryer to 340°F. Return the first batch of shrimp to the air fryer basket with the second batch and air-fry for an additional 2 minutes, just to re-heat everything.
6. Serve with sweet chili sauce, duck sauce or just eat them plain!

Garlic-lemon Scallops

Servings:4
Cooking Time: 12 Minutes
Ingredients:
- ¼ teaspoon salt
- ¼ teaspoon ground black pepper
- 8 sea scallops, rinsed and patted dry
- 4 tablespoons salted butter, melted
- 4 teaspoons finely minced garlic
- Zest and juice of ½ small lemon

Directions:
1. Preheat the air fryer to 375°F.
2. Sprinkle salt and pepper evenly over scallops. Spritz scallops lightly with cooking spray. Place in the air fryer basket in a single layer and cook 12 minutes, turning halfway through cooking time, until scallops are opaque and firm and internal temperature reaches at least 130°F.
3. While scallops are cooking, in a small bowl, mix butter, garlic, lemon zest, and juice. Set aside.
4. When scallops are done, drizzle with garlic–lemon butter. Serve warm.

Parmesan White Fish

Servings: 2 Servings
Cooking Time: 20 Minutes
Ingredients:
- 2 filets of white fish
- ½ cup of grated Parmesan cheese
- ½ teaspoon of smoked paprika
- ½ teaspoon of onion powder
- ½ teaspoon of garlic powder
- 1 tablespoon of olive oil
- Pinch of black pepper and salt, to taste
- Lemon wedges, for serving
- Chopped parsley, for garnishing

Directions:
1. Preheat your air fryer to 380°F.
2. Grease the fish filets with oil. Season both sides with pepper, garlic powder, paprika, onion powder, salt, and pepper. Coat both sides generously with grated cheese.
3. Cover the air fryer basket with the perforated parchment paper. Lightly spray it with oil.
4. Put the coated fillets in the preheated air fryer for 6–12 minutes (the best time is around 8 minutes).
5. Serve with lemon wedges and top with the chopped parsley. Enjoy your Parmesan White Fish!

Yummy White Fish

Servings: 2
Cooking Time: 12 Minutes
Ingredients:
- 12 ounces white fish fillets
- ½ teaspoon onion powder
- ½ teaspoon lemon pepper seasoning
- ½ teaspoon garlic powder
- 1 tablespoon olive oil
- Black pepper
- Salt

Directions:
1. Grease its air fryer basket with cooking spray.
2. At 360 degrees F/ 180 degrees C, preheat your air fryer.
3. Coat fish fillets with olive oil and season with onion powder, lemon pepper seasoning, garlic powder, black pepper, and salt.
4. Place fish fillets in air fryer basket and cook for almost 10-12 minutes.
5. Serve and enjoy.

Crabmeat-stuffed Flounder

Servings: 3
Cooking Time: 12 Minutes
Ingredients:
- 4½ ounces Purchased backfin or claw crabmeat, picked over for bits of shell and cartilage
- 6 Saltine crackers, crushed into fine crumbs
- 2 tablespoons plus 1 teaspoon Regular or low-fat mayonnaise (not fat-free)
- ¾ teaspoon Yellow prepared mustard
- 1½ teaspoons Worcestershire sauce
- ⅛ teaspoon Celery salt
- 3 5- to 6-ounce skinless flounder fillets
- Vegetable oil spray
- Mild paprika

Directions:
1. Preheat the air fryer to 400°F.
2. Gently mix the crabmeat, crushed saltines, mayonnaise, mustard, Worcestershire sauce, and celery salt in a bowl until well combined.
3. Generously coat the flat side of a fillet with vegetable oil spray. Set the fillet sprayed side down on your work surface. Cut the fillet in half widthwise, then cut one of the halves in half lengthwise. Set a scant ⅓ cup of the crabmeat mixture on top of the undivided half of the fish fillet, mounding the mixture to make an oval that somewhat fits the shape of the fillet with at least a ¼-inch border of fillet beyond the filling all around.
4. Take the two thin divided quarters (that is, the halves of the half) and lay them lengthwise over the filling, overlapping at each end and leaving a little space in the middle where the filling peeks through. Coat the top of the stuffed flounder piece with vegetable oil spray, then sprinkle paprika over the stuffed flounder fillet. Set aside and use the remaining fillet(s) to make more stuffed flounder "packets," repeating steps 3 and
5. Use a nonstick-safe spatula to transfer the stuffed flounder fillets to the basket. Leave as much space between them as possible. Air-fry undisturbed for 12 minutes, or until lightly brown and firm (but not hard).
6. Use that same spatula, plus perhaps another one, to transfer the fillets to a serving platter or plates. Cool for a minute or two, then serve hot.

Garlic Tilapia Fillets

Servings: 5
Cooking Time: 10 Minutes
Ingredients:
- 1 tablespoon all-purpose flour
- Sea salt and white pepper, to taste
- 1 teaspoon garlic paste
- 1 tablespoon extra-virgin olive oil
- ½ cup cornmeal
- 5 tilapia fillets, slice into halves

Directions:
1. Prepare a Ziploc bag and mix up the flour, salt, white pepper, garlic paste, olive oil, and cornmeal.
2. Add the fish fillets to the Ziploc bag and coat them well with the spice mixture.
3. Oil the basket of your air fryer with cooking spray and then put the coated fillets in it.
4. Arrange the basket to the air fryer and cook at 400 degrees F/ 205 degrees C for 10 minutes.
5. After 10 minutes, flip the fillets and cook for more 6 minutes.
6. Working in batches is suggested.
7. When done, serve with lemon wedges if desired.
8. Enjoy!

Country Shrimp "boil"

Servings: 4
Cooking Time: 20 Minutes
Ingredients:
- 2 tablespoons olive oil, plus more for spraying
- 1 pound large shrimp, deveined, tail on
- 1 pound smoked turkey sausage, cut into thick slices
- 2 corn cobs, quartered
- 1 zucchini, cut into bite-sized pieces
- 1 red bell pepper, cut into chunks
- 1 tablespoon Old Bay seasoning

Directions:
1. Spray the fryer basket lightly with olive oil.
2. In a large bowl, mix together the shrimp, turkey sausage, corn, zucchini, bell pepper, and Old Bay seasoning, and toss to coat with the spices. Add the 2 tablespoons of olive oil and toss again until evenly coated.
3. Spread the mixture in the fryer basket in a single layer. You will need to cook in batches.
4. Air fry until cooked through, 15 to 20 minutes, shaking the basket every 5 minutes for even cooking.

Great Cat Fish

Servings: 4
Cooking Time: 25 Minutes
Ingredients:
- ¼ cup seasoned fish fry
- 1 tbsp olive oil
- 1 tbsp parsley, chopped

Directions:
1. Preheat your air fryer to 400°F, and add seasoned fish fry, and fillets in a large Ziploc bag; massage well to coat. Place the fillets in your air fryer's cooking basket and cook for 10 minutes. Flip the fish and cook for 2-3 more minutes. Top with parsley and serve.

Roasted Prawns With Firecracker Sauce

Servings: 4
Cooking Time: 10 Minutes
Ingredients:
- Black pepper and salt to taste
- 1 egg
- ½ cup flour
- ¼ cup sesame seeds
- ¾ cup seasoned breadcrumbs
- Firecracker sauce
- ⅓ cup sour cream
- 2 tablespoons buffalo sauce
- ¼ cup spicy ketchup
- 1 green onion, chopped

Directions:
1. At 390 degrees F/ 200 degrees C, preheat your air fryer. Grease its air fryer basket with cooking spray.
2. Beat the eggs in a suitable bowl with salt. In a separate bowl, mix seasoned breadcrumbs with sesame seeds. In a third bowl, pour the flour mixed with black pepper.
3. Dip prawns in the flour and then in the eggs, and finally in the breadcrumb mixture. Spray with cooking spray and add to the cooking basket. Cook for almost 10 minutes, flipping halfway through.
4. Meanwhile, mix well all the sauce ingredients, except for the green onion in a suitable bowl. Serve the prawns with firecracker sauce.

Typical Crab Cakes With Lemon Wedges

Servings: 3
Cooking Time: 10 Minutes
Ingredients:
- 1 egg, beaten
- 2 tablespoons milk
- 2 crustless bread slices
- 1 pound lump crabmeat
- 2 tablespoons scallions, chopped
- 1 garlic clove, minced
- 1 teaspoon deli mustard
- 1 teaspoon Sriracha sauce
- Sea salt, to taste
- Ground black pepper, to taste
- 4 lemon wedges, for serving

Directions:
1. Beat the egg and milk until white and frothy, then add the bread in and let it soak for a few minutes.
2. In addition to the lemon wedges, stir in the remaining ingredients.
3. Form 4 equal-size patties, place the patties in the cooking basket of your air fryer and then spray them with a non-stick cooking spray.
4. Arrange the basket to the air fryer and cook the patties at 400 degrees F/ 205 degrees C for 10 minutes, flipping halfway through.
5. Serve warm, garnished with lemon wedges. Bon appétit!

Old Bay Lobster Tails

Servings: 2
Cooking Time: 20 Minutes
Ingredients:
- ¼ cup green onions, sliced
- 2 uncooked lobster tails
- 1 tbsp butter, melted
- ½ tsp Old Bay Seasoning
- 1 tbsp chopped parsley
- 1 tsp dried sage
- 1 tsp dried thyme
- 1 garlic clove, chopped
- 1 tbsp basil paste
- 2 lemon wedges

Directions:
1. Preheat air fryer at 400°F. Using kitchen shears, cut down the middle of each lobster tail on the softer side. Carefully run your finger between lobster meat and shell to loosen the meat. Place lobster tails, cut side-up, in the frying basket and Air Fry for 4 minutes. Brush the tail meat with butter and season with old bay seasoning, sage, thyme, garlic, green onions, basil paste and cook for another 4 minutes. Scatter with parsley and serve with lemon wedges. Enjoy!

Crab Rangoon

Servings: 4
Cooking Time: 5 Minutes
Ingredients:
- ½ cup imitation crabmeat
- 4 ounces full-fat cream cheese, softened
- ¼ teaspoon Worcestershire sauce
- 8 wonton wrappers

Directions:
1. Preheat the air fryer to 400°F.
2. In a medium bowl, mix crabmeat, cream cheese, and Worcestershire until combined.
3. Place wonton wrappers on work surface. For each rangoon, scoop ½ tablespoon crab mixture onto center of a wonton wrapper. Press opposing edges toward the center and pinch to close. Spray with cooking spray to

coat well. Repeat with remaining crab mixture and wontons.
4. Place in the air fryer basket and cook 5 minutes until brown at the edges. Serve warm.

Timeless Garlic-lemon Scallops
Servings: 2
Cooking Time: 15 Minutes
Ingredients:
- 2 tbsp butter, melted
- 1 garlic clove, minced
- 1 tbsp lemon juice
- 1 lb jumbo sea scallops

Directions:
1. Preheat air fryer to 400ºF. Whisk butter, garlic, and lemon juice in a bowl. Roll scallops in the mixture to coat all sides. Place scallops in the frying basket and Air Fry for 4 minutes, flipping once. Brush the tops of each scallop with butter mixture and cook for 4 more minutes, flipping once. Serve and enjoy!

Masala Fish 'n' Chips
Servings: 4
Cooking Time: 30 Minutes
Ingredients:
- 2 russet potatoes, cut into strips
- 4 pollock fillets
- Salt and pepper to taste
- ½ tsp garam masala
- 1 egg white
- ¾ cup bread crumbs
- 2 tbsp olive oil

Directions:
1. Preheat air fryer to 400°F. Sprinkle the pollock fillets with salt, pepper, and garam masala. In a shallow bowl, beat egg whites until foamy. In a separate bowl, stir together bread crumbs and 1 tablespoon olive oil until completely combined. Dip the fillets into the egg white, then coat with the bread crumbs. In a bowl, toss the potato strips with 1 tbsp olive oil. Place them in the frying basket and Air Fry for 10 minutes. Slide-out the basket, shake the chips and place a metal holder over them. Arrange the fish fillets on the metal holder and cook for 10-12 minutes, flipping once. Serve warm.

Smoked Paprika Cod Goujons
Servings: 2
Cooking Time: 30 Minutes
Ingredients:
- 1 cod fillet, cut into chunks
- 2 eggs, beaten
- ¼ cup breadcrumbs
- ¼ cup rice flour
- 1 lemon, juiced
- ½ tbsp garlic powder
- 1 tsp smoked paprika
- Salt and pepper to taste

Directions:
1. Preheat air fryer to 350°F. In a bowl, stir the beaten eggs and lemon juice thoroughly. Dip the cod chunks in the mixture. In another bowl, mix the bread crumbs, rice flour, garlic powder, smoked paprika, salt, and pepper.
2. Coat the cod with the crumb mixture. Transfer the coated cod to the greased frying basket. Air Fry for 14-16 minutes until the fish goujons are cooked through and their crust is golden, brown, and delicious. Toss the basket two or three times during the cooking time. Serve.

Lobster Tails
Servings: 4
Cooking Time: 10 Minutes
Ingredients:
- 4 lobster tails
- 2 tablespoons salted butter, melted
- 1 tablespoon finely minced garlic
- ¼ teaspoon salt
- ¼ teaspoon ground black pepper
- 2 tablespoons lemon juice

Directions:
1. Preheat the air fryer to 400°F.
2. Carefully cut open lobster tails with kitchen scissors and pull back the shell a little to expose the meat. Drizzle butter over each tail, then sprinkle with garlic, salt, and pepper.
3. Place tails in the air fryer basket and cook 10 minutes until lobster is firm and opaque and internal temperature reaches at least 145°F.
4. Drizzle lemon juice over lobster meat. Serve warm.

Caribbean Skewers
Servings: 4
Cooking Time: 25 Minutes
Ingredients:
- 1 ½ lb large shrimp, peeled and deveined
- 1 can pineapple chunks, drained, liquid reserved
- 1 red bell pepper, chopped
- 3 scallions, chopped
- 1 tbsp lemon juice
- 1 tbsp olive oil
- ½ tsp jerk seasoning
- ⅛ tsp cayenne pepper
- 2 tbsp cilantro, chopped

Directions:
1. Preheat the air fryer to 37-°F. Thread the shrimp, pineapple, bell pepper, and scallions onto 8 bamboo skewers. Mix 3 tbsp of pineapple juice with lemon juice, olive oil, jerk seasoning, and cayenne pepper. Brush every bit of the mix over the skewers. Place 4 kebabs in the frying basket, add a rack, and put the rest of the skewers on top. Bake for 6-9 minutes and rearrange at about 4-5 minutes. Cook until the shrimp curl and pinken. Sprinkle with freshly chopped cilantro and serve.

Panko-breaded Cod Fillets

Servings: 2
Cooking Time: 20 Minutes
Ingredients:
- 1 lemon wedge, juiced and zested
- ½ cup panko bread crumbs
- Salt to taste
- 1 tbsp Dijon mustard
- 1 tbsp butter, melted
- 2 cod fillets

Directions:
1. Preheat air fryer to 350°F. Combine all ingredients, except for the fish, in a bowl. Press mixture evenly across tops of cod fillets. Place fillets in the greased frying basket and Air Fry for 10 minutes until the cod is opaque and flakes easily with a fork. Serve immediately.

Quick Shrimp Scampi

Servings: 2
Cooking Time: 5 Minutes
Ingredients:
- 16 to 20 raw large shrimp, peeled, deveined and tails removed
- ½ cup white wine
- freshly ground black pepper
- ¼ cup + 1 tablespoon butter, divided
- 1 clove garlic, sliced
- 1 teaspoon olive oil
- salt, to taste
- juice of ½ lemon, to taste
- ¼ cup chopped fresh parsley

Directions:
1. Start by marinating the shrimp in the white wine and freshly ground black pepper for at least 30 minutes, or as long as 2 hours in the refrigerator.
2. Preheat the air fryer to 400°F.
3. Melt ¼ cup of butter in a small saucepan on the stovetop. Add the garlic and let the butter simmer, but be sure to not let it burn.
4. Pour the shrimp and marinade into the air fryer, letting the marinade drain through to the bottom drawer. Drizzle the olive oil on the shrimp and season well with salt. Air-fry at 400°F for 3 minutes. Turn the shrimp over (don't shake the basket because the marinade will splash around) and pour the garlic butter over the shrimp. Air-fry for another 2 minutes.
5. Remove the shrimp from the air fryer basket and transfer them to a bowl. Squeeze lemon juice over all the shrimp and toss with the chopped parsley and remaining tablespoon of butter. Season to taste with salt and serve immediately.

Sea Bass With Potato Scales And Caper Aïoli

Servings: 2
Cooking Time: 10 Minutes
Ingredients:
- 2 (6- to 8-ounce) fillets of sea bass
- salt and freshly ground black pepper
- ¼ cup mayonnaise
- 2 teaspoons finely chopped lemon zest
- 1 teaspoon chopped fresh thyme
- 2 fingerling potatoes, very thinly sliced into rounds
- olive oil
- ½ clove garlic, crushed into a paste
- 1 tablespoon capers, drained and rinsed
- 1 tablespoon olive oil
- 1 teaspoon lemon juice, to taste

Directions:
1. Preheat the air fryer to 400°F.
2. Season the fish well with salt and freshly ground black pepper. Mix the mayonnaise, lemon zest and thyme together in a small bowl. Spread a thin layer of the mayonnaise mixture on both fillets. Start layering rows of potato slices onto the fish fillets to simulate the fish scales. The second row should overlap the first row slightly. Dabbing a little more mayonnaise along the upper edge of the row of potatoes where the next row overlaps will help the potato slices stick. Press the potatoes onto the fish to secure them well and season again with salt. Brush or spray the potato layer with olive oil.
3. Transfer the fish to the air fryer and air-fry for 8 to 10 minutes, depending on the thickness of your fillets. 1-inch of fish should take 10 minutes at 400°F.
4. While the fish is cooking, add the garlic, capers, olive oil and lemon juice to the remaining mayonnaise mixture to make the caper aïoli.
5. Serve the fish warm with a dollop of the aïoli on top or on the side.

Outrageous Crispy Fried Salmon Skin

Servings: 4
Cooking Time: 10 Minutes
Ingredients:
- ½ pound salmon skin, patted dry
- 4 tablespoons coconut oil
- Salt and pepper to taste

Directions:
1. Preheat the air fryer for 5 minutes.
2. In a large bowl, combine everything and mix well.
3. Place in the fryer basket and close.
4. Cook for 10 minutes at 400°F.
5. Halfway through the cooking time, give a good shake to evenly cook the skin.

Fish Mania With Mustard

Servings: 4-5
Cooking Time: 10 Minutes
Ingredients:
- 1 cup soft bread crumbs
- 1 teaspoon whole-grain mustard
- 2 cans canned fish
- 2 celery stalks, chopped
- 1 egg, whisked

Air Fryer Cookbook for BEGINNERS

- ½ teaspoon sea salt
- ¼ teaspoon black peppercorns, cracked
- 1 teaspoon paprika

Directions:
1. Thoroughly mix the fish, breadcrumbs, celery and other ingredients in a large bowl.
2. Make four cakes shapes from the mixture and refrigerate for 45-50 minutes.
3. Place the cakes in the basket that has been coated with cooking oil or spray.
4. Arrange it to air fryer and cook for 5 minutes at 360 degrees F/ 180 degrees C.
5. After 5 minutes, flip the cakes gently and cook for another 4 minutes
6. Serve over mashed potatoes.

Blackened Catfish

Servings: 4
Cooking Time: 8 Minutes
Ingredients:
- 1 teaspoon paprika
- 1 teaspoon garlic powder
- 1 teaspoon onion powder
- 1 teaspoon ground dried thyme
- ½ teaspoon ground black pepper
- ⅛ teaspoon cayenne pepper
- ½ teaspoon dried oregano
- ⅛ teaspoon crushed red pepper flakes
- 1 pound catfish filets
- ½ teaspoon sea salt
- 2 tablespoons butter, melted
- 1 tablespoon extra-virgin olive oil
- 2 tablespoons chopped parsley
- 1 lemon, cut into wedges

Directions:
1. In a small bowl, stir together the paprika, garlic powder, onion powder, thyme, black pepper, cayenne pepper, oregano, and crushed red pepper flakes.
2. Pat the fish dry with paper towels. Season the filets with sea salt and then coat with the blackening seasoning.
3. In a small bowl, mix together the butter and olive oil and drizzle over the fish filets, flipping them to coat them fully.
4. Preheat the air fryer to 350°F.
5. Place the fish in the air fryer basket and cook for 8 minutes, checking the fish for doneness after 4 minutes. The fish will flake easily when cooked.
6. Remove the fish from the air fryer. Top with chopped parsley and serve with lemon wedges.

Chili-lime Shrimp

Servings:4
Cooking Time: 10 Minutes
Ingredients:
- 1 pound medium shrimp, peeled and deveined
- ½ cup lime juice
- 2 tablespoons olive oil
- 2 tablespoons sriracha
- 1 teaspoon salt
- ¼ teaspoon ground black pepper

Directions:
1. Preheat the air fryer to 375°F.
2. In an 6" round cake pan, combine all ingredients.
3. Place pan in the air fryer and cook 10 minutes, stirring halfway through cooking time, until the inside of shrimp are pearly white and opaque and internal temperature reaches at least 145°F. Serve warm.

Chapter 9: Vegetable Side Dishes Recipes

Salmon Salad With Steamboat Dressing

Servings: 4
Cooking Time: 18 Minutes
Ingredients:
- ¼ teaspoon salt
- 1½ teaspoons dried dill weed
- 1 tablespoon fresh lemon juice
- 8 ounces fresh or frozen salmon fillet (skin on)
- 8 cups shredded romaine, Boston, or other leaf lettuce
- 8 spears cooked asparagus, cut in 1-inch pieces
- 8 cherry tomatoes, halved or quartered

Directions:
1. Mix the salt and dill weed together. Rub the lemon juice over the salmon on both sides and sprinkle the dill and salt all over. Refrigerate for 15 to 20minutes.
2. Make Steamboat Dressing and refrigerate while cooking salmon and preparing salad.
3. Cook salmon in air fryer basket at 330°F for 18 minutes. Cooking time will vary depending on thickness of fillets. When done, salmon should flake with fork but still be moist and tender.
4. Remove salmon from air fryer and cool slightly. At this point, the skin should slide off easily. Cut salmon into 4 pieces and discard skin.
5. Divide the lettuce among 4 plates. Scatter asparagus spears and tomato pieces evenly over the lettuce, allowing roughly 2 whole spears and 2 whole cherry tomatoes per plate.
6. Top each salad with one portion of the salmon and drizzle with a tablespoon of dressing. Serve with additional dressing to pass at the table.

Shallots Almonds Green Beans

Servings: 6
Cooking Time: 15 Minutes
Ingredients:
- 1/4 cup almonds, toasted
- 1 1/2 lbs green beans, trimmed and steamed
- 2 tbsp olive oil
- 1/2 lb shallots, chopped
- Pepper
- Salt

Directions:
1. Add all ingredients into the large bowl and toss well.
2. Transfer green bean mixture into the air fryer basket and cook at 400ºF for 15 minutes.
3. Serve and enjoy.

Cheese Broccoli With Basil

Servings: 4
Cooking Time: 7 Minutes
Ingredients:
- 1 cup broccoli, chopped, boiled
- 1 teaspoon nut oil
- 1 teaspoon salt
- 1 teaspoon dried basil
- ½ cup Cheddar cheese, shredded
- ½ cup of coconut milk
- ½ teaspoon butter, softened

Directions:
1. In the air fryer basket, place the broccoli, nut oil, dried dill, and salt.
2. Stir together the mixture and then pour in the coconut milk.
3. Drizzle butter and Cheddar cheese on the top of the meal.
4. Before cooking, heat your air fryer to 400 degrees F/ 205 degrees C.
5. Cook the mixture inside the preheated air fryer for 7 minutes.

Yellow Squash And Zucchinis Dish

Servings: 4
Cooking Time:45 Minutes
Ingredients:
- 1 yellow squash; halved, deseeded and cut into chunks
- 6 tsp. olive oil
- 1 lb. zucchinis; sliced
- 1/2 lb. carrots; cubed
- 1 tbsp. tarragon; chopped
- Salt and white pepper to the taste

Directions:
1. In your air fryer's basket; mix zucchinis with carrots, squash, salt, pepper and oil; toss well and cook at 400 °F, for 25 minutes. Divide them on plates and serve as a side dish with tarragon sprinkled on top.

Roasted Broccoli And Red Bean Salad

Servings: 3
Cooking Time: 14 Minutes
Ingredients:
- 3 cups (about 1 pound) 1- to 1½-inch fresh broccoli florets (not frozen)
- 1½ tablespoons Olive oil spray
- 1¼ cups Canned red kidney beans, drained and rinsed
- 3 tablespoons Minced yellow or white onion
- 2 tablespoons plus 1 teaspoon Red wine vinegar
- ¾ teaspoon Dried oregano
- ¼ teaspoon Table salt
- ¼ teaspoon Ground black pepper

Directions:
1. Preheat the air fryer to 375°F .
2. Put the broccoli florets in a big bowl, coat them generously with olive oil spray, then toss to coat all surfaces, even down into the crannies, spraying them a couple of times more.
3. Pour the florets into the basket, spreading them into as close to one layer as you can. Air-fry for 12 minutes, tossing and rearranging the florets twice so that any touching or covered parts are eventually exposed to the

air currents, until light browned but still a bit firm. (If the machine is at 360°F, you may need to add 2 minutes to the cooking time.)
4. Dump the contents of the basket onto a large cutting board. Cool for a minute or two, then chop the florets into small bits. Scrape these into a bowl and add the kidney beans, onion, vinegar, oregano, salt, and pepper. Toss well and serve warm or at room temperature.

Rutabaga Fries

Servings: 4
Cooking Time: 20 Minutes
Ingredients:
- 15 ounces rutabaga, cut into fries
- 4 tablespoons olive oil
- ½ teaspoon chili powder
- A pinch of salt and black pepper

Directions:
1. Mix the rutabaga, olive oil, chili powder, salt, and black pepper in a bowl.
2. Transfer into your air fryer basket.
3. Cook the seasoned rutabaga in your air fryer at 400 degrees F/ 205 degrees C for 20 minutes.
4. Serve on plates as a side dish.

Roasted Ratatouille Vegetables

Cooking Time: 15 Minutes
Servings: 2
Ingredients:
- 1 baby or Japanese eggplant, cut into 1½-inch cubes
- 1 red pepper, cut into 1-inch chunks
- 1 yellow pepper, cut into 1-inch chunks
- 1 zucchini, cut into 1-inch chunks
- 1 clove garlic, minced
- ½ teaspoon dried basil
- 1 tablespoon olive oil
- salt and freshly ground black pepper
- ¼ cup sliced sun-dried tomatoes in oil
- 2 tablespoons chopped fresh basil

Directions:
1. Preheat the air fryer to 400°F.
2. Toss the eggplant, peppers and zucchini with the garlic, dried basil, olive oil, salt and freshly ground black pepper.
3. Air-fry the vegetables at 400°F for 15 minutes, shaking the basket a few times during the cooking process to redistribute the ingredients.
4. As soon as the vegetables are tender, toss them with the sliced sun-dried tomatoes and fresh basil and serve.

Crispy Herbed Potatoes

Servings: 6
Cooking Time: 20 Minutes
Ingredients:
- 3 medium baking potatoes, washed and cubed
- ½ teaspoon dried thyme
- 1 teaspoon minced dried rosemary
- ½ teaspoon garlic powder
- 1 teaspoon sea salt
- ½ teaspoon black pepper
- 2 tablespoons extra-virgin olive oil
- ¼ cup chopped parsley

Directions:
1. Preheat the air fryer to 390°F.
2. Pat the potatoes dry. In a large bowl, mix together the cubed potatoes, thyme, rosemary, garlic powder, sea salt, and pepper. Drizzle and toss with olive oil.
3. Pour the herbed potatoes into the air fryer basket. Cook for 20 minutes, stirring every 5 minutes.
4. Toss the cooked potatoes with chopped parsley and serve immediately.
5. VARY IT! Potatoes are versatile — add any spice or seasoning mixture you prefer and create your own favorite side dish.

Mozzarella Cabbage Wedges

Servings: 4
Cooking Time: 25 Minutes
Ingredients:
- 2 cups Parmesan cheese, chopped
- 4 tablespoons melted butter
- Salt and pepper to taste
- ½ cup blue cheese sauce

Directions:
1. Before cooking, heat your air fryer to 380 degrees F/ 195 degrees C.
2. Coat the cabbage wedges with melted butter, then with the Mozzarella.
3. Place the coated cabbage in the air fryer basket.
4. Cook in your air fryer at 380 degrees F/ 195 degrees C for 20 minutes.
5. Serve the wedges with blue cheese sauce.

Roasted Broccoli

Servings: 4
Cooking Time: 8 Minutes
Ingredients:
- 12 ounces broccoli florets
- 2 tablespoons olive oil
- ½ teaspoon salt
- ¼ teaspoon ground black pepper

Directions:
1. Preheat the air fryer to 360°F.
2. In a medium bowl, place broccoli and drizzle with oil. Sprinkle with salt and pepper.
3. Place in the air fryer basket and cook 8 minutes, shaking the basket twice during cooking, until the edges are brown and the center is tender. Serve warm.

Roasted Salsa

Servings: 2
Cooking Time: 30 Minutes
Ingredients:
- 2 large San Marzano tomatoes, cored and cut into large chunks
- ½ medium white onion, peeled and large-diced
- ½ medium jalapeño, seeded and large-diced

- 2 cloves garlic, peeled and diced
- ½ teaspoon salt
- 1 tablespoon coconut oil
- ¼ cup fresh lime juice

Directions:
1. Place tomatoes, onion, and jalapeño into an ungreased 6" round nonstick baking dish. Add garlic, then sprinkle with salt and drizzle with coconut oil.
2. Place dish into air fryer basket. Adjust the temperature to 300°F and set the timer for 30 minutes. Vegetables will be dark brown around the edges and tender when done.
3. Pour mixture into a food processor or blender. Add lime juice. Process on low speed 30 seconds until only a few chunks remain.
4. Transfer salsa to a sealable container and refrigerate at least 1 hour. Serve chilled.

Grilled Lime Scallions

Servings: 6
Cooking Time: 15 Minutes
Ingredients:
- 2 bunches of scallions
- 1 tbsp olive oil
- 2 tsp lime juice
- Salt and pepper to taste
- ¼ tsp Italian seasoning
- 2 tsp lime zest

Directions:
1. Preheat air fryer to 370°F. Trim the scallions and cut them in half lengthwise. Place them in a bowl and add olive oil and lime juice. Toss to coat. Place the mix in the frying basket and Air Fry for 7 minutes, tossing once. Transfer to a serving dish and stir in salt, pepper, Italian seasoning and lime zest. Serve immediately.

Golden Garlicky Mushrooms

Servings: 4
Cooking Time: 10 Minutes
Ingredients:
- 6 small mushrooms
- 1 tablespoon bread crumbs
- 1 tablespoon olive oil
- 1 ounce (28 g) onion, peeled and diced
- 1 teaspoon parsley
- 1 teaspoon garlic purée
- Salt and ground black pepper, to taste

Directions:
1. Preheat the air fryer to 350°F (177°C).
2. Combine the bread crumbs, oil, onion, parsley, salt, pepper and garlic in a bowl. Cut out the mushrooms' stalks and stuff each cap with the crumb mixture.
3. Air fry in the air fryer for 10 minutes.
4. Serve hot.

Sweet And Spicy Tofu

Servings: 3
Cooking Time: 23 Minutes
Ingredients:
- For Tofu:
- 1 (14-ounce) block firm tofu, pressed and cubed
- ½ cup arrowroot flour
- ½ teaspoon sesame oil
- For Sauce:
- 4 tablespoons low-sodium soy sauce
- 1½ tablespoons rice vinegar
- 1½ tablespoons chili sauce
- 1 tablespoon agave nectar
- 2 large garlic cloves, minced
- 1 teaspoon fresh ginger, peeled and grated
- 2 scallions (green part), chopped

Directions:
1. Mix arrowroot flour, sesame oil, and tofu together in a bowl.
2. Before cooking, heat your air fryer to 360 degrees F/ 180 degrees C.
3. Gently grease an air fryer basket.
4. Place the tofu evenly on the air fryer basket in a layer.
5. Cook in your air fryer for 20 minutes. Halfway through cooking, shake the air fryer basket once.
6. To make the sauce, add soy sauce, rice vinegar, chili sauce, agave nectar, garlic, and ginger in a bowl. Beat the mixture to combine well.
7. When the tofu has cooked, remove from the air fryer and transfer to a skillet.
8. Add the sauce and heat the skillet over medium heat. Cook for about 3 minutes. Stir the meal from time to time.
9. Add the scallions to garnish and serve hot.

Prosciutto Mini Mushroom Pizza

Servings: 3
Cooking Time: 5 Minutes
Ingredients:
- 3 portobello mushroom caps, cleaned and scooped
- 3 tablespoons olive oil
- Pinch of salt
- Pinch of dried Italian seasonings
- 3 tablespoons tomato sauce
- 3 tablespoons shredded Mozzarella cheese
- 12 slices prosciutto

Directions:
1. Preheat the air fryer to 330°F (166°C).
2. Season both sides of the portobello mushrooms with a drizzle of olive oil, then sprinkle salt and the Italian seasonings on the insides.
3. With a knife, spread the tomato sauce evenly over the mushroom, before adding the Mozzarella on top.
4. Put the portobello in the air fryer basket and place in the air fryer.
5. Air fry for 1 minute, before taking the air fryer basket out of the air fryer and putting the prosciutto slices on top.
6. Air fry for another 4 minutes.
7. Serve warm.

Roasted Butternut Squash With Cranberries

Servings: 6
Cooking Time: 35 Minutes
Ingredients:
- 4 cups butternut squash, diced
- ¼ cup dried cranberries
- 3 garlic cloves, minced
- 1 tablespoon soy sauce
- 1 tablespoon balsamic vinegar
- 1 tablespoon olive oil
- 8 ounces mushrooms, quartered
- 1 cup green onions, sliced

Directions:
1. In a suitable mixing bowl, mix together squash, mushrooms, and green onion and set aside.
2. In a suitable bowl, whisk together oil, garlic, vinegar, and soy sauce.
3. Pour oil mixture over squash and toss to coat.
4. Grease its air fryer basket with cooking spray.
5. Add squash mixture into the air fryer basket and cook for 30-35 minutes at 400 degrees F/ 205 degrees C. Shake after every 5 minutes.
6. Toss with cranberries and serve hot.

Fried Eggplant Slices

Servings: 3
Cooking Time: 12 Minutes
Ingredients:
- 1½ sleeves Saltine crackers
- ¾ cup Cornstarch
- 2 Large egg(s), well beaten
- 1 medium (about ¾ pound) Eggplant, stemmed, peeled, and cut into ¼-inch-thick rounds
- Olive oil spray

Directions:
1. Preheat the air fryer to 400°F. Also, position the rack in the center of the oven and heat the oven to 175°F.
2. Grind the saltines, in batches if necessary, in a food processor, pulsing the machine and rearranging the saltine pieces every few pulses. Or pulverize the saltines in a large, heavy zip-closed plastic bag with the bottom of a heavy saucepan. In either case, you want small bits of saltines, not just crumbs.
3. Set up and fill three shallow soup plates or small pie plates on your counter: one for the cornstarch, one for the beaten egg(s), and one for the pulverized saltines.
4. Set an eggplant slice in the cornstarch and turn it to coat on both sides. Use a brush to lightly remove any excess. Dip it into the beaten egg(s) and turn to coat both sides. Let any excess egg slip back into the rest, then set the slice in the saltines. Turn several times, pressing gently to coat both sides evenly but not heavily. Coat both sides of the slice with olive oil spray and set it aside. Continue dipping and coating the remaining slices.
5. Set one, two, or maybe three slices in the basket. There should be at least ½ inch between them for proper air flow. Air-fry undisturbed for 12 minutes, or until crisp and browned.
6. Use a nonstick-safe spatula to transfer the slice(s) to a large baking sheet. Slip it into the oven to keep the slices warm as you air-fry more batches, as needed, always transferring the slices to the baking sheet to stay warm.

Stuffed Peppers With Cottage

Servings: 2
Cooking Time: 20 Minutes
Ingredients:
- 1 red bell pepper, top and seeds removed
- 1 yellow bell pepper, top and seeds removed
- Salt and pepper, to taste
- 1 cup Cottage cheese
- 4 tablespoons mayonnaise
- 2 pickles, chopped

Directions:
1. Lightly grease an air fryer basket.
2. Before cooking, heat your air fryer to 400 degrees F/ 205 degrees C.
3. Arrange evenly the peppers inside the air fryer basket.
4. Then cook in your air fryer for 15 minutes.
5. To season, add salt and pepper.
6. Combine the mayonnaise, chopped pickles, and the cream cheese in a mixing bowl.
7. Fill the pepper with the cheese mixture.
8. Serve immediately.

Dijon Roasted Purple Potatoes

Servings: 4
Cooking Time: 25 Minutes
Ingredients:
- 1 lb purple potatoes, scrubbed and halved
- 1 tbsp olive oil
- 1 tsp Dijon mustard
- 1 tsp lemon juice
- 2 cloves garlic, minced
- Salt and pepper to taste
- 2 tbsp butter, melted
- 1 tbsp chopped cilantro
- 1 tsp fresh rosemary

Directions:
1. Mix the olive oil, mustard, garlic, lemon juice, pepper, salt and rosemary in a bowl. Let chill covered in the fridge until ready to use.
2. Preheat air fryer at 350ºF. Toss the potatoes, salt, pepper, and butter in a bowl, place the potatoes in the frying basket, and Roast for 18-20 minutes, tossing once. Transfer them into a bowl. Drizzle potatoes with the dressing and toss to coat. Garnish with cilantro to serve.

Glazed Carrots

Servings: 4
Cooking Time: 10 Minutes
Ingredients:
- 2 teaspoons honey
- 1 teaspoon orange juice
- ½ teaspoon grated orange rind
- ⅛ teaspoon ginger
- 1 pound baby carrots
- 2 teaspoons olive oil
- ¼ teaspoon salt

Directions:
1. Combine honey, orange juice, grated rind, and ginger in a small bowl and set aside.
2. Toss the carrots, oil, and salt together to coat well and pour them into the air fryer basket.
3. Cook at 390°F for 5minutes. Shake basket to stir a little and cook for 4 minutes more, until carrots are barely tender.
4. Pour carrots into air fryer baking pan.
5. Stir the honey mixture to combine well, pour glaze over carrots, and stir to coat.
6. Cook at 360°F for 1 minute or just until heated through.

Beef Stuffed Bell Peppers

Servings:4
Cooking Time: 30 Minutes
Ingredients:
- 1 pound (454 g) ground beef
- 1 tablespoon taco seasoning mix
- 1 can diced tomatoes and green chilis
- 4 green bell peppers
- 1 cup shredded Monterey jack cheese, divided

Directions:
1. Preheat the air fryer to 350ºF (177ºC).
2. Set a skillet over a high heat and cook the ground beef for 8 minutes. Make sure it is cooked through and browned all over. Drain the fat.
3. Stir in the taco seasoning mix, and the diced tomatoes and green chilis. Allow the mixture to cook for a further 4 minutes.
4. In the meantime, slice the tops off the green peppers and remove the seeds and membranes.
5. When the meat mixture is fully cooked, spoon equal amounts of it into the peppers and top with the Monterey jack cheese. Then place the peppers into the air fryer. Air fry for 15 minutes.
6. The peppers are ready when they are soft, and the cheese is bubbling and brown. Serve warm.

Garlic Parmesan-roasted Cauliflower

Servings:6
Cooking Time: 15 Minutes
Ingredients:
- 1 medium head cauliflower, leaves and core removed, cut into florets
- 2 tablespoons salted butter, melted
- ½ tablespoon salt
- 2 cloves garlic, peeled and finely minced
- ½ cup grated Parmesan cheese, divided

Directions:
1. Toss cauliflower in a large bowl with butter. Sprinkle with salt, garlic, and ¼ cup Parmesan.
2. Place florets into ungreased air fryer basket. Adjust the temperature to 350°F and set the timer for 15 minutes, shaking basket halfway through cooking. Cauliflower will be browned at the edges and tender when done.
3. Transfer florets to a large serving dish and sprinkle with remaining Parmesan. Serve warm.

Potato Wedges

Servings: 4
Cooking Time: 20 Minutes
Ingredients:
- 6 cups water
- 4 large russet potatoes, sliced into wedges
- 2 teaspoons seasoned salt
- ½ cup whole milk
- ½ cup all-purpose flour

Directions:
1. In a large saucepan over medium-high heat, bring water to a boil.
2. Carefully place potato wedges into boiling water and cook 5 minutes.
3. Preheat the air fryer to 400°F.
4. Drain potatoes into a colander, then rinse under cold running water 1 minute until they feel cool to the touch.
5. Place potatoes in a large bowl and sprinkle with seasoned salt. Pour milk into bowl, then toss wedges to coat.
6. Place flour on a large plate. Gently dredge each potato wedge in flour on both sides to lightly coat.
7. Place wedges in the air fryer basket and spritz both sides with cooking spray. Cook 15 minutes, turning after 10 minutes, until wedges are golden brown. Serve warm.

Roasted Potatoes And Asparagus

Servings:4
Cooking Time: 23 Minutes
Ingredients:
- 4 medium potatoes
- 1 bunch asparagus
- ⅓ cup cottage cheese
- ⅓ cup low-fat crème fraiche
- 1 tablespoon wholegrain mustard
- Salt and pepper, to taste
- Cook spray

Directions:
1. Preheat the air fryer to 390ºF (199ºC). Spritz the air fryer basket with cooking spray.
2. Place the potatoes in the basket. Air fry the potatoes for 20 minutes.
3. Boil the asparagus in salted water for 3 minutes.
4. Remove the potatoes and mash them with rest of ingredients. Sprinkle with salt and pepper.
5. Serve immediately.

Crunchy Roasted Potatoes

Servings: 5
Cooking Time: 25 Minutes
Ingredients:
- 2 pounds Small red, white, or purple potatoes
- 2 tablespoons Olive oil
- 2 teaspoons Table salt
- ¾ teaspoon Garlic powder
- ½ teaspoon Ground black pepper

Directions:
1. Preheat the air fryer to 400°F.
2. Toss the potatoes, oil, salt, garlic powder, and pepper in a large bowl until the spuds are evenly and thoroughly coated.
3. When the machine is at temperature, pour the potatoes into the basket, spreading them into an even layer. Air-fry for 25 minutes, tossing twice, until the potatoes are tender but crunchy.
4. Pour the contents of the basket into a serving bowl. Cool for 5 minutes before serving.

Baked Shishito Peppers

Servings: 2
Cooking Time: 15 Minutes
Ingredients:
- 6 oz shishito peppers
- 1 tsp olive oil
- 1 tsp salt
- ¼ cup soy sauce

Directions:
1. Preheat air fryer at 375ºF. Combine all ingredients in a bowl. Place peppers in the frying basket and Bake for 8 minutes until the peppers are blistered, shaking once. Serve with soy sauce for dipping.

Pork Tenderloin Salad

Servings: 4
Cooking Time: 25 Minutes
Ingredients:
- Pork Tenderloin
- ½ teaspoon smoked paprika
- ¼ teaspoon salt
- ¼ teaspoon garlic powder
- ½ teaspoon onion powder
- ⅛ teaspoon ginger
- 1 teaspoon extra-light olive oil
- ¾ pound pork tenderloin
- Dressing
- 3 tablespoons extra-light olive oil
- 2 tablespoons red wine vinegar
- 2 tablespoons Dijon mustard
- 1 tablespoon honey
- Salad
- ¼ sweet red bell pepper
- 1 large Granny Smith apple
- 8 cups shredded Napa cabbage

Directions:
1. Mix the tenderloin seasonings together with oil and rub all over surface of meat.
2. Place pork tenderloin in the air fryer basket and cook at 390°F for 25minutes, until meat registers 130°F on a meat thermometer.
3. Allow meat to rest while preparing salad and dressing.
4. In a jar, shake all dressing ingredients together until well mixed.
5. Cut the bell pepper into slivers, then core, quarter, and slice the apple crosswise.
6. In a large bowl, toss together the cabbage, bell pepper, apple, and dressing.
7. Divide salad mixture among 4 plates.
8. Slice pork tenderloin into ½-inch slices and divide among the 4 salads.
9. Serve with sweet potato or other vegetable chips.

Stuffed Bell Peppers With Mayonnaise

Servings: 2
Cooking Time: 15 Minutes
Ingredients:
- 2 red bell peppers, tops and seeds removed
- 2 yellow bell peppers, tops and seeds removed
- Black pepper and salt, to taste
- 1 cup cream cheese
- 4 tablespoons mayonnaise
- 2 pickles, chopped

Directions:
1. Arrange the black peppers in the lightly greased cooking basket. Cook in the preheated air fryer at about 400 degrees F/ 205 degrees C for almost 15 minutes, flipping them once halfway through the cooking time.
2. Season with black pepper and salt.
3. Then, in a suitable mixing bowl, combine the cream cheese with the mayonnaise and chopped pickles.
4. Stuff the black pepper with the cream cheese mixture and serve.
5. Enjoy!

Roasted Fennel Salad

Servings: 3
Cooking Time: 20 Minutes
Ingredients:
- 3 cups (about ¾ pound) Trimmed fennel, roughly chopped
- 1½ tablespoons Olive oil
- ¼ teaspoon Table salt
- ¼ teaspoon Ground black pepper
- 1½ tablespoons White balsamic vinegar

Directions:
1. Preheat the air fryer to 400°F.
2. Toss the fennel, olive oil, salt, and pepper in a large bowl until the fennel is well coated in the oil.
3. When the machine is at temperature, pour the fennel into the basket, spreading it out into as close to one layer as possible. Air-fry for 20 minutes, tossing and

rearranging the fennel pieces twice so that any covered or touching parts get exposed to the air currents, until golden at the edges and softened.
4. Pour the fennel into a serving bowl. Add the vinegar while hot. Toss well, then cool a couple of minutes before serving. Or serve at room temperature.

Ricotta & Broccoli Cannelloni
Servings: 4
Cooking Time: 35 Minutes
Ingredients:
- 1 cup shredded mozzarella cheese
- ½ cup cooked broccoli, chopped
- ½ cup cooked spinach, chopped
- 4 cooked cannelloni shells
- 1 cup ricotta cheese
- ½ tsp dried marjoram
- 1 egg
- 1 cup passata
- 1 tbsp basil leaves

Directions:
1. Preheat air fryer to 360°F. Beat the egg in a bowl until fluffy. Add the ricotta, marjoram, half of the mozzarella, broccoli, and spinach and stir to combine. Cover the base of a baking dish with a layer of passata. Fill the cannelloni with the cheese mixture and place them on top of the sauce. Spoon the remaining passata over the tops and top with the rest of the mozzarella cheese. Put the dish in the frying basket and Bake for 25 minutes until the cheese is melted and golden. Top with basil.

Mint Lemon Squash
Servings: 4
Cooking Time: 25 Minutes
Ingredients:
- 4 summer squash, cut into wedges
- ¼ cup olive oil
- ¼ cup lemon juice
- ½ cup mint, chopped
- 1 cup mozzarella, shredded
- Black pepper and salt to the taste

Directions:
1. In a suitable pan that fits your air fryer, mix the squash with the rest of the ingredients, toss, introduce the pan in the preheated air fryer and cook at almost 370 degrees F/ 185 degrees C for 25 minutes.
2. Serve.

Sweet Butternut Squash
Servings: 8
Cooking Time: 15 Minutes
Ingredients:
- 1 medium butternut squash, peeled and cubed
- 2 tablespoons salted butter, melted
- ½ teaspoon salt
- 1 ½ tablespoons brown sugar
- ½ teaspoon ground cinnamon

Directions:
1. Preheat the air fryer to 400°F.
2. In a large bowl, place squash and add butter. Toss to coat. Sprinkle salt, brown sugar, and cinnamon over squash and toss to fully coat.
3. Place squash in the air fryer basket and cook 15 minutes, shaking the basket three times during cooking, until the edges are golden and the center is fork-tender. Serve warm.

Healthy Caprese Salad
Servings: 2
Cooking Time: 20 Minutes
Ingredients:
- 1 ball mozzarella cheese, sliced
- 16 grape tomatoes
- 2 tsp olive oil
- Salt and pepper to taste
- 1 tbsp balsamic vinegar
- 1 tsp mix of seeds
- 1 tbsp chopped basil

Directions:
1. Preheat air fryer at 350°F. Toss tomatoes with 1 tsp of olive oil and salt in a bowl. Place them in the frying basket and Air Fry for 15 minutes, shaking twice. Divide mozzarella slices between 2 serving plates, top with blistered tomatoes, and drizzle with balsamic vinegar and the remaining olive oil. Sprinkle with basil, black pepper and the mixed seeds and serve.

Lush Vegetables Roast
Servings: 6
Cooking Time: 20 Minutes
Ingredients:
- 1⅓ cups small parsnips, peeled and cubed
- 1⅓ cups celery
- 2 red onions, sliced
- 1⅓ cups small butternut squash, cut in half, deseeded and cubed
- 1 tablespoon fresh thyme needles
- 1 tablespoon olive oil
- Salt and ground black pepper, to taste

Directions:
1. Preheat the air fryer to 390°F (199°C).
2. Combine the cut vegetables with the thyme, olive oil, salt and pepper.
3. Put the vegetables in the basket and transfer the basket to the air fryer.
4. Roast for 20 minutes, stirring once throughout the roasting time, until the vegetables are nicely browned and cooked through.
5. Serve warm.

Stuffed Peppers

Servings: 1
Cooking Time: 16 Minutes
Ingredients:
- 1 bell pepper
- ½ tablespoon diced onion
- ½ diced tomato, plus one tomato slice
- ¼ teaspoon smoked paprika
- Salt and pepper, to taste
- 1 teaspoon olive oil
- ¼ teaspoon dried basil

Directions:
1. Before cooking, heat your air fryer to 350 degrees F/ 175 degrees C.
2. The bell pepper should be cored and cleaned for stuffing.
3. Using half of the olive oil to brush the pepper on the outside.
4. Combine together the diced onion, the diced tomato, smoked paprika, salt, and pepper in a small bowl.
5. Then stuff the cored pepper with the mixture and add the tomato slice on the top.
6. Using the remaining olive oil, brush the tomato slice.
7. Sprinkle the stuffed pepper with basil.
8. Cook the stuffed peppers in your air fryer for 10 minutes or until thoroughly cooked.

Fried Brussel Sprouts

Servings: 4
Cooking Time: 20 Minutes
Ingredients:
- 1 pound Brussels sprouts, trimmed and halved
- Salt and black pepper to the taste
- 2 tablespoons ghee, melted
- ½ cup coconut cream
- 2 tablespoons garlic, minced
- 1 tablespoon chives, chopped

Directions:
1. Grease the air fryer basket with the melted ghee.
2. Mix the Brussels sprouts with the remaining ingredients in the air fryer basket.
3. Cook in your air fryer at 370 degrees F/ 185 degrees C for 20 minutes.
4. Serve on plates as a side dish.

Kidney Beans Oatmeal In Peppers

Servings: 4
Cooking Time: 6 Minutes
Ingredients:
- 2 large bell peppers, halved lengthwise, deseeded
- 2 tablespoons cooked kidney beans
- 2 tablespoons cooked chick peas
- 2 cups cooked oatmeal
- 1 teaspoon ground cumin
- ½ teaspoon paprika
- ½ teaspoon salt or to taste
- ¼ teaspoon black pepper powder
- ¼ cup yogurt

Directions:
1. Preheat the air fryer to 355°F (179°C).
2. Put the bell peppers, cut-side down, in the air fryer basket. Air fry for 2 minutes.
3. Take the peppers out of the air fryer and let cool.
4. In a bowl, combine the rest of the ingredients.
5. Divide the mixture evenly and use each portion to stuff a pepper.
6. Return the stuffed peppers to the air fryer and continue to air fry for 4 minutes.
7. Serve hot.

Moroccan Cauliflower

Servings: 6
Cooking Time: 15 Minutes
Ingredients:
- 1 tablespoon curry powder
- 2 teaspoons smoky paprika
- ½ teaspoon ground cumin
- ½ teaspoon salt
- 1 head cauliflower, cut into bite-size pieces
- ¼ cup red wine vinegar
- 2 tablespoons extra-virgin olive oil
- 2 tablespoons chopped parsley

Directions:
1. Preheat the air fryer to 370°F.
2. In a large bowl, mix the curry powder, paprika, cumin, and salt. Add the cauliflower and stir to coat. Pour the red wine vinegar over the top and continue stirring.
3. Place the cauliflower into the air fryer basket; drizzle olive oil over the top.
4. Cook the cauliflower for 5 minutes, toss, and cook another 5 minutes. Raise the temperature to 400°F and continue cooking for 4 to 6 minutes, or until crispy.

Asparagus Wrapped In Pancetta

Servings: 4
Cooking Time: 30 Minutes
Ingredients:
- 20 asparagus trimmed
- Salt and pepper pepper
- 4 pancetta slices
- 1 tbsp fresh sage, chopped

Directions:
1. Sprinkle the asparagus with fresh sage, salt and pepper. Toss to coat. Make 4 bundles of 5 spears by wrapping the center of the bunch with one slice of pancetta.
2. Preheat air fryer to 400°F. Put the bundles in the greased frying basket and Air Fry for 8-10 minutes or until the pancetta is brown and the asparagus are starting to char on the edges. Serve immediately.

Swiss Vegetable Casserole

Servings: 6
Cooking Time: 33 Minutes
Ingredients:
- 1 tablespoon olive oil

Air Fryer Cookbook for Beginners

- 1 shallot, sliced
- 2 garlic cloves, minced
- 1 red bell pepper, seeded and sliced
- 1 yellow bell pepper, seeded and sliced
- 1 ½ cups kale
- 1 28-ounce bag frozen tater tots
- 6 eggs
- 1 cup milk
- Salt and black pepper, to your liking
- 1 cup Swiss cheese, shredded
- 4 tablespoons seasoned breadcrumbs

Directions:
1. Sauté the shallot, garlic, and black peppers with oil in a skillet for 2 to 3 minutes.
2. Add the kale and cook until wilted.
3. Arrange the tater tots evenly over the bottom of a lightly greased casserole dish.
4. Spread the sautéed mixture over the top.
5. In a suitable mixing bowl, thoroughly combine the eggs, milk, salt, black pepper, and shredded cheese. Pour the mixture into the casserole dish.
6. Lastly, top with the seasoned breadcrumbs.
7. Air fry at 330 degrees F/ 165 degrees C for 30 minutes or until top is golden brown.
8. Serve!

Turmeric Cauliflower Rice

Servings: 4
Cooking Time: 20 Minutes
Ingredients:
- 1 big cauliflower, florets separated and riced
- 1 and ½ cups chicken stock
- 1 tablespoon olive oil
- Salt and black pepper to the taste
- ½ teaspoon turmeric powder

Directions:
1. In a pan that fits the air fryer, combine the cauliflower with the oil and the rest of the ingredients, toss, introduce in the air fryer and cook at 360ºF for 20 minutes. Divide between plates and serve as a side dish.

Green Beans And New Potatoes

Servings:6
Cooking Time: 22 Minutes
Ingredients:
- Olive oil
- 2 pounds new potatoes, each cut in half
- 2 teaspoons seasoned salt, divided
- 16 ounces fresh green beans, trimmed

Directions:
1. Spray a fryer basket lightly with olive oil.
2. Add the new potatoes to the fryer basket and sprinkle with 1 teaspoon of seasoned salt. Lightly spray the potatoes with olive oil. You may need to cook them in batches.
3. Air fry for 10 minutes. Shake the basket and add the green beans and sprinkle with the remaining 1 teaspoon of seasoned salt. Lightly spray the potatoes and green beans with olive oil.
4. Air fry until the potatoes are fork tender and lightly browned, 8 to 12 more minutes. If you want the potatoes to be extra crispy, add a few minutes to the cook time and spray with a little extra olive oil.

Roasted Bell Peppers

Servings: 3
Cooking Time: 8 Minutes
Ingredients:
- 3 ½ cups bell peppers, cut into chunks
- Black pepper
- Salt

Directions:
1. Grease its air fryer basket with cooking spray.
2. Add bell peppers into the air fryer basket and cook at almost 360 degrees F/ 180 degrees C for 8 minutes.
3. Season bell peppers with black pepper and salt.
4. Serve and enjoy.

Garlic-parmesan Popcorn

Servings: 2
Cooking Time: 15 Minutes
Ingredients:
- 2 tsp grated Parmesan cheese
- ¼ cup popcorn kernels
- 1 tbsp lemon juice
- 1 tsp garlic powder

Directions:
1. Preheat air fryer to 400°F. Line the basket with aluminum foil. Put the popcorn kernels in a single layer and Grill for 6-8 minutes until they stop popping. Remove them into a bowl. Drizzle with lemon juice and toss until well coated. Sprinkle with garlic powder and grated Parmesan and toss to coat. Drizzle with more lemon juice. Serve.

Smashed Fried Baby Potatoes

Servings: 3
Cooking Time: 18 Minutes
Ingredients:
- 1½ pounds baby red or baby Yukon gold potatoes
- ¼ cup butter, melted
- 1 teaspoon olive oil
- ½ teaspoon paprika
- 1 teaspoon dried parsley
- salt and freshly ground black pepper
- 2 scallions, finely chopped

Directions:
1. Bring a large pot of salted water to a boil. Add the potatoes and boil for 18 minutes or until the potatoes are fork-tender.
2. Drain the potatoes and transfer them to a cutting board to cool slightly. Spray or brush the bottom of a drinking glass with a little oil. Smash or flatten the potatoes by pressing the glass down on each potato slowly. Try not to completely flatten the potato or smash it so hard that it breaks apart.

3. Combine the melted butter, olive oil, paprika, and parsley together.
4. Preheat the air fryer to 400°F.
5. Spray the bottom of the air fryer basket with oil and transfer one layer of the smashed potatoes into the basket. Brush with some of the butter mixture and season generously with salt and freshly ground black pepper.
6. Air-fry at 400°F for 10 minutes. Carefully flip the potatoes over and air-fry for an additional 8 minutes until crispy and lightly browned.
7. Keep the potatoes warm in a 170°F oven or tent with aluminum foil while you cook the second batch. Sprinkle minced scallions over the potatoes and serve warm.

Easy Homemade Veggie Burger
Servings: 5
Cooking Time: 26 Minutes
Ingredients:
- Olive oil
- 1 medium carrot, chopped very small
- Salt
- Freshly ground black pepper
- 8 ounces fresh mushrooms, stems removed, chopped very small
- 1 (15-ounce) can black beans, drained and rinsed
- 1 egg, beaten
- 2 tablespoons tomato paste
- 2 teaspoons minced garlic
- ½ teaspoon onion powder
- ¼ teaspoon salt
- ½ cup whole-wheat bread crumbs
- 5 whole-wheat hamburger buns

Directions:
1. Spray a fryer basket lightly with olive oil.
2. Place the carrots in the fryer basket. Lightly spray with oil and season with salt and pepper.
3. Air fry for 8 minutes.
4. Add the mushrooms to the fryer basket with the carrots. Lightly spray with oil and season with a little more salt and pepper, if desired.
5. Air fry for 5 more minutes.
6. While the vegetables are roasting, spread the rinsed black beans out on a paper towel and dry them off. It is important to remove as much excess moisture as possible.
7. Place the black beans in a large bowl and mash them with a fork. If you like your veggie burger a little chunkier, leave some of the beans only partially mashed.
8. Add the egg, tomato paste, garlic, onion powder, salt, cooked carrots, and mushrooms to the bowl and mix together very well. Mash up the veggies with a fork if you prefer. Add the bread crumbs and stir to combine.
9. Form the mixture into 5 patties.
10. Add the patties to the fryer basket, leaving a little room between each patty. You may need to cook them in batches.
11. Air fry for 5 minutes. Flip the patties over and lightly spray with olive oil. Air fry for another 5 to 7 minutes.
12. Serve on whole-wheat buns.

Sweet Corn Fritters With Avocado
Servings: 3
Cooking Time: 8 Minutes
Ingredients:
- 2 cups sweet corn kernels
- 1 small-sized onion, chopped
- 1 garlic clove, minced
- 2 eggs, whisked
- 1 teaspoon baking powder
- 2 tablespoons fresh cilantro, chopped
- Salt and black pepper, to taste
- 1 avocado, peeled, pitted and diced
- 2 tablespoons sweet chili sauce

Directions:
1. In a suitable mixing bowl, thoroughly combine the corn, onion, garlic, eggs, baking powder, cilantro, salt, and black pepper.
2. Shape the corn mixture into 6 patties and transfer them to the lightly greased air fryer basket.
3. Cook in the preheated air fry at 370 degrees F/ 185 degrees C or 8 minutes; turn them over and cook for 7 minutes longer.
4. Serve the fritters with the avocado and chili sauce.

Garlicky Vegetable Rainbow Fritters
Servings: 2
Cooking Time: 12 Minutes
Ingredients:
- 1 zucchini, grated and squeezed
- 1 cup corn kernels
- ½ cup canned green peas
- 4 tablespoons all-purpose flour
- 2 tablespoons fresh shallots, minced
- 1 teaspoon fresh garlic, minced
- 1 tablespoon peanut oil
- Salt and black pepper, to taste
- 1 teaspoon cayenne pepper

Directions:
1. In a suitable mixing bowl, thoroughly combine all the recipe ingredients until everything is well incorporated.
2. Shape the mixture into patties.
3. Grease its air fryer basket with cooking spray.
4. Cook the patties in the preheated air fryer at about 365 degrees F/ 185 degrees C for 6 minutes almost.
5. Flip and cook for a 6 minutes more.
6. Serve immediately and enjoy!

Roasted Asparagus
Servings: 4
Cooking Time: 12 Minutes
Ingredients:
- 1 tablespoon olive oil
- 1 pound asparagus spears, ends trimmed
- ¼ teaspoon salt
- ¼ teaspoon ground black pepper

- 1 tablespoon salted butter, melted

Directions:
1. In a large bowl, drizzle olive oil over asparagus spears and sprinkle with salt and pepper.
2. Place spears into ungreased air fryer basket. Adjust the temperature to 375°F and set the timer for 12 minutes, shaking the basket halfway through cooking. Asparagus will be lightly browned and tender when done.
3. Transfer to a large dish and drizzle with butter. Serve warm.

Cheese Spinach

Servings: 6
Cooking Time: 16 Minutes
Ingredients:
- 1-pound fresh spinach
- 6 ounces gouda cheese, shredded
- 8 ounces cream cheese
- 1 teaspoon garlic powder
- 1 tablespoon onion, minced
- Black pepper
- Salt

Directions:
1. At 370 degrees F/ 185 degrees C, preheat your air fryer.
2. Grease its air fryer basket with cooking spray and set aside.
3. Spray a large pan with cooking spray and heat over medium heat.
4. Add spinach to the same pan and cook until wilted.
5. Add cream cheese, garlic powder, and onion and stir until cheese is melted.
6. Remove pan from heat and add Gouda cheese and season with black pepper and salt.
7. Transfer spinach mixture to the prepared baking dish and place into the air fryer.
8. Cook for 16 minutes.
9. Serve and enjoy.

Chapter 10: Desserts And Sweets Recipes

Cherry Cheesecake Rolls

Servings: 6
Cooking Time: 30 Minutes
Ingredients:
- 1 can crescent rolls
- 4 oz cream cheese
- 1 tbsp cherry preserves
- 1/3 cup sliced fresh cherries
- Cooking spray

Directions:
1. Roll out the dough into a large rectangle on a flat work surface. Cut the dough into 12 rectangles by cutting 3 cuts across and 2 cuts down. In a microwave-safe bowl, soften cream cheese for 15 seconds. Stir together with cherry preserves. Mound 2 tsp of the cherries-cheese mix on each piece of dough. Carefully spread the mixture but not on the edges. Top with 2 tsp of cherries each. Roll each triangle to make a cylinder.
2. Preheat air fryer to 350°F. Place the first batch of the rolls in the greased air fryer. Spray the rolls with cooking oil and Bake for 8 minutes. Let cool in the air fryer for 2-3 minutes before removing. Serve.

Fudgy Chocolate Brownies

Servings: 6
Cooking Time: 16 Minutes
Ingredients:
- 3 eggs
- ½ teaspoon baking powder
- ¾ cup erythritol
- 2 oz. dark chocolate
- ¾ cup butter softened
- ½ cup almond flour
- ¼ cup of cocoa powder

Directions:
1. At 325 degrees F/ 160 degrees C, preheat your air fryer.
2. Grease its air fryer basket with cooking spray and set aside.
3. In a suitable bowl, mix together chocolate and butter and microwave for 30 seconds or until melted. Stir well.
4. Mix together almond flour, baking powder, cocoa powder, and sweetener.
5. In a suitable bowl, beat eggs using a hand mixer. Add chocolate-butter mixture and beat until combined.
6. Slowly stir in dry recipe ingredients and mix until well combined.
7. Pour batter into the prepared dish and place into the air fryer.
8. Cook for 16 minutes.
9. Slice and serve.

Pecan Snowball Cookies

Servings: 12
Cooking Time: 24 Minutes
Ingredients:
- 1 cup chopped pecans
- ½ cup salted butter, melted
- ½ cup coconut flour
- ¾ cup confectioners' erythritol, divided
- 1 teaspoon vanilla extract

Directions:
1. In a food processor, blend together pecans, butter, flour, ½ cup erythritol, and vanilla 1 minute until a dough forms.
2. Form dough into twelve individual cookie balls, about 1 tablespoon each.
3. Cut three pieces of parchment to fit air fryer basket. Place four cookies on each ungreased parchment and place one piece parchment with cookies into air fryer basket. Adjust air fryer temperature to 325°F and set the timer for 8 minutes. Repeat cooking with remaining batches.
4. When the timer goes off, allow cookies to cool 5 minutes on a large serving plate until cool enough to handle. While still warm, dust cookies with remaining erythritol. Allow to cool completely, about 15 minutes, before serving.

Pineapple Chips With Cinnamon

Servings: 4
Cooking Time: 20 Minutes
Ingredients:
- 4 pineapple slices
- 1 teaspoon cinnamon
- 2 tablespoons erythritol

Directions:
1. In a zip-lock bag, add the cinnamon, sweetener, and pineapple slices. Seal the bag and shake. Then cool the bag in the refrigerator for 30 minutes.
2. Before cooking, heat your air fryer to 350 degrees F/ 175 degrees C.
3. In the air fryer basket, arrange the pineapple slices.
4. Cook in the preheated air fryer at 350 degrees F/ 175 degrees C for 20 minutes. Flip the slices halfway through cooking.
5. When cooked, remove from the air fryer and serve.

Fruity Oatmeal Crisp

Servings: 6
Cooking Time: 25 Minutes
Ingredients:
- 2 peeled nectarines, chopped
- 1 peeled apple, chopped
- 1/3 cup raisins
- 2 tbsp honey
- 1/3 cup brown sugar
- ¼ cup flour
- ½ cup oatmeal
- 3 tbsp softened butter

Directions:
1. Preheat air fryer to 380°F. Mix together nectarines, apple, raisins, and honey in a baking pan. Set aside. Mix brown sugar, flour, oatmeal and butter in a medium bowl until crumbly. Top the fruit in a greased pan with the crumble. Bake until bubbly and the topping is golden, 10-12 minutes. Serve warm and top with vanilla ice cream if desired.

Apple-blueberry Hand Pies

Servings: 4
Cooking Time: 7 To 9 Minutes
Ingredients:
- 1 medium Granny Smith apple, peeled and finely chopped
- ½ cup dried blueberries
- 1 tablespoon freshly squeezed orange juice
- 1 tablespoon packed brown sugar
- 2 teaspoons cornstarch
- 4 sheets frozen phyllo dough, thawed
- 8 teaspoons unsalted butter, melted
- 8 teaspoons sugar
- Nonstick cooking spray, for coating the phyllo dough

Directions:
1. In a medium bowl, mix the apple, blueberries, orange juice, brown sugar, and cornstarch.
2. Place 1 sheet of phyllo dough on a work surface with the narrow side facing you. Brush very lightly with 1 teaspoon of butter and sprinkle with 1 teaspoon of sugar. Fold the phyllo sheet in half from left to right.
3. Place one-fourth of the fruit filling at the bottom of the sheet in the center. Fold the left side of the sheet over the filling. Spray lightly with cooking spray. Fold the right side of the sheet over the filling. Brush with 1 teaspoon of butter and sprinkle with 1 teaspoon of sugar.
4. Fold the bottom right corner of the dough up to meet the left side of the pastry sheet to form a triangle. Continue folding the triangles over to enclose the filling, as you would fold a flag. Seal the edge with a bit of water. Spray lightly with cooking spray. Repeat with the remaining 3 sheets of the phyllo, butter, sugar, and cooking spray, making four pies.
5. Place the pies in the air fryer basket. Bake for 7 to 9 minutes, or until golden brown and crisp. Remove the pies and let cool on a wire rack before serving.

Cheese Muffins With Cinnamon

Servings: 10
Cooking Time: 16 Minutes
Ingredients:
- 2 eggs
- ½ cup erythritol
- 8 ounces cream cheese
- 1 teaspoon ground cinnamon
- ½ tsp vanilla

Directions:
1. Before cooking, heat your air fryer to 325 degrees F/ 160 degrees C.
2. Mix together vanilla, erythritol, eggs, and cream cheese until smooth.
3. Divide the batter into the silicone muffin molds. Top the muffins with cinnamon.
4. In the air fryer basket, transfer the muffin molds.
5. Cook in your air fryer for 16 minutes.
6. Serve and enjoy!

Strawberry Donuts

Servings: 4
Cooking Time: 55 Minutes
Ingredients:
- ¾ cup Greek yogurt
- 2 tbsp maple syrup
- 1 tbsp vanilla extract
- 2 tsp active dry yeast
- 1 ½ cups all-purpose flour
- 3 tbsp milk
- ½ cup strawberry jam

Directions:
1. Preheat air fryer to 350°F. Whisk the Greek yogurt, maple syrup, vanilla extract, and yeast until well combined. Then toss in flour until you get a sticky dough. Let rest covered for 10 minutes. Flour a parchment paper on a flat surface, lay the dough, sprinkle with some flour, and flatten to ½-inch thick with a rolling pin.
2. Using a 3-inch cookie cutter, cut the donuts. Repeat the process until no dough is left. Place the donuts in the basket and let rise for 15-20 minutes. Spread some milk on top of each donut and Air Fry for 4 minutes. Turn the donuts, spread more milk, and Air Fry for 4 more minutes until golden brown. Let cool for 15 minutes. Using a knife, cut the donuts 3/4 lengthwise, brush 1 tbsp of strawberry jam on each and close them. Serve.

Black Forest Pies

Servings: 6
Cooking Time: 15 Minutes
Ingredients:
- 3 tablespoons milk or dark chocolate chips
- 2 tablespoons thick, hot fudge sauce
- 2 tablespoons chopped dried cherries
- 1 (10-by-15-inch) sheet frozen puff pastry, thawed
- 1 egg white, beaten
- 2 tablespoons sugar
- ½ teaspoon cinnamon

Directions:
1. Preheat the air fryer to 350ºF (177ºC).
2. In a small bowl, combine the chocolate chips, fudge sauce, and dried cherries.
3. Roll out the puff pastry on a floured surface. Cut into 6 squares with a sharp knife.
4. Divide the chocolate chip mixture into the center of each puff pastry square. Fold the squares in half to make triangles. Firmly press the edges with the tines of a fork to seal.
5. Brush the triangles on all sides sparingly with the beaten egg white. Sprinkle the tops with sugar and cinnamon.
6. Put in the air fryer basket and bake for 15 minutes or until the triangles are golden brown. The filling will be hot, so cool for at least 20 minutes before serving.

Air Fryer Cookbook for Beginners

Lemony Apple Butter

Servings: 1
Cooking Time: 1 Hour
Ingredients:
- Cooking spray
- 2 cups unsweetened applesauce
- ⅔ cup packed light brown sugar
- 3 tablespoons fresh lemon juice
- ½ teaspoon kosher salt
- ¼ teaspoon ground cinnamon
- ⅛ teaspoon ground allspice

Directions:
1. Preheat the air fryer to 340ºF (171ºC).
2. Spray a metal cake pan with cooking spray. Whisk together all the ingredients in a bowl until smooth, then pour into the greased pan. Set the pan in the air fryer and bake until the apple mixture is caramelized, reduced to a thick purée, and fragrant, about 1 hour.
3. Remove the pan from the air fryer, stir to combine the caramelized bits at the edge with the rest, then let cool completely to thicken.
4. Serve immediately.

Pineapple Galette

Servings: 2
Cooking Time: 40 Minutes
Ingredients:
- ¼ medium-size pineapple, peeled, cored, and cut crosswise into ¼-inch-thick slices
- 2 tablespoons dark rum
- 1 teaspoon vanilla extract
- ½ teaspoon kosher salt
- Finely grated zest of ½ lime
- 1 store-bought sheet puff pastry, cut into an 8-inch round
- 3 tablespoons granulated sugar
- 2 tablespoons unsalted butter, cubed and chilled
- Coconut ice cream, for serving

Directions:
1. Preheat the air fryer to 310ºF (154ºC).
2. In a small bowl, combine the pineapple slices, rum, vanilla, salt, and lime zest and let stand for at least 10 minutes to allow the pineapple to soak in the rum.
3. Meanwhile, press the puff pastry round into the bottom and up the sides of a round metal cake pan and use the tines of a fork to dock the bottom and sides.
4. Arrange the pineapple slices on the bottom of the pastry in more or less a single layer, then sprinkle with the sugar and dot with the butter. Drizzle with the leftover juices from the bowl. Put the pan in the air fryer and bake until the pastry is puffed and golden brown and the pineapple is lightly caramelized on top, about 40 minutes.
5. Transfer the pan to a wire rack to cool for 15 minutes. Unmold the galette from the pan and serve warm with coconut ice cream.

Oreo-coated Peanut Butter Cups

Servings: 8
Cooking Time: 4 Minutes
Ingredients:
- 8 Standard ¾-ounce peanut butter cups, frozen
- ⅓ cup All-purpose flour
- 2 Large egg white(s), beaten until foamy
- 16 Oreos or other creme-filled chocolate sandwich cookies, ground to crumbs in a food processor
- Vegetable oil spray

Directions:
1. Set up and fill three shallow soup plates or small pie plates on your counter: one for the flour, one for the beaten egg white(s), and one for the cookie crumbs.
2. Dip a frozen peanut butter cup in the flour, turning it to coat all sides. Shake off any excess, then set it in the beaten egg white(s). Turn it to coat all sides, then let any excess egg white slip back into the rest. Set the candy bar in the cookie crumbs. Turn to coat on all parts, even the sides. Dip the peanut butter cup back in the egg white(s) as before, then into the cookie crumbs as before, making sure you have a solid, even coating all around the cup. Set aside while you dip and coat the remaining cups.
3. When all the peanut butter cups are dipped and coated, lightly coat them on all sides with the vegetable oil spray. Set them on a plate and freeze while the air fryer heats.
4. Preheat the air fryer to 400°F.
5. Set the dipped cups wider side up in the basket with as much air space between them as possible. Air-fry undisturbed for 4 minutes, or until they feel soft but the coating is set.
6. Turn off the machine and remove the basket from it. Set aside the basket with the fried cups for 10 minutes. Use a nonstick-safe spatula to transfer the fried cups to a wire rack. Cool for at least another 5 minutes before serving.

Gingerbread

Servings: 6
Cooking Time: 20 Minutes
Ingredients:
- cooking spray
- 1 cup flour
- 2 tablespoons sugar
- ¾ teaspoon ground ginger
- ¼ teaspoon cinnamon
- 1 teaspoon baking powder
- ½ teaspoon baking soda
- ⅛ teaspoon salt
- 1 egg
- ¼ cup molasses
- ½ cup buttermilk
- 2 tablespoons oil
- 1 teaspoon pure vanilla extract

Directions:
1. Preheat air fryer to 330°F.

2. Spray 6 x 6-inch baking dish lightly with cooking spray.
3. In a medium bowl, mix together all the dry ingredients.
4. In a separate bowl, beat the egg. Add molasses, buttermilk, oil, and vanilla and stir until well mixed.
5. Pour liquid mixture into dry ingredients and stir until well blended.
6. Pour batter into baking dish and cook at 330°F for 20minutes or until toothpick inserted in center of loaf comes out clean.

Enticing Cappuccino Muffins

Servings: 12
Cooking Time: 20 Minutes
Ingredients:
- 4 eggs
- 2 cups almond flour
- ½ teaspoon vanilla
- 1 teaspoon espresso powder
- ½ cup sour cream
- 1 teaspoon cinnamon
- 2 teaspoons baking powder
- ¼ cup coconut flour
- ½ cup Swerve
- ¼ teaspoon salt

Directions:
1. Before cooking, heat your air fryer to 325 degrees F/ 160 degrees C.
2. In a blender, mix together vanilla, espresso powder, eggs, and sour cream until smooth.
3. Then blend again with cinnamon, coconut flour, baking powder, salt, and sweetener until smooth.
4. Divide the batter into the silicone muffin molds.
5. Cook in batches in the preheated air fryer for 20 minutes.
6. Serve and enjoy!

Cinnamon Almonds

Servings:4
Cooking Time: 8 Minutes
Ingredients:
- 1 cup whole almonds
- 2 tablespoons salted butter, melted
- 1 tablespoon sugar
- ½ teaspoon ground cinnamon

Directions:
1. Preheat the air fryer to 300°F (149°C).
2. In a medium bowl, combine the almonds, butter, sugar, and cinnamon. Mix well to ensure all the almonds are coated with the spiced butter.
3. Transfer the almonds to the air fryer basket and shake so they are in a single layer. Bake for 8 minutes, stirring the almonds halfway through the cooking time.
4. Let cool completely before serving.

Eggless & Vegan Cake

Servings: 8
Cooking Time: 10 Minutes
Ingredients:
- 2 tablespoons olive oil
- ¼ cup all-purpose flour
- 2 tablespoons cocoa powder
- ⅛ teaspoon baking soda
- 3 tablespoons sugar
- 1 tablespoon of warm water
- 3 tablespoons milk:
- 2 drops of vanilla extract
- 4 raw almonds for decoration roughly chopped
- a pinch of salt

Directions:
1. Let the air fryer preheat to 390 degrees F/ 200 degrees C for at least 2 minutes.
2. In a suitable bowl, add sugar, milk, water, and oil. Whisk until a smooth batter forms.
3. Now add salt, all-purpose flour, cocoa powder, and baking soda, sift them into wet ingredients, mix to form a paste.
4. Spray the four-inch baking pan with oil and pour the batter into it. Then add in the chopped up almonds on top of it.
5. Put the baking pan in the preheated air fryer. And cook for 10 minutes.
6. Take out from the air fryer.
7. Let it cool completely before slicing.

Orange-chocolate Cake

Servings: 6
Cooking Time: 35 Minutes
Ingredients:
- ¾ cup flour
- ½ cup sugar
- 7 tbsp cocoa powder
- ½ tsp baking soda
- ½ cup milk
- 2 ½ tbsp sunflower oil
- ½ tbsp orange juice
- 2 tsp vanilla
- 2 tsp orange zest
- 3 tbsp butter, softened
- 1 ¼ cups powdered sugar

Directions:
1. Use a whisk to combine the flour, sugar, 2 tbsp of cocoa powder, baking soda, and a pinch of salt in a bowl. Once combined, add milk, sunflower oil, orange juice, and orange zest. Stir until combined. Preheat the air fryer to 350°F. Pour the batter into a greased cake pan and Bake for 25 minutes or until a knife inserted in the center comes out clean.
2. Use an electric beater to beat the butter and powdered sugar together in a bowl. Add the remaining cocoa powder and vanilla and whip until fluffy. Scrape the sides occasionally. Refrigerate until ready to use. Allow the cake to cool completely, then run a knife around the edges of the baking pan. Turn it upside-down on a plate so it can be frosted on the sides and top. When the frosting is no longer cold, use a butter knife or small spatula to frost the sides and top. Cut into slices and enjoy!

Wild Blueberry Sweet Empanadas

Servings: 12
Cooking Time: 8 Minutes
Ingredients:
- 2 cups frozen wild blueberries
- 5 tablespoons chia seeds
- ¼ cup honey
- 1 tablespoon lemon or lime juice
- ¼ cup water
- 1½ cups all-purpose flour
- 1 cup whole-wheat flour
- ½ teaspoon salt
- 1 tablespoon sugar
- ½ cup cold unsalted butter
- 1 egg
- ½ cup plus 2 tablespoons milk, divided
- 1 cup powdered sugar
- 1 teaspoon vanilla extract

Directions:
1. To make the wild blueberry chia jam, place the blueberries, chia seeds, honey, lemon or lime juice, and water into a blender and pulse for 2 minutes. Pour the chia jam into a glass jar or bowl and cover. Store in the refrigerator at least 4 to 8 hours or until the jam is thickened.
2. In a food processor, place the all-purpose flour, whole-wheat flour, salt, sugar, and butter and process for 2 minutes, scraping down the sides of the food processor every 30 seconds. Add in the egg and blend for 30 seconds. Using the pulse button, add in ½ cup of the milk 1 tablespoon at a time or until the dough is moist enough to handle and be rolled into a ball. Let the dough rest at room temperature for 30 minutes.
3. On a floured surface, cut the dough in half; then form a ball and cut each ball into 6 equal pieces, totaling 12 equal pieces. Work with one piece at a time, and cover the remaining dough with a towel. Roll out the dough into a 6-inch round, much like a tortilla, with ¼ inch thickness. Place 4 tablespoons of filling in the center of round, fold over to form a half-circle. Using a fork, crimp the edges together and pierce the top with a fork for air holes. Repeat with the remaining dough and filling.
4. Preheat the air fryer to 350°F.
5. Working in batches, place 3 to 4 empanadas in the air fryer basket and spray with cooking spray. Cook for 8 minutes. Repeat in batches, as needed. Allow the sweet empanadas to cool for 15 minutes. Meanwhile, in a small bowl, whisk together the powdered sugar, the remaining 2 tablespoons of milk, and the vanilla extract. Then drizzle the glaze over the surface and serve.

Hot Coconut 'n Cocoa Buns

Servings: 8
Cooking Time: 15 Minutes
Ingredients:
- ¼ cup cacao nibs
- 1 cup coconut milk
- 1/3 cup coconut flour
- 3 tablespoons cacao powder
- 4 eggs, beaten

Directions:
1. Preheat the air fryer for 5 minutes.
2. Combine all ingredients in a mixing bowl.
3. Form buns using your hands and place in a baking dish that will fit in the air fryer.
4. Bake for 15 minutes for 375°F.
5. Once air fryer turns off, leave the buns in the air fryer until it cools completely.

Creamy Cheesecake Bites

Servings: 16
Cooking Time: 2 Minutes
Ingredients:
- 8 ounces cream cheese, softened
- 2 tablespoons erythritol
- ½ cup almond flour
- ½ tsp vanilla
- 4 tablespoons heavy cream
- ½ cup erythritol

Directions:
1. In a stand mixer, mix cream cheese, 2 tbsp. heavy cream, vanilla, and ½ cup erythritol until smooth.
2. Line a plate with parchment paper and spread the cream cheese onto the parchment.
3. Refrigerate for 1 hour.
4. Mix together 2 tbsp. Erythritol and almond flour in a small bowl.
5. Drip the remaining heavy cream over the cheesecake bites and dip in the almond flour mixture to coat.
6. Arrange evenly the cheesecake bites inside the air fryer basket and cook in the air fryer at 350 degrees F/ 175 degrees C for 2 minutes.
7. Halfway cooking, check the cheesecake bites to ensure they are still frozen.
8. Serve with chocolate syrup on the top.

Maple Cinnamon Cheesecake

Servings: 4
Cooking Time: 12 Minutes
Ingredients:
- 6 sheets of cinnamon graham crackers
- 2 tablespoons butter
- 8 ounces Neufchâtel cream cheese
- 3 tablespoons pure maple syrup
- 1 large egg
- ½ teaspoon ground cinnamon
- ¼ teaspoon salt

Directions:
1. Preheat the air fryer to 350°F.
2. Place the graham crackers in a food processor and process until crushed into a flour. Mix with the butter and press into a mini air-fryer-safe pan lined at the bottom with parchment paper. Place in the air fryer and cook for 4 minutes.

3. In a large bowl, place the cream cheese and maple syrup. Use a hand mixer or stand mixer and beat together until smooth. Add in the egg, cinnamon, and salt and mix on medium speed until combined.
4. Remove the graham cracker crust from the air fryer and pour the batter into the pan.
5. Place the pan back in the air fryer, adjusting the temperature to 315°F. Cook for 18 minutes. Carefully remove when cooking completes. The top should be lightly browned and firm.
6. Keep the cheesecake in the pan and place in the refrigerator for 3 or more hours to firm up before serving.

Berry Tacos

Servings: 2
Cooking Time: 5 Minutes
Ingredients:
- 2 soft shell tortillas
- 4 tablespoons strawberry jelly
- ¼ cup fresh blueberries
- ¼ cup fresh raspberries
- 2 tablespoons powdered sugar

Directions:
1. Spread 2 tablespoons of strawberry jelly over each tortilla.
2. Top each with berries evenly and sprinkle with powdered sugar.
3. Arrange the tortillas in air fry basket and insert it in the air fryer.
4. Cook in your air fryer at 300 degrees F/ 150 degrees C for 5 minutes.
5. Serve.

Rustic Berry Layer Cake

Servings: 6
Cooking Time: 45 Minutes
Ingredients:
- 2 eggs, beaten
- ½ cup milk
- 2 tbsp Greek yogurt
- ¼ cup maple syrup
- 1 tbsp apple cider vinegar
- 1 tbsp vanilla extract
- ¾ cup all-purpose flour
- 1 tsp baking powder
- ½ tsp baking soda
- ¼ cup dark chocolate chips
- 1/3 cup raspberry jam

Directions:
1. Preheat air fryer to 350°F. Combine the eggs, milk, Greek yogurt, maple syrup, apple vinegar, and vanilla extract in a bowl. Toss in flour, baking powder, and baking soda until combined. Pour the batter into a 6-inch round cake pan, distributing well, and Bake for 20-25 minutes until a toothpick comes out clean. Let cool completely.
2. Turn the cake onto a plate, cut lengthwise to make 2 equal layers. Set aside. Add chocolate chips to a heat-proof bowl and Bake for 3 minutes until fully melted. In the meantime, spread raspberry jam on top of the bottom layer, distributing well, and top with the remaining layer. Once the chocolate is ready, stir in 1 tbsp of milk. Pour over the layer cake and spread well. Cut into 6 wedges and serve immediately.

Strawberry Pastry Rolls

Servings: 4
Cooking Time: 6 Minutes
Ingredients:
- 3 ounces low-fat cream cheese
- 2 tablespoons plain yogurt
- 2 teaspoons sugar
- ¼ teaspoon pure vanilla extract
- 8 ounces fresh strawberries
- 8 sheets phyllo dough
- butter-flavored cooking spray
- ¼–½ cup dark chocolate chips (optional)

Directions:
1. In a medium bowl, combine the cream cheese, yogurt, sugar, and vanilla. Beat with hand mixer at high speed until smooth, about 1 minute.
2. Wash strawberries and destem. Chop enough of them to measure ½ cup. Stir into cheese mixture.
3. Preheat air fryer to 330°F.
4. Phyllo dough dries out quickly, so cover your stack of phyllo sheets with waxed paper and then place a damp dish towel on top of that. Remove only one sheet at a time as you work.
5. To create one pastry roll, lay out a single sheet of phyllo. Spray lightly with butter-flavored spray, top with a second sheet of phyllo, and spray the second sheet lightly.
6. Place a quarter of the filling (about 3 tablespoons) about ½ inch from the edge of one short side. Fold the end of the phyllo over the filling and keep rolling a turn or two. Fold in both the left and right sides so that the edges meet in the middle of your roll. Then roll up completely. Spray outside of pastry roll with butter spray.
7. When you have 4 rolls, place them in the air fryer basket, seam side down, leaving some space in between each. Cook at 330°F for 6 minutes, until they turn a delicate golden brown.
8. Repeat step 7 for remaining rolls.
9. Allow pastries to cool to room temperature.
10. When ready to serve, slice the remaining strawberries. If desired, melt the chocolate chips in microwave or double boiler. Place 1 pastry on each dessert plate, and top with sliced strawberries. Drizzle melted chocolate over strawberries and onto plate.

Healthy Berry Crumble

Servings: 4
Cooking Time: 30 Minutes
Ingredients:
- ½ cup fresh blackberries
- ½ cup chopped strawberries
- 1/3 cup frozen raspberries

- ½ lemon, juiced and zested
- 1 tbsp honey
- 2/3 cup flour
- 3 tbsp sugar
- 2 tbsp butter, melted

Directions:
1. Add the strawberries, blackberries, and raspberries to a baking pan, then sprinkle lemon juice and honey over the berries. Combine the flour, lemon zest, and sugar, then add the butter and mix; the mixture won't be smooth. Drizzle this all over the berries. Preheat air fryer to 370°F. Put the pan in the fryer and Bake for 12-17 minutes. The berries should be softened and the top golden. Serve hot.

Lava Cakes

Servings: 2
Cooking Time: 9 Minutes
Ingredients:
- 1 tablespoon cocoa powder
- 2 tablespoons coconut oil, softened
- 2 tablespoons Erythritol
- 1 teaspoon peppermint
- 3 eggs, beaten
- 1 teaspoon spearmint, dried
- 4 teaspoons almond flour
- Cooking spray

Directions:
1. To melt the coconut oil, microwave it for 10 seconds, then add in the cocoa powder, almond flour, Erythritol, peppermint, spearmint and eggs.
2. Whisk the mixture well until smooth.
3. Spray the ramekins with cooking spray and pour the chocolate mixture inside.
4. Cook the lava cakes in your air fryer at 375 degrees F/ 190 degrees C for 9 minutes.
5. When the cooking is finished, remove and rest for 5 minutes.
6. Serve and enjoy.

Peanut Butter-banana Roll-ups

Servings: 4
Cooking Time: 20 Minutes
Ingredients:
- 2 ripe bananas, halved crosswise
- 4 spring roll wrappers
- ¼ cup molasses
- ¼ cup peanut butter
- 1 tsp ground cinnamon
- 1 tsp lemon zest

Directions:
1. Preheat air fryer to 375°F. Place the roll wrappers on a flat surface with one corner facing up. Spread 1 tbsp of molasses on each, then 1 tbsp of peanut butter, and finally top with lemon zest and 1 banana half. Sprinkle with cinnamon all over. For the wontons, fold the bottom over the banana, then fold the sides, and roll-up. Place them seam-side down and Roast for 10 minutes until golden brown and crispy. Serve warm.

Vanilla Cupcakes With Chocolate Chips

Servings: 2
Cooking Time: 25 Minutes + Cooling Time
Ingredients:
- ½ cup white sugar
- 1 ½ cups flour
- 2 tsp baking powder
- ½ tsp salt
- 2/3 cup sunflower oil
- 1 egg
- 2 tsp maple extract
- ¼ cup vanilla yogurt
- 1 cup chocolate chips

Directions:
1. Preheat air fryer to 350°F. Combine the sugar, flour, baking powder, and salt in a bowl and stir to combine. Whisk the egg in a separate bowl. Pour in the sunflower oil, yogurt, and maple extract, and continue whisking until light and fluffy. Spoon the wet mixture into the dry ingredients and stir to combine. Gently fold in the chocolate chips with a spatula. Divide the batter between cupcake cups and Bake in the air fryer for 12-15 minutes or until a toothpick comes out dry. Remove the cupcakes let them cool. Serve.

Enticing Grain-free Cakes

Servings: 2
Cooking Time: 4 Minutes
Ingredients:
- 2 large eggs
- ½ cup of chocolate chips, you can use dark chocolate
- 2 tablespoons of coconut flour
- 2 tablespoons of honey as a sugar substitute
- A dash of salt
- ½ teaspoon of baking soda
- Butter and cocoa powder for 2 small ramekins
- ¼ cup of butter or grass-fed butter

Directions:
1. At 370 degrees F/ 185 degrees C, preheat your air fryer.
2. Grease the ramekins with soft butter and sprinkle with cocoa powder. It will stick to the butter.
3. Turn the ramekins upside down, so excess cocoa powder will fall out. Set it aside.
4. In a double boiler or microwave-safe bowl, melt the butter and chocolate chips together, stir every 15 seconds. Make sure to mix well to combine.
5. In a suitable bowl, crack the eggs and whisk with either honey or sugar, mix well.
6. Add in the salt, baking soda, and coconut flour.
7. Then add the melted chocolate chip and butter mixture to the egg, flour, and honey mixture. Mix well, so everything combines.

8. Pour the batter in those 2 prepared ramekins.
9. Let them air fry for 10 minutes. Then take them out from the air fryer and let it cool for 3 to 4 minutes.
10. Top with mint leaves and coconut cream, raspberries, if you want.
11. Serve right away and enjoy.

Almond Pecan Muffins
Servings: 12
Cooking Time: 15 Minutes
Ingredients:
- 4 eggs
- 1 teaspoon vanilla
- ¼ cup almond milk
- 2 tablespoons butter, melted
- ½ cup swerve
- 1 teaspoon psyllium husk
- 1 tablespoon baking powder
- ½ cup pecans, chopped
- ½ teaspoon ground cinnamon
- 2 teaspoons allspice
- 1 ½ cups almond flour

Directions:
1. Before cooking, heat your air fryer to 370 degrees F/ 185 degrees C.
2. In a bowl, beat the butter, sweetener, almond milk, whisked eggs, and vanilla together with a hand mixer until smooth.
3. Then mix all the remaining ingredients together until well combined.
4. Divide the batter into the silicone muffin molds.
5. Cook in batches in the preheated air fryer for 15 minutes.
6. Serve and enjoy!

Marshmallow Pastries
Servings:8
Cooking Time:5 Minutes
Ingredients:
- 4-ounce butter, melted
- 8 phyllo pastry sheets, thawed
- ½ cup chunky peanut butter
- 8 teaspoons marshmallow fluff
- Pinch of salt

Directions:
1. Preheat the Air fryer to 360°F and grease an Air fryer basket.
2. Brush butter over 1 filo pastry sheet and top with a second filo sheet.
3. Brush butter over second filo pastry sheet and repeat with all the remaining sheets.
4. Cut the phyllo layers in 8 strips and put 1 tablespoon of peanut butter and 1 teaspoon of marshmallow fluff on the underside of a filo strip.
5. Fold the tip of the sheet over the filling to form a triangle and fold repeatedly in a zigzag manner.
6. Arrange the pastries into the Air fryer basket and cook for about 5 minutes.
7. Season with a pinch of salt and serve warm.

Cinnamon And Pecan Pie
Servings:4
Cooking Time: 25 Minutes
Ingredients:
- 1 pie dough
- ½ teaspoons cinnamon
- ¾ teaspoon vanilla extract
- 2 eggs
- ¾ cup maple syrup
- ⅛ teaspoon nutmeg
- 3 tablespoons melted butter, divided
- 2 tablespoons sugar
- ½ cup chopped pecans

Directions:
1. Preheat the air fryer to 370ºF (188ºC).
2. In a small bowl, coat the pecans in 1 tablespoon of melted butter.
3. Transfer the pecans to the air fryer and air fry for about 10 minutes.
4. Put the pie dough in a greased pie pan and add the pecans on top.
5. In a bowl, mix the rest of the ingredients. Pour this over the pecans.
6. Put the pan in the air fryer and bake for 25 minutes.
7. Serve immediately.

Vanilla Butter Cake
Servings: 6
Cooking Time: 20-24 Minutes
Ingredients:
- ¾ cup plus 1 tablespoon All-purpose flour
- 1 teaspoon Baking powder
- ¼ teaspoon Table salt
- 8 tablespoons (½ cup/1 stick) Butter, at room temperature
- ½ cup Granulated white sugar
- 2 Large egg(s)
- 2 tablespoons Whole or low-fat milk (not fat-free)
- ¾ teaspoon Vanilla extract
- Baking spray (see here)

Directions:
1. Preheat the air fryer to 325°F (or 330°F, if that's the closest setting).
2. Mix the flour, baking powder, and salt in a small bowl until well combined.
3. Using an electric hand mixer at medium speed, beat the butter and sugar in a medium bowl until creamy and smooth, about 3 minutes, occasionally scraping down the inside of the bowl.
4. Beat in the egg or eggs, as well as the white or a yolk as necessary. Beat in the milk and vanilla until smooth. Turn off the beaters and add the flour mixture. Beat at low speed until thick and smooth.
5. Use the baking spray to generously coat the inside of a 6-inch round cake pan for a small batch, a 7-inch round cake pan for a medium batch, or an 8-inch round cake

pan for a large batch. Scrape and spread the batter into the pan, smoothing the batter out to an even layer.
6. Set the pan in the basket and air-fry undisturbed for 20 minutes for a 6-inch layer, 22 minutes for a 7-inch layer, or 24 minutes for an 8-inch layer, or until a toothpick or cake tester inserted into the center of the cake comes out clean. Start checking it at the 15-minute mark to know where you are.
7. Use hot pads or silicone baking mitts to transfer the cake pan to a wire rack. Cool for 5 minutes. To unmold, set a cutting board over the baking pan and invert both the board and the pan. Lift the still-warm pan off the cake layer. Set the wire rack on top of the cake layer and invert all of it with the cutting board so that the cake layer is now right side up on the wire rack. Remove the cutting board and continue cooling the cake for at least 10 minutes or to room temperature, about 30 minutes, before slicing into wedges.

Blueberry Vanilla Muffins

Servings: 12
Cooking Time: 20 Minutes
Ingredients:
- 3 large eggs
- ⅓ cup coconut oil, melted
- 1 ½ teaspoons gluten-free baking powder
- ½ cup erythritol
- 2 ½ cups almond flour
- ¾ cup blueberries
- ½ teaspoon vanilla
- ⅓ cup unsweetened almond milk

Directions:
1. Before cooking, heat your air fryer to 325 degrees F/ 160 degrees C.
2. Stir together the baking powder, erythritol, and almond flour in a large bowl.
3. Mix vanilla, almond milk, coconut oil, and the whisked eggs in the bowl. Then add in the strawberries and fold together.
4. Divide the batter into the silicone muffin molds.
5. Cook in batches in the preheated air fryer for 20 minutes.
6. Serve and enjoy!

Mango Cobbler With Raspberries

Servings: 4
Cooking Time: 30 Minutes
Ingredients:
- 1 ½ cups chopped mango
- 1 cup raspberries
- 1 tbsp brown sugar
- 2 tsp cornstarch
- 1 tsp lemon juice
- 2 tbsp sunflower oil
- 1 tbsp maple syrup
- 1 tsp vanilla
- ½ cup rolled oats
- 1/3 cup flour
- 3 tbsp coconut sugar
- 1 tsp cinnamon
- ¼ tsp nutmeg
- ⅛ tsp salt

Directions:
1. Place the mango, raspberries, brown sugar, cornstarch, and lemon juice in a baking pan. Stir with a rubber spatula until combined. Set aside.
2. In a separate bowl, add the oil, maple syrup, and vanilla and stir well. Toss in the oats, flour, coconut sugar, cinnamon, nutmeg, and salt. Stir until combined. Sprinkle evenly over the mango-raspberry filling. Preheat air fryer to 320°F. Bake for 20 minutes or until the topping is crispy and golden. Enjoy warm.

Black And Blue Clafoutis

Servings: 2
Cooking Time: 15minutes
Ingredients:
- 6-inch pie pan
- 3 large eggs
- ½ cup sugar
- 1 teaspoon vanilla extract
- 2 tablespoons butter, melted 1 cup milk
- ½ cup all-purpose flour*
- 1 cup blackberries
- 1 cup blueberries
- 2 tablespoons confectioners' sugar

Directions:
1. Preheat the air fryer to 320°F.
2. Combine the eggs and sugar in a bowl and whisk vigorously until smooth, lighter in color and well combined. Add the vanilla extract, butter and milk and whisk together well. Add the flour and whisk just until no lumps or streaks of white remain.
3. Scatter half the blueberries and blackberries in a greased (6-inch) pie pan or cake pan. Pour half of the batter (about 1¼ cups) on top of the berries and transfer the tart pan to the air fryer basket. You can use an aluminum foil sling to help with this by taking a long piece of aluminum foil, folding it in half lengthwise twice until it is roughly 26-inches by 3-inches. Place this under the pie dish and hold the ends of the foil to move the pie dish in and out of the air fryer basket. Tuck the ends of the foil beside the pie dish while it cooks in the air fryer.
4. Air-fry at 320°F for 15 minutes or until the clafoutis has puffed up and is still a little jiggly in the center. Remove the clafoutis from the air fryer, invert it onto a plate and let it cool while you bake the second batch. Serve the clafoutis warm, dusted with confectioners' sugar on top.

Coconut-custard Pie

Servings: 4
Cooking Time: 20 Minutes
Ingredients:
- 1 cup milk
- ¼ cup plus 2 tablespoons sugar
- ¼ cup biscuit baking mix
- 1 teaspoon vanilla
- 2 eggs
- 2 tablespoons melted butter
- cooking spray
- ½ cup shredded, sweetened coconut

Directions:
1. Place all ingredients except coconut in a medium bowl.
2. Using a hand mixer, beat on high speed for 3minutes.
3. Let sit for 5minutes.
4. Preheat air fryer to 330°F.
5. Spray a 6-inch round or 6 x 6-inch square baking pan with cooking spray and place pan in air fryer basket.
6. Pour filling into pan and sprinkle coconut over top.
7. Cook pie at 330°F for 20 minutes or until center sets.

Party S´mores

Servings: 6
Cooking Time: 15 Minutes
Ingredients:
- 2 dark chocolate bars, cut into 12 pieces
- 12 buttermilk biscuits
- 12 marshmallows

Directions:
1. Preheat air fryer to 350°F. Place 6 biscuits in the air fryer. Top each square with a piece of dark chocolate. Bake for 2 minutes. Add a marshmallow to each piece of chocolate. Cook for another minute. Remove and top with another piece of biscuit. Serve warm.

Strawberry-rhubarb Crumble

Servings: 6
Cooking Time:12 To 17 Minutes
Ingredients:
- 1½ cups sliced fresh strawberries
- ¾ cup sliced rhubarb
- ⅓ cup sugar
- ⅔ cup quick-cooking oatmeal
- ½ cup whole-wheat pastry flour
- ¼ cup packed brown sugar
- ½ teaspoon ground cinnamon
- 3 tablespoons unsalted butter, melted

Directions:
1. In a 6-by-2-inch metal pan, combine the strawberries, rhubarb, and sugar.
2. In a medium bowl, mix the oatmeal, pastry flour, brown sugar, and cinnamon.
3. Stir the melted butter into the oatmeal mixture until crumbly. Sprinkle this over the fruit. Bake for 12 to 17 minutes, or until the fruit is bubbling and the topping is golden brown. Serve warm.

Vanilla Coconut Pie

Servings: 6
Cooking Time: 12 Minutes
Ingredients:
- 2 eggs
- ½ cup coconut flour
- ½ cup erythritol
- 1 cup shredded coconut
- 1 ½ tsp vanilla
- ¼ cup butter
- 1 ½ cups coconut milk

Directions:
1. Beat the 2 eggs in a large bowl and mix them with coconut flour, erythritol, shredded coconut, vanilla, butter, and coconut milk until well combined.
2. Using cooking spray, spray a baking dish that fits in your air fryer.
3. Transfer the batter onto the greased baking dish.
4. Cook in your air fryer at 350 degrees F/ 175 degrees C for 10 to 12 minutes.
5. Before serving, slice into your desired size.
6. Serve and enjoy!

Air Fryer Cookbook for Beginners

Recipes Index

A

Air Fried Cod With Basil Vinaigrette 73
Air Fried Grilled Steak 53
Air-fried Pork With Wine Sauce 50
Almond Pecan Muffins 99
Almond-pumpkin Porridge 19
Apple-blueberry Hand Pies 93
Asian Meatball Tacos 61
Asian Steamed Tuna 71
Asparagus And Bell Pepper Strata 14
Asparagus Wrapped In Pancetta 87
Avocado Tempura 11

B

Bacon Tater Tots 27
Bacon With Chocolate Coating 28
Bacon-y Cauliflower Skewers 27
Baharat Lamb Kebab With Mint Sauce 48
Baked Shishito Peppers 85
Balsamic Marinated Rib Eye Steak With Balsamic Fried Cipollini Onions 47
Banana-blackberry Muffins 13
Barbecue Chicken Nachos 29
Basic Chicken Breasts(2) 59
Bbq Chips 27
Beef & Mushrooms 45
Beef And Bean Chimichangas 53
Beef And Mushroom Meatballs 46
Beef Chuck Cheeseburgers 54
Beef Chuck With Brussels Sprouts 47
Beef Loin With Thyme And Parsley 46
Beef Steak Sliders 22
Beef Stuffed Bell Peppers 84
Bell Pepper & Lentil Tacos 39
Bengali Samosa With Mango Chutney 37
Berry Tacos 97
Black And Blue Clafoutis 100
Black Forest Pies 93
Black's Bangin' Casserole 11
Blackened Catfish 78
Blackened Shrimp Tacos 69
Blueberry Scones 18
Blueberry Vanilla Muffins 100
Bread Boat Eggs 19
Breadcrumbs Stuffed Mushrooms 37
Breaded Chicken Patties 62
Breaded Homestyle Chicken Strips 61
Breaded Pork Cutlets 52
Breakfast Burrito With Sausage 15
Breakfast Frittata 13
Brussels Sprouts With Balsamic Oil 37
Buffalo Cauliflower Wings 23

Buffalo Chicken Sandwiches 59
Butter And Bacon Chicken 57
Buttermilk-fried Drumsticks 58
Buttery Scallops 12

C

Cajun Flounder Fillets 71
Caponata Salsa 29
Caramelized Carrots 36
Caribbean Skewers 76
Carrot Orange Muffins 11
Cauliflower Pizza Crust 37
Cheddar Chicken Fajitas 58
Cheese Beef Roll 49
Cheese Broccoli With Basil 80
Cheese Muffins With Cinnamon 93
Cheese Spinach 90
Cheeseburger Sliders With Pickle Sauce 53
Cheeseburger-stuffed Bell Peppers 46
Cheesy Cauliflower "hash Browns" 20
Cheesy Chicken-avocado Paninis 62
Cheesy Green Dip 25
Cheesy Hash Brown Bruschetta 30
Cheesy Jalapeño Poppers 31
Cheesy Mustard Toasts 15
Cherry Cheesecake Rolls 92
Chewy Glazed Parsnips 40
Chicken Tenders With Veggies 65
Chicken Wings With Lemon Pepper 57
Chicken Wings With Sauce 61
Chili-lime Shrimp 78
Chinese-style Lamb Chops 49
Chipotle Drumsticks 67
Chives Meatballs 32
Chocolate Chip Scones 17
Cinnamon Almonds 95
Cinnamon And Pecan Pie 99
Cinnamon Rolls With Cream Cheese Glaze 16
Classic Hash Browns 13
Coconut & Peanut Rice Cereal 18
Coconut Chicken With Apricot-ginger Sauce 65
Coconut Shrimp 73
Coconut-custard Pie 101
Country Shrimp "boil" 74
Crab Cake Bites 26
Crab Rangoon 75
Crabmeat-stuffed Flounder 74
Cream Cheese Danish 14
Creamy Cheesecake Bites 96
Creamy Chicken Tenders 67
Crispy Chicken Nuggets With Turnip 63
Crispy Chicken Strips 62
Crispy Cod Sticks 69

Crispy Curried Sweet Potato Fries 31
Crispy Fish Sticks 14
Crispy Fried Pickle Chips 24
Crispy Herbed Potatoes 81
Crispy Lamb Shoulder Chops 48
Crispy Paprika Chips 22
Crispy Sweet-and-sour Cod Fillets 72
Crumbed Golden Filet Mignon 47
Crunchy Chicken And Ranch Wraps 63
Crunchy Chicken Strips 59
Crunchy Roasted Potatoes 85
Crustless Spinach And Cheese Frittata 41
Cucumber Sushi 29
Curried Potato, Cauliflower And Pea Turnovers 41

D

Delectable Beef With Kale Pieces 48
Delectable Pork Chops 52
Dijon Roasted Purple Potatoes 83
Double Cheese & Beef Burgers 52

E

Easy Air Fried Salmon 69
Easy Asian Turkey Meatballs 66
Easy Cheese & Spinach Lasagna 34
Easy Corn Dog Cupcakes 11
Easy Homemade Veggie Burger 89
Egg In A Hole 18
Eggless & Vegan Cake 95
Eggplant Parmesan 34
English Breakfast 19
Enticing Cappuccino Muffins 95
Enticing Grain-free Cakes 98

F

Falafels 40
Fancy Chicken Piccata 66
Favorite Blueberry Muffins 13
Fish And Vegetable Tacos 69
Fish Mania With Mustard 77
Fish Sticks For Kids 71
Fish Tacos With Hot Coleslaw 70
Flavorful Espresso-grilled Pork Tenderloin 53
Fried Brussel Sprouts 87
Fried Dill Pickle Chips 26
Fried Eggplant Slices 83
Fried Ranch Pickles 28
Fried String Beans With Greek Sauce 28
Fruity Oatmeal Crisp 92
Fudgy Chocolate Brownies 92

G

Garlic Beef Cubes 45
Garlic Beef Meatloaf 53
Garlic Chicken Popcorn 66
Garlic Chicken 64
Garlic Fillets 45
Garlic Parmesan–roasted Cauliflower 84

Garlic Spinach Dip 31
Garlic Tilapia Fillets 74
Garlic Turkey With Tomato Mix 56
Garlicky Radish Chips 25
Garlicky Vegetable Rainbow Fritters 89
Garlic-lemon Scallops 73
Garlic-lemon Steamer Clams 71
Garlic-parmesan Popcorn 88
Gingerbread 94
Gingery Turkey Meatballs 59
Glazed Carrots 84
Glazed Chicken Drumsticks With Herbs 63
Glazed Chicken Wings 23
Golden Breaded Mushrooms 36
Golden Garlicky Mushrooms 82
Gourmet Wasabi Popcorn 36
Great Cat Fish 75
Greek-style Pork Stuffed Jalapeño Poppers 51
Green Bean Sautée 38
Green Beans And New Potatoes 88
Grilled Chicken Pesto 62
Grilled Lime Scallions 82
Grilled Pork & Bell Pepper Salad 52

H

Ham And Cheddar Gritters 11
Ham And Cheese Sliders 31
Ham And Egg Toast Cups 12
Hash Browns 17
Hawaiian Pineapple Chicken Kebabs 56
Healthy Berry Crumble 97
Healthy Caprese Salad 86
Healthy Salmon With Cardamom 69
Healthy Vegetable Patties 65
Herbed Omelet 17
Herb-roasted Turkey Breast 67
Herby Breaded Artichoke Hearts 25
Home-style Buffalo Chicken Wings 22
Hot Coconut 'n Cocoa Buns 96

I

Indian Cauliflower Tikka Bites 32
Indian Fry Bread Tacos 50
Italian Chicken Parmesan 62
Italian Sausage Rolls 44
Italian-style Fried Cauliflower 40

J

Jalapeño And Bacon Breakfast Pizza 19
Jerk Chicken Kebabs 57
Jerk Pork Butt Pieces 51

K

Kale & Lentils With Crispy Onions 38
Kale & Rice Chicken Rolls 64
Katsu Chicken Thighs 64
Kidney Beans Oatmeal In Peppers 87
Kochukaru Pork Lettuce Cups 45

Air Fryer Cookbook for Beginners

L

Lava Cakes	98
Layered Ravioli Bake	40
Lemon-garlic Strip Steak	48
Lemon-roasted Salmon Fillets	70
Lemony Apple Butter	94
Lemony Pear Chips	28
Lobster Tails	76
Lush Vegetables Roast	86

M

Mahi Mahi With Cilantro-chili Butter	69
Mango Cobbler With Raspberries	100
Maple Cinnamon Cheesecake	96
Marshmallow Pastries	99
Masala Fish `n´ Chips	76
Mayonnaise Salmon With Spinach	72
Mediterranean-style Beef Steak	46
Mexican Sheet Pan Dinner	64
Mexican-inspired Chicken Breasts	57
Middle Eastern Roasted Chickpeas	27
Mint Lemon Squash	86
Montreal Steak	51
Moroccan Cauliflower	87
Moroccan-style Steak With Salad	44
Mozzarella Cabbage Wedges	81
Mozzarella Rolls	20
Mushroom & Turkey Bread Pizza	57
Mushroom And Beef Meatloaf	49
Mushroom And Fried Onion Quesadilla	35
Mushroom Lasagna	39
Mushroom, Zucchini And Black Bean Burgers	34
Mustard Pork Meatballs	26
Mustard Pork	54

N

Not-so-english Muffins	17

O

Old Bay Lobster Tails	75
Orange-chocolate Cake	95
Oreo-coated Peanut Butter Cups	94
Outrageous Crispy Fried Salmon Skin	77

P

Panko-breaded Cod Fillets	77
Parmesan Portobello Mushroom Caps	34
Parmesan Spinach Muffins	18
Parmesan White Fish	73
Parmesan-lemon Chicken	66
Party S´mores	101
Peanut Butter-banana Roll-ups	98
Pecan Snowball Cookies	92
Peppery Chicken Meatballs	23
Pineapple Chips With Cinnamon	92
Pineapple Galette	94
Pita And Pepperoni Pizza	20
Pizza Dough	40
Popcorn Chicken Bites	28
Pork Tenderloin Salad	85
Pork Tenderloin With Apple Juice	54
Pork Tenderloins	44
Portobello Mini Pizzas	42
Potato And Prosciutto Salad	51
Potato Bread Rolls	15
Potato Chip-crusted Cod	71
Potato Chips	23
Potato Wedges	84
Prosciutto Mini Mushroom Pizza	82
Prosciutto Mozzarella Bites	30
Puffed Egg Tarts	12

Q

Quick Shrimp Scampi	77

R

Ranch Broccoli With Cheddar	24
Rib Eye Steak Seasoned With Italian Herb	45
Rice & Bean Burritos	39
Rich Turkey Burgers	61
Ricotta & Broccoli Cannelloni	86
Roasted Asparagus	89
Roasted Bell Peppers	88
Roasted Broccoli And Red Bean Salad	80
Roasted Broccoli	81
Roasted Butternut Squash With Cranberries	83
Roasted Fennel Salad	85
Roasted Jalapeño Salsa Verde	24
Roasted Potatoes And Asparagus	84
Roasted Prawns With Firecracker Sauce	75
Roasted Ratatouille Vegetables	81
Roasted Salsa	81
Roasted Vegetable, Brown Rice And Black Bean Burrito	37
Rustic Berry Layer Cake	97
Rutabaga Fries	81

S

Sage & Paprika Turkey Cutlets	58
Salmon Bites With Coconut	25
Salmon Nachos	27
Salmon On Bed Of Fennel And Carrot	72
Salmon Salad With Steamboat Dressing	80
Savory Herb Cloud Eggs	36
Savory Sausage Balls	30
Sea Bass With Potato Scales And Caper Aïoli	77
Seasoned Chicken Breast	56
Shallots Almonds Green Beans	80
Shrimp Pirogues	26
Simple Cherry Tarts	16
Simple Cinnamon Toasts	13
Simple Pork Chops	52
Smashed Fried Baby Potatoes	88
Smoked Paprika Cod Goujons	76
Snapper Scampi	72

Snow Crab Legs	71
Spiced Duck Legs	63
Spiced Sweet Potato Fries	24
Spiced Vegetable Galette	35
Spicy Cocktail Wieners	31
Spicy Coconut Chicken Wings	60
Spicy Honey Mustard Chicken	59
Spicy Pork Rind Fried Chicken	58
Spicy Turkey Meatballs	32
Spinach And Feta Chicken Meatballs	56
Spinach And Mushroom Mini Quiche	20
Spinach And Mushroom Steak Rolls	51
Spinach And Provolone Steak Rolls	46
Spinach Bacon Spread	12
Spinach Eggs And Cheese	19
Spinach With Scrambled Eggs	19
Sriracha Pork Strips With Rice	44
Steak Fingers	54
Strawberry Donuts	93
Strawberry Pastry Rolls	97
Strawberry-rhubarb Crumble	101
Stress-free Beef Patties	49
Stuffed Baby Bella Caps	22
Stuffed Bell Peppers With Mayonnaise	85
Stuffed Jalapeno Poppers	23
Stuffed Mushrooms	36
Stuffed Peppers With Cottage	83
Stuffed Peppers	87
Sun-dried Tomato Crusted Chops	50
Super Crunchy Flounder Fillets	70
Sweet And Spicy Tofu	82
Sweet Butternut Squash	86
Sweet Corn Fritters With Avocado	89
Sweet Marinated Chicken Wings	60
Sweet Plantain Chips	30
Sweet-and-sour Polish Sausage	54
Swiss Vegetable Casserole	87

T

Tacos Norteños	49
Tempero Baiano Brazilian Chicken	67
Tender Pork Ribs With Bbq Sauce	47
The Ultimate Chicken Bulgogi	59
Thick-crust Pepperoni Pizza	29
Thyme Beef & Eggs	12
Thyme Sweet Potato Chips	22
Timeless Garlic-lemon Scallops	76
Tofu & Spinach Lasagna	35
Tuna Wraps	72
Turmeric Cauliflower Rice	88
Tuscan Stuffed Chicken	60
Two-cheese Grilled Sandwiches	41
Typical Crab Cakes With Lemon Wedges	75

U

Uncle´s Potato Wedges	25

V

Vanilla Butter Cake	99
Vanilla Coconut Pie	101
Vanilla Cupcakes With Chocolate Chips	98
Vegan Buddha Bowls(1)	41
Vegetable Burgers	39
Vodka Basil Muffins With Strawberries	18

W

Western Frittata	14
Wild Blueberry Sweet Empanadas	96

Y

Yellow Squash And Zucchinis Dish	80
Yummy Bagel Breakfast	17
Yummy White Fish	74

Z

Zucchini & Bell Pepper Stir-fry	41
Zucchini Chips	24
Zucchini Muffins With Cinnamon	16
Zucchini Tamale Pie	38

Air Fryer Cookbook for Beginners

Printed in Great Britain
by Amazon